RAVE REVIEWS FOR
A GATHERING OF SAINTS

A
Gathering
of Saints

A True Story
of Money, Murder
and Deceit

Robert Lindsey

A DELL BOOK

Published by
Dell Publishing
a division of
Bantam Doubleday Dell Publishing Group, Inc.
666 Fifth Avenue
New York, New York 10103

ISBN: 0-440-20558-1

Reprinted by arrangement with Simon & Schuster.
Printed in the United States of America

Published simultaneously in Canada

April 1990

10 9 8 7 6 5 4 3 2 1
KRI

To Richard Witkin

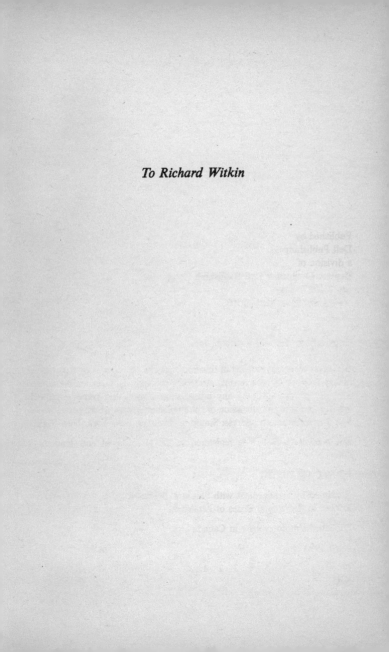

THE MORMONS

Brent Ashworth
Steven F. Christensen
Terri Romney Christensen
Shannon Flynn
Doralee Olds Hofmann
Mark W. Hofmann
Lyn Jacobs
Brent Metcalfe
James Gary Sheets
Kathleen Webb Sheets

THE DEALERS

ALTON BAY, NEW HAMPSHIRE
Elwyn Doubleday

CORTLAND, NEW YORK
William Thoman

NEW YORK CITY
Charles Hamilton
Justin Schiller
Raymond Wapner

NEWTON, MASSACHUSETTS
Kenneth Rendell

SALT LAKE CITY
Curt Bench
Alvin Rust
Gaylen Rust

THE GENERAL AUTHORITIES

PRESIDENT, PROPHET, SEER AND REVELATOR
Spencer Woolley Kimball
Ezra Taft Benson

Gordon B. Hinckley
Dallin H. Oaks
Hugh W. Pinnock

THE INVESTIGATORS

SALT LAKE CITY POLICE DEPARTMENT
James Bell
Kenneth Farnsworth

SALT LAKE COUNTY ATTORNEY'S OFFICE
Richard Forbes
Michael George
George Throckmorton

ARIZONA DEPARTMENT OF PUBLIC SAFETY
William Flynn

THE PROSECUTORS

Theodore L. Cannon
David Biggs
Gerry D'Elia
Robert Stott

THE ANTI-MORMONS

Jerald Tanner
Sandra Tanner

Who controls the past controls the future: who controls the present controls the past.

George Orwell

Prologue

Prologue

       A chilly wind swept over the Salt Lake Valley of Utah at dawn on the morning of October 15, 1985, moving westward from the Rockies with an icy warning that a long and pleasant Indian summer was almost over. At 6 the sun began to climb over the tops of the mountains, bathing the dark and crooked rim of the Wasatch Front in a purple glow. As shafts of morning light cascaded down the jagged wall of mountains that rise east of the Valley, the foothills were covered with an autumnal quilt of red, yellow and gold, and on the freeways the first commuters of the day were heading for Salt Lake City. The street lamps began to flicker off, the street sweepers headed for home and from the tallest spire in Temple Square, a gilded angel looked out benignly on a city coming to life after a holiday weekend, unprepared for what lay ahead.

The downtown streets were still filled with the shadows of day-break when a tall, brown-haired woman in her early thirties parked outside the Judge Building in Salt Lake City shortly before 7 o'clock. Janet McDermott-Reynolds was following her routine as a service representative for the Minnesota Mutual Life Insurance

Company: arrive at the office early, check the mail, deal with paperwork and leave about 8 o'clock for her first appointments.

As the doors of the elevator closed behind her on the sixth floor of the Judge Building, two things distracted her: A cardboard box was propped against the door of the suite across from her office, and a pudgy man with dark hair was striding away from her at the end of the hall. Perhaps he was as startled as she was. When he heard the elevator doors close, he swung around and looked at her with dark eyes set between rounded cheeks. The eyes, she thought, were curiously empty of emotion. He turned around and disappeared down a flight of stairs, leaving her alone in the hall. The experience gave her a chill. Usually, the only people in the Judge Building so early in the day were maintenance men, and she knew he was not one of the janitors.

She placed her briefcase, purse and raincoat outside her office and stepped across the hall to pick up the package. Several tenants on the sixth floor—including Janet McDermott, the name most of the tenants knew her by—had unpredictable schedules, and whenever a parcel arrived for an absent tenant, it was customary to take it in for safekeeping.

She bent over to pick up the package but then hesitated; it didn't seem like an ordinary business parcel. It was addressed by hand with a Magic Marker pen and there was no return address on it. Deciding it was a gift or personal package for her neighbor, she left it propped against the door. Then she saw the stranger with the plump cheeks in the hallway again and quickly entered her office.

An hour later, as Janet McDermott stood outside her door, ready to leave for her first appointment, she noticed that the package was still there. She again considered taking charge of it, but before she could make a decision she saw the dark-haired young man who occupied Suite 609 striding toward her with a bag of doughnuts and a carton of canned soft drinks.

Remembering that she had forgotten to inform her answering service that she was leaving the office, she reopened the door, picked up the phone and began to dial.

In the weeks that followed, Janet McDermott would be unable to remember whether it was the thunder of the bomb exploding in her ears or the sight of her office wall hurtling toward her that first made her realize something was terribly wrong.

Before she could think, an invisible force hurled her backward, tied itself around her legs and dragged her down. As the shock wave of the bomb pushed her to the floor, the office door slammed open with a bang, and for an instant Janet McDermott looked at the telephone in her hand and wondered if by touching it she had made the wall of her office assault her with shards of plaster, glass and wood.

She let the phone drop and crawled behind her desk. Someone was trying to kill her, she decided.

She listened.

For a moment, the room was silent. Then she heard a baby. It was a *little girl*, moaning with agonizing, tortured cries of pain.

Suddenly, she realized what had happened: Someone outside the office—the man with the fat cheeks—had shot a baby girl and she was dying.

"You have used your allotted time for dialing. If you want to place a call, please hang up and dial again or call your operator for assistance."

The recorded voice ascended mechanically from the smoke, debris and stench of burnt powder and sent a wave of terror through her body: The killer was in the hallway. He would hear the voice from the telephone and know she was in the office.

She cowered closer to her desk, trying to vanish, listening for footsteps.

But all she heard were the frail cries of a dying baby.

Something then possessed her to flee: Perhaps the smell of powder, possibly a fire alarm was ringing somewhere. Fear of fire overpowered her fear of the killer, and she grabbed her briefcase and purse and looked out the gaping hole that had been her office doorway.

Chunks of plaster, splinters of broken wood, nails, scorched cans of Tab diet cola, scraps of doughnuts littered the carpeted floor. As she struggled to make sense of this chaos, Janet McDermott felt instinctively that the threat to her had passed. And she sensed she was not alone in the hallway.

She looked around for the baby and couldn't find her. But she still heard the terrible sounds, and then she looked directly across the hallway and saw where the sounds were coming from.

The tenant of Suite 609 was sprawled across the doorway to his office. His face was covered with blood and black soot, as if he had been made up for a hideous role in blackface. There was a huge, bloody hole in his chest. Half of one of his shoes was lying upside down on the carpet. Instinctively, she looked around for the other half of the shoe. His necktie, still neatly tied, was lying on the floor beside him. His right eye was a dark hole. As she looked out of her office, she realized the moans now sounded different. The sound was heavier, deeper, huskier. They were not the cries of a baby. She realized they were the sounds of a dying man.

While Janet McDermott was listening to life ebb from the young man who was lying face up on the sixth floor of the Judge Building, another woman was getting ready to take a walk on the other side of the Salt Lake Valley.

Kathleen Webb Sheets worried a lot about getting fat—too much, her friends and daughters said. At fifty, she had the same vivacious personality, with strong measures of optimism and independence, that had elected her senior class president and made her a popular member of Kappa Kappa Gamma at the University of Utah almost thirty years before. She might have been slightly overweight based on the weight/height charts that she habitually clipped from magazines, but only slightly so, and none of her friends thought of her as overweight. Nevertheless, she fretted often that it was becoming harder and harder to lose weight as she got older. The morning walks and tennis helped, but they weren't enough.

Two weeks earlier, before she had gone with her husband to New York City on a business trip, her doctor had broken the news that she half-expected but dreaded: She would probably have to have a hysterectomy soon.

Perhaps, she thought, it would help her cope with the depression she felt so often now.

Kathy Sheets and her husband, James Gary Sheets, lived with the two youngest of their four children, Jim, who was fifteen, and Gretchen, who was a nineteen-year-old student at the University of Utah, in a sprawling home with a swimming pool next to a stream in Holladay, a wooded suburb of Salt Lake City. Rising behind them were the soaring Wasatch Mountains, dominated by the peak pioneers had called Mount Olympus. To the west stretched the city Kathy Sheets loved.

After they had become millionaires, Kathy and Gary Sheets could have afforded to move up the slopes to a grander house even higher above the Valley, as many other Utahans did to send a signal that they had succeeded in a culture that very much revered success. But they were content to remain where they were—in their own ward, in the home they had worked and planned for together.

In so many ways Kathy and Gary had accomplished things she had never dreamed of, accumulated things she had never thought of wanting. In so many ways their life had been a success, and not only because of Gary's success in business. They had been married —sealed for time and all eternity—in the Salt Lake Temple the year after her graduation from the university. Then, as Gary established himself, applying the drive and energy that always amazed her and always made her proud, she worked as a teacher, then assumed the only role that she ever expected in life, her *duty,* as wife, mother, homemaker.

There were other reasons to be proud: The Church had called Gary as a bishop; she had served as president of the Relief Society and the Primary Association. The Church had given her everything she had ever wanted from it and more. Perhaps their marriage was not all that Kathy Sheets wanted. But whatever disappointments she had had were more than compensated for by her children and, especially, her grandchildren, Danny, Elizabeth and Molly.

She had never set out to become rich. Her family and the Church were the important things in her life. But she did not want to be poor again. She enjoyed her home. She enjoyed the cabin in the canyon. She enjoyed being able to buy gifts for her children and grandchildren. She loved to travel. In New York she Christmas-shopped until her feet were raw. At night she and Gary saw *The Odd Couple* and enjoyed New York's restaurants. They people-watched on Fifth Avenue, enjoyed themselves and tried to pretend nothing was wrong. But she knew the life that she loved was slipping away from her.

In her hotel in New York City she wrote in her journal:

Scared and uncertain. . . .Will we ever have money again? I'm
so scared. I want to escape. . . .

At 8:15 A.M. on October 15, 1985, as a man lay sprawled across
the doorway to his office in downtown Salt Lake City, Kathy
Sheets cleaned up a mess around her family's garbage cans left the
night before by prowling dogs. She passed the small sign she had
posted in her kitchen, *Avenge Yourself: Live long enough to be a
problem to your children,* and drove out the driveway in her red
Audi with license plates that read URPBAG, a word Kathy Sheets
used to describe anything disagreeable, the comic origins of which
were lost somewhere in family history.

She went to a neighbor's home to pick up her walking partner,
Faye Kotter. As they strolled beneath a canopy of cottonwood
trees a few blocks from their neighborhood, Kathy Sheets reported
on her adventures in New York and, bundled up against the morning chill in a quilted jacket, savored one of her favorite times of the
year, the season when the Salt Lake Valley's crisp Indian summer
gave way to autumn.

After the walk, she stopped at the drive-in window of her bank,
deposited $800 and told the teller how much enjoyment she was
getting from her youngest granddaughter, Molly. At 9:45, she arrived home and parked the Audi in the driveway. A brown box was
lying near the garage. She picked it up, tucked it under her arm
and walked toward the house. She saw a copy of *The Salt Lake
Tribune* on the ground and bent over to pick it up.

At that moment, a neighbor, Jane Forsgren, was thinking about
awakening her sons. She had let them sleep later than usual because the family had returned late the previous night from a Columbus Day outing.

"My gosh," she told her husband, "that sounds like a sonic
boom."

They looked out the window but did not see anything out of the
ordinary and decided to wake the kids.

Stephanie St. James, another neighbor, also heard a sharp noise.
She looked over toward Kathy Sheets's house and saw hundreds of
leaves swirling in the air as if they had been caught up in a whirlpool.

When a friend arrived at her home for a visit an hour later,

Kathy Sheets was lying on her back, her green eyes, glazed and half-opened, staring blankly into the sun.

The blast had torn open her stomach and chest, disemboweled her, removed parts of several fingers and severed her left arm at the elbow, leaving her forearm connected to the rest of her body by only two scorched strands of cartilage.

A jagged piece of wood from the garage roof was lying across her pink jumpsuit like a starched and weathered shroud, and on the ground all around her were the red, gold and orange leaves of autumn.

As Gerry D'Elia steered his pickup truck through the high mountain pass that isolated the ski resort of Park City from the Salt Lake Valley, his thoughts were foggy from a hangover.

His parents had come from New York for a Columbus Day weekend visit, and everyone had partied too late and drunk too much wine.

Maybe, he thought, Italians enjoyed wine too much.

If it had been necessary on the morning of October 15, 1985, to produce a man from Mars in Utah, Gerry D'Elia might have qualified. Born in Jersey City and reared in New York, he had dropped out of college, worked as a construction steel rigger, then moved to Utah because he loved to ski. There was a joke he had heard, not necessarily true, but one often repeated: There are two reasons to move to Utah—one, if you're a Mormon; two, if you love to ski. D'Elia was not a Mormon, but an alien who loved to ski. In a community founded on religious piety, he was a fallen-away Catholic turned atheist.

D'Elia landed in Utah with dreams of becoming an astronaut. He studied physics and mathematics at the University of Utah and envisioned himself working in a space station. But after offering himself to NASA, he was advised that at twenty-eight he was too old to enter a crowded job market requiring sophisticated graduate training or experience as a pilot. He enrolled at the University of Utah College of Law, obtained a law degree and, to acquire some courtroom experience, took a job as a prosecutor for Salt Lake County.

The chill that had cooled the Salt Lake Valley at dawn was giving way to brilliant skies and rising temperatures as D'Elia's pickup truck pulled away from his home in Park City. As the Valley unfolded beneath him, he heard a bulletin on the radio—a report of a fatal bombing in Salt Lake City. Forgetting his hangover, he drove faster to the office. He was the arson specialist for the County Attorney's office. He had worked too many homicides in which the cops had screwed up the evidence and made the case difficult to prosecute. He wanted to be in on this case from the start.

While D'Elia drove on Interstate 80 toward the city, a noisy Dodge Omni came to a stop near the Judge Building, and two detectives on the Salt Lake City Police Department homicide detail got out and threaded their way through a thicket of fire trucks, police cars, ambulances and emergency vans with chattering radios and flashing red lights.

Kenneth Farnsworth was a tall, slender man of forty with a dark mustache and a deep cleft in his chin. James Bell, his partner, was a wiry, taciturn Canadian with black hair and droopy eyes. They had been alerted that a boiler had exploded at the Judge Building and that many people were injured. As they ducked beneath the yellow tape that had been strung outside the building to keep out sightseers, a man in the crowd turned to a friend and said: "The guy who got killed was the guy who bought the salamander letter."

In a building two blocks away, an aide informed Salt Lake County Attorney Theodore L. Cannon about the bombing. Cannon looked out the window past the offices of Coordinated Financial Services Corporation but did not see any smoke rising from the Judge Building. He approved the assignment of D'Elia and David Biggs, a new lawyer on his staff, to the case, then turned his thoughts back to a topic that was increasingly on his mind. He was thinking about being a judge. Almost ten years before, Cannon had vaulted to political prominence in Salt Lake County as a militant battler of pornography in a community that valued such a record more than most. He had twice been elected County Attorney and had helped win convictions in a string of grotesque murder cases. He was politically secure. But soon he would have to decide whether to seek a third term, and the more he thought about it, the more Ted Cannon liked the idea of becoming a judge instead.

David Biggs looked down at Kathleen Sheets and thought that he had never seen such a look of surprise on any face. Her eyes were frozen as they looked into the sun. Her mouth was wide open. There was little blood around her: She had died so quickly that her heart must have stopped pumping almost immediately. Life had been jerked out of her so quickly, he thought, that if there was a spirit liberated at death it must have continued walking up to her front door holding her newspaper after the bomb exploded.

Biggs was distracted by a shadow blocking the sun and he looked up. He saw the left arm of Kathy Sheets's quilted jacket dangling from the limb of a tree like a piece of clothing hung out to dry.

Fearing a madman was loose, hundreds of people in the Salt Lake Valley requested police protection on the afternoon of October 15, 1985. Others fled the Valley by plane or automobile. Telephoned bomb threats to newspapers and police agencies and rumors of religious death squads added to a haunting sense of fear that gripped the community.

As television cameras and news reporters circled them, police officials tried to restore calm: "We want to assure people we don't have a mad person on the street indiscriminately killing people," police chief Bud Willoughby said at a press conference.

"These were highly sophisticated bombs used by assassins. Someone was brought in to kill these people."

Salt Lake County Sheriff N. D. (Pete) Hayward, in whose jurisdiction the murder of Mrs. Sheets occurred, agreed: "The way the bomb was made, the way it was handled and detonated, the individual had to be a professional."

Do you suspect the Mafia? Hayward was asked.

"That's a strong possibility," he said. Agents of the federal Bureau of Alcohol, Tobacco and Firearms sent a report to Washington that the two bombings appeared to be related. Both victims, ATF agents reported, were part of an investment firm in which investors had lost tens of millions of dollars, and the apparent motive for the killings was revenge.

By dawn the following day, the largest criminal investigation in the history of Utah had begun. Nevertheless, most residents of the Valley had to resume the routine tasks of ordinary life. For Christine Hays, that meant patrolling downtown streets in a Jeep and ticketing overtime parkers. For Brad Christensen, a red-haired student who at twenty-three was already energized with the sense of ambition and drive that seemed to propel a disproportionate number of people in his community, it meant restocking a new flower shop that he had recently opened.

Shortly after 2:30 P.M., Christine Hays spun the Jeep around to make a U-turn on Main Street two blocks north of Temple Square, the headquarters of the Mormon church. In her rearview mirror she saw a stocky, dark-haired man crossing the street toward a blue sports car, then resumed her search for chalk marks that incriminated overtime parkers. As she did, she checked her rearview mirror again, and the image that was reflected in the glass astonished her: The man she had seen moments earlier was several feet off the ground, airborne and flying backward. As he fell to the pavement, a clap of thunder rumbled down the narrow street, becoming louder and louder as it ricocheted between the concrete buildings on each side of the street.

Brad Christensen had been standing across the street, hands on his hips, trying to catch his breath after walking up the hill, when he saw the man unlock the blue Toyota. The florist had entered the intersection and was walking toward his delivery truck when the bomb exploded. As he spun around, chunks of chrome and upholstery erupted from the Toyota like flaming lava from a volcano. The roof of the car was gone, and above it sheets of paper were circling in the air like a flock of seagulls.

Christensen sprinted across the street. The man he had seen a few moments earlier was a motionless heap. His face was blue.

Blood was streaming from a large hole in his head. There was another large and bloody hole in his right knee. Several bones on his right hand were exposed and one finger was gone.

He looked as if he were dead.

As Christensen wondered what he should do to help him, the car exploded into a scorching inferno.

Within an instant the flames engulfed the car and pushed him away from the man on the ground.

"Let's get him out of there," he said as two other pedestrians ran up behind him.

Braving the heat and flames, they lifted the man off the asphalt and carried him to a nearby lawn and loosened his tie and shirt. As they did, Brad Christensen saw something beneath the man's shirt that propelled him into action as if it had been a jolt of electricity.

Christensen removed a vial of consecrated oil from his pocket. While all three men laid their hands on the man, one of the pedestrians daubed oil on his forehead and Christensen prayed.

"I command you to live," he said.

"I command you to live in the name of Jesus Christ . . ."

After a moment, the man started to move.

I

For my own part, I am happily disappointed in the appearance of the Valley of the Salt Lake, but if the land be as rich as it has the appearance of being, I have no fears but the Saints can live here and do well while we will do right.

The journal of William Clayton, July 22, 1847

1

The final push began on the Nebraska plains on an April morning in 1847. William Clayton, a handsome Lancashire bookkeeper who had crossed the Atlantic in pursuit of salvation, recorded the composition of the party in his journal: 143 men and boys, 3 women, 2 children, "72 wagons, 93 horses, 52 mules, 66 oxen, 19 cows, and 17 dogs, and chickens."

They were, he recorded, "148 souls who have decided to go west of the mountains as pioneers to find a home where the Saints can live in peace and enjoy the fruits of their labors and where we shall not be under the dominion of gentile governments, subject to the wrath of mobs and where the standards of peace can be raised, the Ensign to the nations reared and the kingdom of God flourish until truth shall prevail. . . ."

As they struggled down the canyons of the Wasatch Front, a dazzling and bleak panorama unfolded before them. It was a desert valley barren of timber and dominated by a shimmering lake stretching north as far as they could see. "This is truly a wild looking place," wrote Clayton.

The journey to the Salt Lake Valley had begun seventeen years

earlier and almost two thousand miles away on a farm in upstate
New York.

On April 6, 1830, six men led by a twenty-four-year-old farmer's
son named Joseph Smith, Jr., incorporated a new religious faith,
the Church of Christ. In itself, the event was not extraordinary. In
western New York, new churches were sprouting like birch trees
and competing for disciples in a crowded forest of religious experi-
mentation. From New England, the restless, the have-nots, the
adventurous were moving west in search of land and a better life
while leaving behind, along with everything else, the austere faith
and Puritan values of their past. A Babel of voices had emerged
offering new answers to mankind's age-old questions about God.
While the Methodists, Baptists and other religious groups splin-
tered into feuding sects, rival saviors of many varieties bloomed on
the frontier, each courting man's innate dread of death with his
own vision and promise of eternity.

Although the meeting in April 1830 at a Fayette, New York,
farmhouse was not in itself extraordinary, the story told by their
leader was: Joseph Smith, Jr., told his followers that in September
1823 an angel had visited him several times while he was working
the fields near his home. The angel, whom Smith subsequently
called Moroni, led him to a cache of gold tablets. He said the angel
told him that he had buried the plates near Smith's home fourteen
hundred years ago. He said they contained a written history of an
ancient civilization that had once thrived in America but later
came upon hard and turbulent times and vanished except for a
handful of survivors who were the ancestors of the American Indians. Although the angel withheld the gold tablets from him,
Moroni reappeared on the anniversary of their first meeting during
each of the succeeding three years. Finally, Smith said that on
September 22, 1827, the angel appeared again and granted him
temporary possession of the plates, along with two magical stones
called Urim and Thummim that Smith could use to translate the
ancient people's language on the tablets into English. The treasure
was buried in a small, rounded hill, the Hill Cumorah, that rose
above the sparsely cultivated farmland three miles from Smith's
log cabin.

Joseph Smith said he then spent many months deciphering the

plates, which he said had been written in "reformed Egyptian characters," in the alphabet of an ancient language that, according to Moroni, had been "handed down and altered by us, according to our manner of speech."

The story Smith described was essentially a history of the American Indians that he said was written by prophets and divided into books.

It recounted how a band of Hebrews, led by a great prophet named Lehi, had abandoned Jerusalem six hundred years before the birth of Christ because of its wickedness and migrated by boat to the Americas. In the New World, Lehi's family split into two warring factions: One, a mostly righteous group, was led by his son Nephi; the other, a wicked faction, was led by his son Laman. Because of their sins, God cursed the followers of Laman and gave them dark skin. Smith said the record he translated described centuries of warfare between the Nephites and the Lamanites that was unremitting except for a period of two hundred years or so following the Resurrection of Jesus, when He came to the New World, visited Lehi's descendants, delivered a discourse similar to the Sermon on the Mount and directed them to preach His gospel. Later, hostilities erupted again until a climactic battle in A.D. 421 near the Hill Cumorah that ended with a conquest of the Nephites by the Lamanites. The Nephites' only survivor was Moroni, who buried in the hill plates containing a history of their civilization recorded by his father, a prophet named Mormon. The Lamanites survived, but because they kept no written history or genealogical records, time washed away all memories of their Hebrew origins and they became the progenitors of the aboriginal Indians Columbus found when he arrived in the New World.

Joseph Smith entitled the book he translated the Book of Mormon.

In 1827, Martin Harris, a farmer and wealthy neighbor of Smith's, was impressed by his story of finding a "gold bible" and gave him $50 to feed his family while he completed its translation. In February of the following year, Harris decided to travel to New York City to consult experts about the exciting and mysterious discovery. He took with him a sheet of paper upon which Smith said he had copied a few of the characters from the gold plates and showed them to Charles Anthon, a Columbia College classics scholar. When Harris returned to Palmyra, the village in western New York where he lived, he reported that Anthon said they were similar to Egyptian hieroglyphics or Arabic symbols but that he had been unable to decipher them. Nor could Dr. Samuel Mitchell, a physician and the vice-president of Rutgers University.

Smith said it didn't surprise him that the two scholars could not translate the hieroglyphics. The prophet Isaiah had predicted twenty-five centuries before that in time a great book would be brought forth and delivered "to one that is learned, saying, 'Read this, I pray thee'; and he saith, 'I cannot; for it is sealed.' "

Harris became Smith's first disciple and transcribed the words of the Book of Mormon as Smith translated them. Smith placed the two special stones into his hat, buried his face in the hat and then, shrouded under a blanket, dictated to Harris the writings that he said were on the gold plates. To impress his family with the importance of his holy work, Martin Harris took home the first 116 pages that Smith had translated and had called the Book of Lehi. The pages were never seen again, their fate obscured by time and conflicting legends. According to one legend, Harris's wife, Lucy, was so outraged when he told her that he wanted to give Smith more money that she burned the manuscript. Others said religious rivals of Smith stole the Book of Lehi; still others said Harris simply lost the 116 pages out of carelessness. Whatever the answer, the fate of the first 116 pages of the Book of Mormon would remain a mystery that endured long after Martin Harris died in 1875.

Joseph Smith said that when he finished translating the gold plates, the angel Moroni took them away from him.

On March 26, 1830, five thousand copies of the Book of Mormon (minus the Book of Lehi) were published in Palmyra by a local printer, Egbert B. Grandin, financed by a $3,000 mortgage on Harris's 240-acre farm. Because few copies were sold, Harris was unable to pay his debt and lost his farm.

Almost from the day it was published the Book of Mormon came under attack and ridicule. Neighbors of Smith claimed that it was a figment of his imagination, that he initially told them it was a novel he had written in order to ease his family's poverty and that he had been surprised when some people regarded it not only as truthful but as divine scripture.

As word of Smith's gold bible spread over western New York, its dramatic account of bloody warfare, family intrigue, and a daring flight across the seas, together with an optimistic spiritual message that promised true believers riches and a good life, began to attract disciples to the church that Smith and his friends had organized. The book provided what to many frontiersmen sounded like a plausible explanation for the origins of the Indians, still very much a presence on the frontier. Once a potential convert accepted the Book of Mormon as truthful, it was only a short step to acceptance of a claim by Joseph Smith that his church was "the only true and living church upon the face of the whole earth."

To those who accepted the Book of Mormon, the message was clear: God had sent a latter-day prophet, Joseph Smith, Jr., to reestablish His Old Testament church, and those who followed him were an elite people whose help God would need to prepare earth for the second coming of Christ, when he would rule for a thousand years of light and holiness.

During this imminent Millennium, Smith preached, God would turn to members of His only true church to rule His earthly principalities. The Mormonites, as they were first called on the frontier, were God's *chosen people,* the sons and daughters of Israel. Only they had a covenant with God.

Only they were the Lord's Elect.

Despite little education and humble beginnings, Smith proved to be an articulate, charismatic leader. Soon, people began to flock around him. Tall, well-built and handsome, brimming with intelligence and self-confidence, he had a thick head of black hair brushed back from his forehead and a powerful voice that well equipped him for his role as a modern Moses. To distinguish his church from sects with similar names, Smith changed its name to the Church of Jesus Christ of Latter-day Saints: Those who obeyed God's original gospel in the last days before the Millennium were saints of the latter days. Everyone else was a gentile.

There was something distinctively American about the new church that helped it grow. It was an appeal rooted in the same sense of optimism and confidence in individual enterprise that was persuading many people to pull up stakes and move West to build a better life in Jacksonian America, the age of the common man.

In a country whose religious experience had been shaped by a Calvinist vision of a vengeful God convinced of man's inherent evil, determined to make him atone for Adam's original sin and menacing him with visions of a fiery hell, Smith broke the tether to Calvinism and seldom mentioned hell. He said man alone, by his good works, determined his fate after death.

And in a new country where young people were taught that anyone could aspire to become the President, Joseph Smith said any man could become a god.

After examining scrolls of papyrus found buried with an Egyptian museum mummy, Smith said that they were lost writings of the Old Testament prophet Abraham that gave him new insight into God's blueprint for the universe. He said he had translated the papyri just as he had translated the gold plates and determined that man's life on earth was only one step in a long progression leading up to his deification.

There was not *one* God in the universe, he said, but many. Every man was a *god in embryo.* Every man could rule his own planet as God ruled earth. Indeed, "God Himself was once as we are now," a man with flesh and bones. "Now he is an exalted man and sits enthroned in yonder heavens." Smith said God had revealed to him the plan by which men could become gods: Before birth every human existed in a premortal state known as "spirit child." Mortal men and women were obligated to liberate these spirits by conceiving children. At the close of their earthly lives, each spirit would await the Millennium, when families would be reunited. Marriages were to be "for time and all eternity," not "until death doth you part." Families, like life itself, were to last into eternity. In temple rituals children were to be "sealed" to their parents, assuring they would rejoin them in eternity. When Jesus returned, Mormons who had led worthy lives would be risen from the dead and joined with their spirits and would enter the Kingdom of God, an exalted place with three levels, each offering more glory and privilege than the one below it. Those judged to have led the worthiest lives would be admitted to the loftiest tier in the Celestial Kingdom, be reunited with their families and ultimately become gods—like Jesus, each a ruler of his own star, planets and principalities.

As the church attracted more members, its claim to being God's *only* true church and whispers that it purported to turn men into gods brought it under increasing attack from members of other faiths. Criticism soon turned to harassment on the frontier and then often to vicious mob attacks. Less than a year after the church was organized, Joseph Smith said he had received a divine revelation directing that there should be a gathering of the Lord's Elect.

At their gathering place, Joseph Smith said members of the Elect could live together in peace isolated from their persecutors in the gentile world, share their wealth and await the Millennium, preparing, as God's acolytes, to bring godliness to a chaotic world.

Abandoning New York, Joseph Smith led the Saints to Ohio, then Missouri, then Illinois in his search for a gathering place. Mobs—increasingly propelled as much by fear of economic and political competition from the close-knit Mormons as by their doctrines—pursued them wherever they went.

The blood of hundreds of Mormons and that of their enemies moistened the plains as they moved westward. There was also bloody strife in the Mormon camp, often stirred by rebellion over Smith's authoritarian rule. To smother dissent, some Saints close to the Prophet formed a secret society called the Danites to execute, in the name of the Lord, those who challenged him.

Hostility, persecution and internal strife only seemed to push Smith harder to build his church, and as his flock expanded on the American frontier, he sent missionaries abroad to begin the task of bringing the restored gospel to the rest of the world.

Declaring that he received revelations directly from God and was God's surrogate on earth, Smith promulgated new doctrines and secret rituals adapted from those of the Masonic Lodge. He disclosed that when he was fourteen he had been visited by God the Father and Jesus who came to him in a "pillar of light" and that later John the Baptist had come to him on earth and personally ordained him a priest.

As his missionaries began to send converts across the Atlantic to join him, Smith found the Zion for which he had been searching: In 1840, the Illinois legislature allowed him to build a settlement near a small town called Commerce, at the western edge of the state, that Smith renamed Nauvoo. It was a Hebrew word meaning "beautiful plantation." Before long, Nauvoo was a thriving community on the Mississippi that each month welcomed hundreds of new converts. Within a year, the church claimed a membership of more than twenty thousand and Nauvoo was the largest city in Illinois.

The happy idyll in Nauvoo, however, was brief.

Smith had long had a reputation for possessing a physical as well as a spiritual interest in women other than his wife, Emma. Many Mormon women responded to the handsome Prophet with the booming voice and stirring gift of persuasion. In 1842, Smith promulgated a secret new principle of Mormonism—one he had personally been practicing for several years—called "Celestial Marriage." Other people called it polygamy.

Every man, Smith said, had a right to marry ten virgins. Many Old Testament prophets, he said, had taken more than one wife, and it was equally appropriate for latter-day members of God's chosen people to do as much. Some women objected to Smith's demand that they bed down with him, but Smith employed a tool of seduction that other men might have envied: He *commanded* women to lie with him because he said it was necessary for their *salvation.* For a Mormon woman the path to salvation was through the priesthood of her husband. He was offering Mormon women an opportunity to share with him "time and all eternity" in the Celestial Kingdom. Estimates of the number of Joseph Smith's wives ranged from a dozen to more than sixty.

Despite his entreaties to keep Celestial Marriage a secret, rumors of the Mormons' polygamous sexual couplings escaped from Nauvoo. There were also rumors from Nauvoo that the Mormons were conducting "baptisms of the dead," rituals in which living church members, acting as proxies, were rebaptized so that their ancestors born before 1830 could enter the Celestial Kingdom.

Another rumor struck their enemies as even more ominous: The Mormons were said to be plotting to take political control of Illinois and eventually the whole country. Joseph Smith fueled these suspicions early in 1844 when he announced his candidacy for President of the United States and formed a secret organization— the Council of Fifty—to establish a "Kingdom of God" on earth led by Smith as "Prophet, Priest and King."

On June 7, 1844, the *Nauvoo Expositor,* a newspaper founded by Mormons who were unhappy with Smith's sexual and political activities, published its first—and only—edition. It was an exposé of polygamy that obliquely attacked the Prophet as a corrupt land speculator and licentious charlatan determined to be the political dictator of a religious state. Four days later, at Smith's direction, the Nauvoo City Council declared the newspaper was libelous and a public nuisance, and Smith's militia destroyed its presses and burned the remaining copies of its first edition.

Smith's suppression of the *Expositor* ignited smoldering embers of anti-Mormonism that advanced over the prairie like a brushfire. At the borders of a young nation that valued freedom of expression as much as it prized freedom of religion, the attack on the newspaper turned pent-up anti-Mormonism into an ugly and deadly force. As mobs assembled outside Nauvoo for an attack on the Mormon community, Smith and his brother Hyrum were arrested for ordering the raid on the *Expositor* and jailed in nearby Carthage.

Two days later, on June 27, 1844, one of the mobs stormed the Carthage Jail and Joseph Smith and his brother were shot to death.

Three years later, 143 men and boys, 3 women and 2 children descended the steep canyons of the Wasatch Mountains and entered the Salt Lake Valley.

The Saints at last had found their gathering place.

2

Led by Brigham Young, a former carpenter who was one of Joseph Smith's first converts, the Saints arrived in the Salt Lake Valley determined to build their martyred Prophet's "Kingdom of God," a religious state where spiritual, political and economic power were combined for the common good. In the months that followed, they laid out broad avenues for a grand city, built irrigation systems to channel water from the mountains, started construction of a temple and enjoyed a first harvest coaxed from the Valley's hard soil.

Envisaging a Mormon nation called Deseret stretching from the Rockies to California, Young, a charismatic man gifted with organizational skills, dispatched wagonloads of settlers to points throughout the West, where they established hundreds of Mormon colonies. In Salt Lake City and other settlements they built stores, printed their own money and opened banks and cooperatives to serve the new Mormon nation's economic needs.

Still awaiting an imminent Millennium, the Saints had found Zion but they had not yet found peace. Nor was their running over.

For much of the next half-century, they warred with the federal

government over their refusal to abandon polygamy, a source of
moral outrage in the East perhaps matched in equal measure by
growing apprehension over the church's rising political and economic power in the West.

Brigham Young also faced challenges within Mormonism. After
Smith's murder, his scepter as Prophet, Seer and Revelator was
claimed by several Saints, and a bitter battle of succession ensued.
Many Mormons who opposed polygamy remained in Nauvoo and
claimed Smith, before his death, had proclaimed that God wanted
a member of his family to succeed him, not Brigham Young.

As Young struggled against the parched soil of the desert, along
with floods, disease, Indian raiding parties, federal troops, anti-
Mormon bigots and rival prophets to build the Kingdom of God, a
book written by Joseph Smith's mother, Lucy Mack Smith, presented him with another crisis. It was a sweeping history of the
Smith family told with brushstrokes larger than life that sent the
Utah Mormons a clear message: Joseph Smith's family was the
royal family of Mormonism. It had given birth to Mormonism, and
a Smith should be at the head of the church. As the book's popu-
larity spread, one rival faction, calling itself the Reorganized
Church of Jesus Christ of Latter-day Saints, persuaded Smith's
son, Joseph Smith III, to serve as Prophet of its church.

His acceptance, it said, was proof that *its* church was the legitimate successor of the one founded by his father.

Brigham Young found a simple way to deal with the seditious
book in an approach to dealing with disagreeable aspects of history
that would be echoed in the Salt Lake Valley more than a century
later. He ordered the book "gathered up and destroyed, so that no
copies should be left." Anyone who read it, he said, jeopardized his
or her exaltation in the Celestial Kingdom.

After federal troops came to the Utah Territory and arrested
Young and other church leaders, others, pursued by federal marshals, fled to Mexico or Canada. As the boundaries of the country,
energized by a sense of Manifest Destiny, pushed westward, it soon
became apparent that the dream of an independent Mormon religious, economic and political kingdom was doomed. In 1890, thirteen years after the death of Brigham Young, his successors bowed
to the rest of the country's antipathy toward polygamy and re-

nounced its practice on earth while insisting it would resume after death in the Celestial Kingdom.

Within six years, Utah was granted statehood. It was the Mormons' reward for abandoning the temporal practice of polygamy.

In the spiritual ferment that marked the first half of the nineteenth century, hundreds of gurus, seekers, prophets and saviors competed to offer the people of a new nation a new religious vision. Most withered and died like weeds on the plains of the frontier. Of all these cults and sects and schismatic splinter groups, only one—the Church of Jesus Christ of Latter-day Saints—was a significant religious force a century later.

It more than merely survived: By the final quarter of the twentieth century, the once isolated and persecuted frontier sect was America's fastest-growing major religious denomination and a powerful international religious force with branches in more than a hundred countries.

It was also an institution curiously preoccupied—and even haunted—by its own history.

In one of his first revelations, Joseph Smith said God had directed members of the Lord's Elect to make a record of their time on earth, not only a history of the church, but a record of "their manner of life, their faith, and works." Once reassembled, he said, the tribes of Israel were not to make the same mistake as the Lamanites and lose sight of their roots. It was, Smith said, a sacred duty for Mormons to keep diaries, family histories, letters and other documents for future generations. As they trekked across the plains, thousands of Mormons, often working by candlelight, religiously kept journals of their experiences, producing a mother lode of raw material for future historians.

History itself was accorded sacred status in the church.

As an institution, it tied its legitimacy to specific historical events, including Joseph Smith's vision of God and Moroni's revelation of the gold tablets that became the Book of Mormon. On these events rested its claim to being God's only true church.

Unlike Judaism, Roman Catholicism and the other faiths it challenged, Mormonism was born during the era of printing. Its claims, it said, could be proved by records and the tangible history of an ancient people given to Joseph Smith that he called "the most correct of any book on earth and the keystone of our religion."

During the twentieth century, when the outer world began to intrude on the Saints' remote western kingdom, their history was part of the glue that helped bind them together. Mormons were taught that Joseph Smith was a latter-day prophet of biblical stature and Brigham Young was compared to Moses leading his people out of Egypt into the Promised Land.

As the church sent missionaries abroad, history became a critical element in the marketing of the faith born on the American frontier: The Book of Mormon, missionaries argued, was evidence that God selected a young American farm boy, Joseph Smith, to restore His Old Testament church to earth and it was proof that only Mormons had the special knowledge needed to lead others into the most exalted levels of the Kingdom of God. Brigham Young said the choice was simple:

"Every spirit that confesses that Joseph Smith is a Prophet, that he lived and died a Prophet and that the Book of Mormon is true, is of God," he said. "Every spirit that does not is anti-Christ." Any other church, Young said, is "an abomination in God's eyes."

As time passed, the church would learn that history could be a bane as well as a blessing.

3

More than a century after the first pioneers struggled down the canyons of the Wasatch Front, a six-year-old boy, standing within the shadow of the mountain range, looked out at a tableau of faces and declared solemnly:

"I testify to you, I know the Book of Mormon is true. I know Joseph Smith was a prophet of God. I know the Church of Jesus Christ of Latter-day Saints is the only true and living church on the face of the earth."

On the same Sunday in another part of Salt Lake City, another boy, slightly younger, faced a sea of faces and said:

"I testify to you, I know the Book of Mormon is true. I know Joseph Smith was a prophet of God. I know the Church of Jesus Christ of Latter-day Saints is the only true and living church on the face of the earth."

Steven Fred Christensen and Mark William Hofmann were born in Salt Lake City in 1954, eleven months apart, heirs to the society founded by the faith-inspired people who battled nature and some of the most vicious religious persecution in the history of America to build a gathering place for the Lord's Elect.

Christensen was the son of Fred MacRay Christensen, a merchant well known to residents of the Salt Lake Valley as a television pitchman for his own chain of clothing stores. After working as a salesman for a church-owned department store, Mac Christensen had opened his own store, then another, and ultimately became proprietor of a prosperous group of men's stores called Mr. Mac's. In achieving great material success, he had fulfilled a goal that had been part and parcel of Mormonism since its beginnings: to make money. Indeed, the Book of Mormon promised earthly prosperity to those who lived by its truths: *After ye have obtained a hope in Christ ye shall obtain riches, if ye seek them.*

Mark Hofmann was a sixth-generation Mormon whose family's history distilled the travails and triumphs of his faith. His father, William Hofmann, was a native of Switzerland who had been brought by his parents to Salt Lake City as an infant. William's father, Karl Edward Hofmann, a German-born architect, and his Swiss wife, Margrethe Albisser, had heeded the call of Mormon missionaries in Zurich shortly after the turn of the century and, after undertaking their own missions for the church, emigrated to Utah in 1929. Mark's mother, Lucille Sears, was the youngest of ten children born into a polygamous family long after the church had officially renounced polygamy. As a child, Isaac Sears, one of her grandfathers, had joined the great nineteenth-century flood of converts from England to the Salt Lake Valley. Sears's wife, Sarah Gailey, was among the first children born to the pioneers in the Valley. Lucille's other grandfather—Anson Bowen Call, a bookkeeper—was one of hundreds of Mormons who chose to flee to Mexico after 1890 rather than give up polygamy; her maternal grandmother, Mary Theresa Thompson, was one of his five wives. In 1906, at the age of eighteen, Mark's grandmother, Athelia Call, became the second wife of William Gailey Sears, a thirty-three-year-old merchant. That his mother was the product of a polygamous Mormon union sixteen years after the 1890 church manifesto abolishing polygamy and a 1904 proclamation that reinforced it was a secret that members of Mark's family seldom discussed.

Bill Hofmann, after his marriage to Lucille Sears in 1947, left Salt Lake City on a mission for the church in Europe that kept them apart almost three years. In 1953, their first child, a daughter, was born, followed a year later by the birth of Mark and five years later by the arrival of a second daughter. After his mission,

Bill Hofmann worked briefly as a mortician, then started a career as a salesman that in 1960 took the family to the southern California town of Buena Park. After four years they returned to Utah and Mark's father became a salesman for the Pitney Bowes Company, a producer of office machines. While he never achieved the great wealth that many Mormons sought, he was secure in the belief that he was raising a loving family devoted to the values of his religion.

Both of Mark's parents had strong personalities, but as in many Mormon homes, his father ruled as patriarch, and he did so with a firm but kind hand. He had grown up in an austere and regimented household and established much the same atmosphere in the home where Mark was raised, and he saw to it that his children read the Book of Mormon and abided by its principles. As did his wife, Bill Hofmann embraced his faith without doubt or reservation. He was a member of the Lord's Elect; he knew he was one of God's chosen people.

It would be many years before Steve Christensen and Mark Hofmann met. But as they grew to manhood on opposite sides of the Salt Lake Valley, they walked parallel paths in a world of absolutes, certainties, obedience and knowledge that if they obeyed the commandments and led worthy lives, they could become gods.

If there was a part of America that embodied the values that Ronald Reagan would bring to Washington a few years later, it was the Salt Lake Valley during the years of Steve Christensen's and Mark Hofmann's childhoods. By and large, it was a community of pious, hard-working, self-reliant and politically conservative people who regarded helping one another as a sacred obligation and who, more often than not, tried to incorporate the values and morals advocated by their faith into their daily lives.

It was a world in which when people mentioned "the church," there was only one church they could mean. It was a world in which the United States Constitution was considered divinely inspired, laissez-faire capitalism was revered and life centered on the church and old-fashioned families in which the husbands brought home the bacon and their wives stayed home to cook it and raise their children—as many children as possible. It was a woman's sacred duty to marry and bear children, liberating them from the spirit world and preparing them for their progression toward the Celestial Kingdom. As a result, Utah's birth rate was double that in the rest of America.

A church founded by men who commanded young women to bed down with them with the threat of eternal damnation if they refused had produced one of the most prudish of twentieth-century societies: Premarital sex and masturbation were forbidden; adultery was a sin considered so serious that only murder was more grievous; an admission of homosexual acts brought excommunication; and worthy members of the church shunned tobacco, coffee, tea, alcohol and soft drinks containing caffeine.

Although the pioneers of 1847 failed to fulfill Joseph Smith's vision of creating an earthly Kingdom of God, they left as their legacy the nearest thing to a theocracy America had produced, a state in which political, economic and religious power were so intertwined that they seemed one and the same. More than sixty-five percent of the Salt Lake Valley's residents were Mormons. Virtually all of Utah's senior elected officials were members of the church, and so were most of its judges, police officials and professional and business leaders.

Directly or indirectly the church dominated the Valley's economic life in addition to its political life. The church was the city's most important property owner and proprietor of many of its largest and most successful businesses. Private business meetings began with a prayer soliciting God's assistance in making a profit, and church membership was a bond of fraternity that formed the foundation of countless deals and partnerships. Membership in the church engendered trust that helped the community prosper. But the community's spirit of trust—along with the scriptural promise that hardworking members of God's chosen people *deserved* earthly rewards—made many Mormons easy targets for con men and promoters of get-rich-quick schemes. In the 1960s federal investigators began to refer to Utah as the fraud capital of America.

Along with most of their playmates, Steve Christensen and Mark Hofmann were taught early in their lives that they were members of the Lord's Elect.

To grow up in a practicing Mormon family in Salt Lake City during the 1960s was to be enclosed in a hermetically sealed chamber that enveloped children at infancy and continued most of their waking hours. From nursery school onward, they were instructed about the divine origin and absolute truth of the Book of Mormon and taught that *their* church was God's *only* true church and that they were members of a chosen people. *Perfection* was a word they heard often. Beginning in nursery school, they were told that if they strove to lead perfect lives, they were destined to become gods and goddesses.

The Book of Mormon and Joseph Smith's story of its origin formed the foundation of the culture in which they lived. It was the cement that bound everything else together. "Mormonism must stand or fall on the story of Joseph Smith," Joseph Fielding Smith, a grandnephew of the church founder and one of his successors as Prophet, Seer and Revelator, said. "He was either a prophet of God, divinely called, or he was one of the biggest frauds this world has ever seen."

At the grass-roots level, the church was divided into wards of about six hundred people—congregations similar to Roman Catholic parishes—and stakes, larger administrative units comprising several wards that were similar to Catholic dioceses. Each ward was headed by a lay bishop and several counselors. Collectively, the stakes of the church were said to hold up the tent of Zion.

For young Mormons, the sabbath was almost fully occupied by the church: Sunday school at the ward meeting house, sacrament meeting where hymns were sung and faith-inspiring commentaries from members of the ward were heard, then often more meetings that lasted through the day.

On the first Sunday of each month, children fasted along with their parents and the money they would have otherwise spent for food was given to the poor. Then they listened to members of the ward offer their testimony of faith in the church, Joseph Smith and the Book of Mormon.

As soon as they felt ready to do so, children—some as young as five years—were encouraged by their parents to stand up and express *their* testimony of belief in the Book of Mormon.

* * *

On days other than Sunday the church sought to occupy much of its members' time. In many families, parents were absent at night because of meetings or their obligations as home teachers, which required them to visit other members of the ward to ensure that their faith was strong and that they were not in need of spiritual or secular sustenance. Or they were attending a fireside—a group discussion or informal speech at another member's home. On Monday night, however, no meetings could be held because the church directed children and parents to meet for a family home evening to discuss among themselves matters of life, faith and family love.

The church and its teachings were seldom far from the lives of Steve Christensen and Mark Hofmann. At three, the first song Steve memorized was "The Golden Plates." At five, the heroes of his life were the teenage priests, called deacons, who served the sacrament on Sunday mornings. At six, Mark Hofmann thrilled his parents by reciting, verbatim, long passages of Mormon scripture, and singing "I want to go on a mission."

For grade school pupils, there was a never-ending round of instruction on Mormonism. As soon as they could turn words into sentences, children watched and later participated in pageants in which Joseph Smith and the angel Moroni brought forth the Book of Mormon from the Hill Cumorah.

On Saturday mornings, the story was repeated at cartoon shows and children went on overnight "pioneer treks" in the mountains above the Valley to retrace the steps of their forebears. Cub Scout packs and Boy Scout troops were run by the church's Primary Association, which was responsible for the children's religious education starting at the age of eighteen months and integrated religious teachings into scouting and other recreational activities. After-school classes sponsored by the Mutual Improvement Association introduced Mormon girls to the skills that they would need in their designated mission in life: mother and homemaker.

At eight, Steve Christensen and Mark Hofmann, along with other children of the same age, were baptized. At twelve, they were ordained as deacons in the Aaronic priesthood, beginning what they were told was lifelong participation in the priesthood of the church. If a Mormon boy accepted the priesthood and later denied it, they were taught, he had little chance of ever entering the Celestial Kingdom and becoming a god.

As they grew older, the presence of the church grew even larger in the lives of Christensen and Hofmann. Mormons were excused from classes at public high schools for instruction at church-owned seminaries located next to the school. Instruction continued at church-owned institutes of religion at their colleges and universities. As they completed more religious instruction, Mormon boys were elevated in the priesthood: at fourteen to the rank of teacher, at sixteen to priest, with increasing responsibilities to strengthen the faith of other Saints. Then, usually at nineteen, they were ordained as Elders in the Melchizedek priesthood. In a ninety-minute endowment ceremony in a Mormon temple, they learned more about the church, moving from a simulated Garden of Eden into multiple levels of heaven, progressing from "one degree of glory to another," to a lavishly appointed room symbolizing the Celestial Kingdom. They learned secret passwords, signs and handclasps; they were given sacred garments that were to protect them from harm, which they were to wear beneath their clothing for life; and they were assured of their exaltation to godhood on Judgment Day if they led worthy lives, kept the temple rituals secret, obeyed the commandments and married in the temple.

To those who might argue that so pervasive a campaign to implant the articles of faith in children so young constituted an effort to gain permanent control over their minds and produce programmed and obedient adults, it could be said that other religions, secular as well as spiritual, had attempted to do as much for centuries. For its part, the church could respond that one of its articles of faith declared that every man and woman was a free agent, that God had given each the right to make a personal choice between good and evil.

And, as events would show, not all Mormons in the generation into which Steve Christensen and Mark Hofmann were born accepted without question the lessons of their youth.

4

In 1954, the year Steve Christensen and Mark Hofmann were born, the Mormon church's membership passed 1.3 million. A decade later, it was nearing 2.3 million. As bicycle-riding missionaries pedaled their way around the world, converts by the thousands joined the flock each year. A church born in conflict on the American frontier became an international organization, and in its native country an institution whose leaders were once pursued across the plains by federal marshals began to enter the mainstream of American life.

In 1952, Ezra Taft Benson, a high priest and Apostle of the church, had been appointed Secretary of Agriculture by President Eisenhower. In 1962, George Romney, a Mormon, had been elected to the first of three terms as Governor of Michigan and was soon touted as a Republican presidential candidate. Mormons such as hotel tycoon J. Willard Marriott moved into prominent positions in American business. And in national radio broadcasts and tours in which it inevitably brought down the house by singing "The Battle Hymn of the Republic," the Mormon Tabernacle Choir added luster to the image of an organization that was eager to lose its reputation as a strange, eccentric cult with roots in polygamy.

As the church's membership and respectability grew, so did its wealth. Many of the businesses the church established after the settlers' arrival in the Salt Lake Valley had matured into large and prosperous enterprises. With its heritage in the optimism and capitalist fervor of nineteenth-century America, the church had made the pursuit of wealth an almost sacred goal of its members and shared, like a silent partner, in their success. To obtain their bishop's annual Temple Recommend—a slip of paper allowing them to participate in the temple rites that advanced them and their ancestors toward eternal salvation—Mormons had to contribute ten percent of their incomes to the church. Tithing, together with profits from the businesses it owned, delivered a cascade of money to the church in Salt Lake City that by the 1960s had made it one of the richest institutions on earth—the owner of shopping centers, office towers, huge farms, industrial parks, hotels, insurance companies, television stations and other property worth billions of dollars.

Yet, for all of the success, there was an uneasiness within the hierarchy of the church.

The Saints had long since lost the physical isolation that once sequestered them from the gentile world. But they had managed during the first half of the twentieth century to remain largely apart from the rest of the country, bonded not by physical isolation but by the shared belief in their uniqueness as members of the Lord's Elect, by their moral code and emphasis on the family as an everlasting unit and, to some extent, by the hostility of others.

In the 1950s and 1960s, however, it became increasingly difficult to isolate the Saints from the influences of the outer world.

Transported by television, the jet plane and the interstate highway, the forces of social change that were reshaping life in all of America arrived in the Salt Lake Valley. From a new acceptance of abortion and homosexuality to a new skepticism about authority produced by the civil rights and antiwar movements, the church's influence over the lives and virtue of its members seemed by its leaders to be under assault.

Among many legacies that Joseph Smith bequeathed to his people were two that in the postwar years began to cause problems for those leaders of the church who wanted to maintain an authoritarian rule over the lives of its members: The first was his insistence that Mormons keep histories of their time on earth; the second was an emphasis on education as an essential ingredient in man's eternal progression toward perfection. "A man is saved no faster," the Mormon Prophet said, "than he gets education."

Smith's account of receiving the gold plates from Moroni on the Hill Cumorah, their subsequent translation and his testimony that God had directed him to restore His Old Testament church to earth had been challenged almost since the day the Book of Mormon was published. Critics ranged from early apostates to Sir Arthur Conan Doyle.

In a caustically anti-Mormon book published in 1834, *Mormonism Unveiled,* E. D. Howe, an investigative journalist of the day, published a collection of affidavits from friends and neighbors of Smith who described him as a lackadaisical and lying religious con man who claimed supernatural powers that enabled him to find buried treasure in ancient Indian burial mounds with stones and divining rods.

When Doyle, a mildly successful British mystery writer, decided to introduce to his readers a new hero called Sherlock Holmes almost half a century after Joseph Smith's death, he chose the Mormons as his first villains. Holmes's *A Study in Scarlet* depicted Utah's Mormons as a murderous and licentious cult ruled by terror and the Danite band.

Church leaders called such attacks the work of Satan, unprincipled muckrakers, bigots and embittered former Mormons. But in 1945, an attack on the Book of Mormon came from close range: A young Mormon historian, Fawn M. Brodie, a niece of David O. McKay, a church Elder who later became its Prophet, Seer and Revelator, wrote a biography of Joseph Smith, *No Man Knows My History,* that, in more than four hundred pages of clinical detail, purported to expose the story of the birth of the church and the translation of the Book of Mormon as a fraud. Much of the material she cited in support of her thesis had been drawn from diaries and other documents kept by early Mormons in compliance with Smith's history-keeping mandate, offering evidence to modern Mormon leaders that history was a sword with two edges.

Joseph Smith's emphasis on education produced during the twentieth century a large system of schools, seminaries, religious institutes and colleges, including the flagship of the system, Brigham Young University in Provo, Utah. And it would also produce conflicts in the minds of many young Mormons that would tear at their hearts and souls.

Among the new generation of lawyers, physicians, professors, scientists and businessmen who had been indoctrinated in the principles of Mormonism starting in nursery school were some who began to ask skeptical questions about the church's teachings.

Church authorities told them to accept what they were told on faith. "When our leaders speak," a handbook for Mormon teachers declared, "the thinking has been done. When they propose a plan, it is God's plan. When they point the way, there is no other which is safe."

"Knowledge," said Apostle Bruce R. McConkie, "is gained by obedience. It comes by obedience to the laws and ordinances of the gospel."

But questioning by the new generation of educated Mormons persisted nevertheless, and during the 1950s there were the beginnings of an intellectual movement within the church.

Some scholars reared as Mormons suggested that perhaps not every word of the Book of Mormon and the story of its origins need be regarded as the literal truth. Others, applying the discipline of academic scholarship, began to reevaluate the lives of early church leaders and to study church practices such as polygamy that leaders of the modern church, who were seeking broader acceptance for it, preferred to say as little about as possible.

Adding to the ferment was the unhappiness of some Mormons over the church's refusal to accept blacks into its priesthood, a barrier imposed because Joseph Smith and Brigham Young had said they bore the biblical "mark of Cain."

In 1960, the church acted decisively to protect the faith of its members from intrusions by the outer world, to halt the challenges to the truthfulness of the Book of Mormon and to increase obedience to the church hierarchy. The job was given to an organization called the Correlation Committee. It was assigned to review, correlate and change church publications and statements to ensure they were consistent "for doctrinal soundness and correctness of doctrinal interpretation." There was to be one consistent story. To deviate in any way was heresy.

The Correlation Committee, however, was unable to stifle the incipient intellectual movement, and a conservative wing of church leaders led by Ezra Taft Benson demanded a stronger crackdown. Mrs. Brodie was excommunicated for heresy; much of the church's historical archives was placed off-limits to scholars and when historians were admitted to less-restricted archives they were monitored by church representatives who reviewed their notes to ensure that they had recorded nothing that was harmful to the church or otherwise veered from orthodoxy. In some communities teenage Mormon elders went to local libraries and removed Mrs. Brodie's book and others that were considered critical of the church. At Brigham Young University in 1964, professors who accepted the theory of evolution without reservation or expressed views considered religiously or politically subversive were monitored and reported on by a ring of student spies organized by a senior administrator at the university.

In many ways, the atmosphere imposed by the church's most conservative leaders would evoke comparisons with the world depicted by George Orwell in *1984*. Orwell's totalitarian world was ruled by a Thought Police that indoctrinated children in what they were to believe beginning in infancy and then forced adults to accept unquestioningly whatever their leaders told them was the truth because only the leaders were in possession of absolute truth. It was a world in which history books were burned, history was rewritten and the past was defined by what the rulers said it was.

"Who controls the past controls the future," Orwell's ruling party said: "who controls the present controls the past."

Yet the fledgling Mormon intellectual movement persisted.

In 1966, a group of scholars established a new organization, the Mormon History Association, and publicly sought access to the thousands of diaries of early Mormons and other historical documents that the church had placed off-limits. Several church members established *Dialogue: A Journal of Mormon Thought,* which printed interpretive articles that were generally in accord with orthodox Mormon dogma but occasionally pointed to apparent inconsistencies or puzzles in it.

At the same time that the intellectuals were pressing for more freedom of thought, the task of managing the church's rapid growth and far-flung economic interests had begun to overwhelm its spiritual leaders. Most had been elevated to positions of ecclesiastical authority after proving themselves in successful careers in business. But as the church grew, many acknowledged that they were out of their depth in managing its activities. In a sweeping reorganization of the church's bureaucracy, they decided to professionalize management operations in Salt Lake City. As part of this program, the hierarchy in 1972 appointed Leonard Arrington, a Utah State University economist and author of *Great Basin Kingdom,* a 1958 book that was considered a classic among Western histories, as Church Historian. Until then, only high-ranking spiritual leaders of the church had served as Historian.

The appointment of Arrington, who had been one of the founders of the Mormon History Association, initiated a period of intellectual freedom in the church that Mormon historians would later call Camelot.

It was an appointment the church hierarchy would regret.

5

Dear Elder Christensen:

You are hereby called to be a missionary of The Church of Jesus Christ of Latter-day Saints to labor in the Australia Melbourne Mission. . . . It will be your duty to live righteously, to keep the commandments of the Lord, to honor the Holy Priesthood which you bear, to increase your testimony of the divinity of the Restored Gospel of Jesus Christ, to be an exemplar in your life of all the Christian virtues, and so to conduct yourself as a devoted servant of the Lord that you may be an effective advocate and messenger of the Truth. . . .

At high school in the Salt Lake City suburb of Bountiful, Steve Christensen was an honor student and student body officer. He also found time to work forty hours a week at his father's store, to fulfill his priesthood responsibilities and to pursue what would become a lifelong obsession: reading and collecting history books, especially histories of his church.

There were five sons and three daughters in Mac Christensen's family, all of whom, to a greater or lesser degree, felt the outsized presence of a demanding and hard-charging father who set high standards for himself and those around him, especially members of his own family. His wife, Joan, by contrast, was easygoing, calmer, introverted.

Steve Christensen had his father's drive and religious piety but his mother's personality. Dark-haired and good-looking, popular with girls, he was warm and outgoing, but at the same time reticent and introspective: He was as content to stay up all night with a new book as he was to go to a dance. He preferred the debate team to the football team, the library to the basketball court, reading to almost anything.

There had never been any doubt in Steve Christensen's home that he would go on a mission.

The church asked all spiritually worthy young men to accept the call and even enlisted Mormon girls—from nursery school onward —to convince boys that it was their duty to go on a mission. Still, only about one third of the boys went abroad on a mission. To accept a call was not a decision to be taken lightly, for it could cause economic hardship for a young man's family, whose duty it was to pay the expenses of his mission. And as other youths went off to college, got married, started careers, began families, it meant knocking on hostile doors in virtually any corner of the world and receiving far more rejections than conversions to Mormonism.

Steve Christensen did not hesitate when the letter arrived at his home in 1973 shortly after his nineteenth birthday. After six weeks at the church's missionary training center, he began searching for converts among Italian-speaking Australians. The most stirring spiritual experience of his young life, he would say later, was standing with a group of Italian immigrants in Melbourne and singing a Mormon hymn, "The Poor Wayfaring Man of Grief." He knew then, he said, that Jesus was the true savior and that Joseph Smith was a true prophet of God.

After almost two years in Australia, Christensen returned to Salt Lake City to get on with the rest of his life. He enrolled at the University of Utah, went back to work at his father's clothing store and then he fell in love. The girl was Terri Romney, a distant relative of George Romney's who was three years younger than Christensen. They were members of the same ward and had known each other as children. When he left on his mission she was thin, gawky, adolescent. When he returned she was beautiful, with dark eyes and blonde hair that swept to her shoulders. Two months after his return from Australia, Christensen spoke about his mission at a fireside in the ward. She was in the audience, and later he called her and asked for a date.

On September 16, 1976, they were sealed for time and all eternity in the Salt Lake Temple, and within two weeks Terri was pregnant. Nothing could have given her more joy. She had begun to fulfill the role that she had been told since childhood was her duty to fill: It was the duty God had intended for her.

"It was all I ever wanted," she would recall several years later. "I just wanted to stay home and be a mother."

Ten days before Mark Hofmann's nineteenth birthday, on November 27, 1973, he received his call to serve a mission and he responded just as promptly as Steve Christensen:

"Please be assured of my eagerness to serve in the England Southwest Mission," he replied. "I have a strong testimony and promise to serve my Heavenly Father diligently and represent my family, church and mission well. I sustain the leaders of the church," he said, "and all those in authority within my mission. I pray that we may lead many people to the truths of the Gospel."

It was perhaps when Mark left for England that Bill and Lucille Hofmann first began to consider the possibility that their son might someday become a General Authority, one of the eighty-five men who ran the Church of Jesus Christ of Latter-day Saints. At the top of the hierarchy was the President, Prophet, Seer and Revelator, who as the lineal successor of Joseph Smith could speak with the authority of God. Next came his two counselors who shared the Office of the First Presidency. Ranked beneath them was the Council of Twelve Apostles, considered successors to the twelve Apostles of Jesus Christ; finally there was the First Quorum of the Seventy, seventy men who administered its ecclesiastical and economic interests.

Mark, Bill Hofmann said, was destined to be a General Authority. Perhaps, his wife suggested, he might even become Prophet.

Like Steve Christensen, Hofmann was bookish and introverted and fascinated by history. And like Christensen, he had few close friends and seldom confided his thoughts to anyone. But in other ways the two young men were different: Mark's interests were broader than Steve Christensen's; he had many hobbies including magic, chemistry, electronics and stamp and coin collecting, and he earned a letter as a long-distance runner on the high school cross-country team. He was not as good a student as Steve. When he was graduated from Olympus High School in Salt Lake City, in June 1973, he ranked 573rd in a class of seven hundred.

The following spring, Mark, who like other Mormon missionaries was deferred from the draft as a minister of religion, arrived in England. It was a country that had been the setting for some of his church's greatest missionary triumphs.

Mormon missionaries arrived in England in 1837, offering the subjects of a poverty-troubled land not only membership in the Lord's Elect but an invitation to join a visionary communal society in the New World. Their success was spectacular. Almost half the eighty thousand Mormons who made their way across the plains to Utah between 1847 and 1870 were from England and Ireland.

Mark Hofmann, one of almost ten thousand missionaries sent abroad by the church in 1974, was assigned to the port city of Bristol. Wearing a dark suit, white shirt and tie—the universal uniform of the Mormon missionary—he and a succession of male companions traveling in tandem roamed southwestern England and Wales. Later, Mark boasted to his family that he had baptized several converts to the church, the ultimate achievement of a mission. He did not tell them that in his spare time, he spent a lot of time reading Fawn Brodie's book, *No Man Knows My History.*

Along with his mission companions, he visited medieval castles, Stonehenge, the Cotswolds and the Roman ruins at Bath. Wherever they went, Hofmann headed first for a library, then a bookstore. Along with other missionaries, he removed anti-Mormon books and sometimes left a Book of Mormon in their place.

To his pleasure, he discovered books that were centuries old could be purchased for a few dollars and his visits to the bookshops soon took on the excitement of a treasure hunt: He bought old copies of the Book of Mormon and anti-Mormon books and told his friends if they looked long enough in the musty bookshops they might find a rarity that would make them rich and famous.

Despite his efforts, however, Hofmann never made his great discovery, and in the spring of 1976 he returned from his mission and enrolled at Utah State University in Logan, a small town nestled beneath the Wasatch Front in the Cache Valley seventy miles north of Salt Lake City.

Before long, he, too, fell in love.

6

Her name was Judy Smith, and she was the first girl he ever kissed, the first girl he ever dated. They met when he was her home teacher for the student ward and he called to audit her faithfulness to the church. At colleges with large numbers of Mormons, student wards helped the church maintain ties to students and provided a venue for social events that usually produced several marriages each year.

Two months after they met, Mark asked her for a date, and seven months later, as they sat alone in a park, he asked her:

"Do you love me?"

"Yes," she said.

"Enough to marry me?"

"Yes," she answered, and Mark gave her a diamond engagement ring, financed by the sale of some of the coins from his collection.

Dark-haired and slender, filled with the energy and dreams of youth, they were a handsome couple with clean-cut, innocent looks like those often seen on college campuses in Utah.

But in many ways it was an incongruous pairing: Even after confronting unfriendly strangers for almost two years in England, Mark was shy and ill at ease with people. An introverted pre-med

student who wore the same dark suit and tie to classes that he wore
as a missionary, he spent hours alone in the library, reading history
books and old historical documents.

By contrast, Judy Smith was vivacious, stylish and extroverted,
an officer in her sorority who had many friends to his few. But she
found in Mark's shyness a tenderness and sensitivity that made her
fall in love, and after she accepted his ring, they decided to marry
in five months, on September 7, 1977.

The wedding, however, never took place.

Just why Mark's parents did not warm to the prospect of Judy
Smith as a daughter-in-law would later become blurred by conflicting recollections, but one thing was certain: They did not regard
her as sufficiently committed to the church to help their son rise in
the church hierarchy and become a General Authority.

It was a joke at some Utah campuses, partially based on truth,
that one reason some Mormon women went to college was to earn
an "R.M." (Returned Missionary) degree. Their obligation in life
was to marry and bear children, not to become career women.
Judy Smith, however, intended to work as a journalist after her
graduation, and this plan was not received with enthusiasm by
Mark's parents. His mother said that Judy should serve as a volunteer in the Relief Society, as she and many other women in the
church did. Other stresses also tore at the engagement. Judy and
Mark began to argue about church history and the Book of Mormon, and the differences became a source of increasing tension
between them.

Two months before the wedding, Judy returned Mark's ring,
then took it back a few days later after he sent her roses and asked
for another chance. But eight days before the wedding was to take
place in the Salt Lake Temple, she returned the ring for good and
the wedding was canceled.

As romances are sometimes wont to do, theirs did not die when
it appeared to end. They dated sporadically for almost two years
before they finally drifted apart and Mark, to Judy's surprise, told
her he had made other plans for his life. On September 14, 1979,
only six weeks after his last date with Judy, Mark married Doralee
Olds, a bright home-economics student with long, light-brown hair
that cascaded below her shoulders.

Dorie Olds, like Terri Christensen, wanted to fulfill her calling as

wife and mother, and Bill and Lue Hofmann said she would be a
perfect wife for a future leader of the church.

After marrying in the Salt Lake Temple, Mark and Dorie posed
outside the temple for pictures, then returned to Logan. Mark
reappeared at his haunts in the university library and wondered
how to make his mark on life.

What had ended his relationship with Judy Smith was a sense of
disillusionment in his church. If there was a Rosetta stone that
others could turn to later to understand Mark Hofmann, perhaps it
was a college essay, prepared in the style of a letter to his mother,
that he wrote in 1979 a few months before his relationship with
Judy finally came to an end.

During his visit home for Easter dinner, Hofmann recalled in
the letter to his mother, he had criticized the church for concealing
embarrassing historical documents, and his mother had defended
the practice, saying that if there were documents that undermined
members' faith, they should not be made public.

This led Mark to describe to his mother a dilemma he was confronting:

The Mormon is taught from Primary on up that he, unlike his
non-Mormon friends, "knows" with absolute certainty the answers to the knottiest problems of existence, that in fact his
search has come to an end, and that his main task in life is to
present these truths to others so that they too may end their
quest. In reality, however, Mormons are also subject to uncertainties and doubts.

He said that he had admitted having doubts about aspects of
church doctrine to his religious instructors and later his bishop.
But he said he was told to forget them and then questioned about
his personal life, as if his questions revealed something was wrong
with *him*. He said his bishop told him to go to the temple once a
month and to study the scriptures an hour daily—a procedure he
said he had tried but found a "perfect waste of time" as far as
resolving the conflicts stirring in him.

"Academia teaches the student to be critical of everything including itself," Hofmann said in the essay.

The student is taught to accept nothing without first questioning. Mormonism, on the other hand, teaches that spiritual things are to be accepted on faith. At church the LDS student is taught (both verbally and by other more subtle but equally effective means) not to question the church for doubts are inspired by the devil and "faithful members of the church never doubt." Indeed, I have talked to young church members who have the idea that thinking is actually a sin.

I am learning at the university to think, investigate, read, and then form an opinion. The church, however, seems to be saying to me to ask the leaders and trust their answer. Why should I be inquisitive and doubting at the university and not at church? . . . The individual's conscience and the weight of authority or public opinion, are thus pitted against each other so that the individual either denies them to himself at the expense of personal honesty or hides them from others and lives in two worlds.

Hofmann did not inform his mother, but he had decided to live in two worlds.

7

On weekday mornings, Steve Christensen studied business and finance at the University of Utah; afternoons and Saturdays, he sold suits at his father's store; evenings and in the early morning hours, he read and catalogued his growing collection of books about religion and church history. And he wondered when he would be able to escape the shadow of his father, who preferred to run things his way, not Steve's way.

One customer, a close friend of his father's, was a tall businessman with prematurely gray hair who liked expensive suits. His name was J. Gary Sheets.

Sheets was already a legend in his ward and rapidly becoming one in Salt Lake City's financial community. Born into a poor Vermont family, he had never known his mother, who died of pneumonia when he was three, and had seen little of his father as a child. He worked his way through the University of Utah, where he joined Sigma Chi and became engaged to Kathy Webb, a member of Kappa Kappa Gamma. After their marriage in the Salt Lake Temple in 1958 he sold encyclopedias, then insurance, and in 1971 he founded his own company, Coordinated Financial Services.

He had a vision of a new kind of financial planning company—a

one-stop center where moneyed clients could buy tax shelters, insurance, securities and real estate and make other investments that
were coordinated with the objective of reducing their taxes. Sheets
attracted his first clients with an unusual gimmick: He sent a dollar
bill to doctors, lawyers, business proprietors and other affluent professionals—most of whom were members of the church—along
with a letter offering the dollar in exchange for their time while
they read how he could lower their taxes. To those who replied, he
promised tax-sheltered investments that could yield earnings up-
ward of twenty percent a year.

Sheets's salesmanship, along with good timing, enabled his clients to share in a spectacular boom in Western real estate during
the 1970s, and before long Sheets himself was a multi-millionaire.
It was a classic success story, the kind of story Utahans expected to
hear, because it validated their belief that members of the Lord's
Elect who worked hard and led worthy lives would prosper.

Gary Sheets liked the soft-spoken and serious young man who
fitted him for suits at Mr. Mac's, and he knew Steve Christensen
was anxious to strike out on his own. He told Steve that he didn't
want to steal an employee from one of his best friends, but if he
ever decided to leave his father's employment, he should look him
up.

As Steve Christensen and Mark Hofmann searched for com-
passes to help them set the course of their lives, the breezes of
intellectual freedom that washed over the Mormon Church during
the early 1970s were running into increasing resistance.

Leonard Arrington, the professor who was appointed Church
Historian in 1972, had recruited a team of young historians who
had launched an unprecedented effort to chronicle the saga of the
Saints, using as raw materials millions of previously locked-up
pages of diaries, letters and other documents accumulated in the
church archives since 1830. They produced a stream of scholarly
papers that illuminated the lives of ordinary Mormons as they
pushed handcarts over gutted prairie trails to Zion, and they embarked on more ambitious writing projects, including a detailed
sixteen-volume history of the church, each volume by a different
author, that was to be published beginning in 1980, the 150th anniversary of the church's founding.

Perhaps it was inevitable that the spiritually committed leaders of a religion that had fought mobs, skeptics and virulent bigotry for almost 150 years would grow uneasy about such a sudden and enthusiastic probing into its past. They suspected that around every corner were enemies waiting to bludgeon the church and its claim to being God's *only* true church. And they expected these enemies to use whatever weapon they could to do so. They believed —as did perhaps the Roman Catholic cardinals who for centuries had limited access to the Vatican archives—that admitting friendly or even neutral scholars into the filing cabinets of the church was also to risk admitting its enemies.

The race to explore its frontier past was occurring at a time when the church was succeeding on other fronts in cultivating a more appealing and modern image. Its welfare system, which provided food and other assistance to needy Mormons, was winning national praise; more and more Mormons were moving into positions of power in business, entertainment, sports and other fields; and in 1978 the church acted to end one of its most serious public relations problems: Prophet Spencer W. Kimball said God had revealed to him that the church should now accept blacks to its priesthood.

Word was passed to Arrington's historians that they were going too far, that some of their research was bordering on betrayal of the church. The historians began suspecting they were being spied on by conservative General Authorities. One librarian underlined their writings that he considered threatening to the faith of Mormons and sent the annotated historical research to members of the hierarchy. Soon, General Authorities complained directly to the historians that their scholarship too often depicted early leaders of the church in ways that they said would diminish their stature in the eyes of contemporary Mormons. Smudging the reputations of dead church leaders was just as wrong as criticizing those who were still alive. Joseph Smith's occasional wine drinking, his land speculation, his prodigious appetite for young wives were topics best left unexplored. A chapter on polygamy was ordered excised from one publication after General Authorities said that not only would it be embarrassing to the church, which looked on that phase of Mormonism as a closed chapter, but it would encourage modern Mormon fundamentalists who claimed the right to practice polygamy because Joseph Smith and Brigham Young had done so.

Arrington's team was attacked for publishing articles in what their conservative critics considered subversive publications: *Dialogue* and *Sunstone Review,* another journal of Mormon intellectuals. Ezra Taft Benson, a longtime church Apostle whose good health, age and seniority seemed to ensure he would some day reach the top of the hierarchy as Prophet, Seer and Revelator, objected to use of the words "communal life" and "communitarianism" in articles describing Joseph Smith's attempts to create a communal economy for the frontier Saints. It smacked too much, he said, of *communism,* of which Benson was a vociferous and widely known enemy.

Benson also denounced Arrington's scholars for a "humanistic emphasis on history." He attacked historians who "underplay revelation and God's intervention in significant events and . . . inordinately humanize the prophets of God so that their human frailties become more evident than their spiritual qualities."

Probing into the church's past by the historians finally became too much for the General Authorities. They canceled Arrington's plans for a sixteen-volume history of the church and other projects, and Boyd K. Packer, a conservative Apostle who rose to power as an administrator of the church's religious institutes and seminaries, announced that objectivity was not required in Mormon scholars.

"In an effort to be objective, impartial and scholarly," he told an audience of students and faculty at Brigham Young University, "a writer or teacher may unwittingly be giving equal time to the adversary."

Packer told Arrington's historians: "Those of you who are employed by the church have a special responsibility to *build faith,* not destroy it. If you do not do that, but in fact accommodate the enemy, you become in a sense a traitor to the cause you have made covenants to protect."

8

Leonard Arrington was gathering up his notes after finishing a lecture at Utah State University in April 1980 when a former student approached him from the audience.

"I have something interesting I want to talk to you about after this session is over," Jeff Simmonds whispered. "Don't run off before I get a chance to see you."

A. J. Simmonds, curator of the university's special collection of early Western books and rare documents, told Arrington a tantalizing story:

The previous day, Mark Hofmann, a U.S.U. pre-med student who collected Mormon coins and currency, had brought him a 1668 Cambridge edition of the King James Bible and asked him to examine it, along with a piece of paper that was stuck between its pages when he bought it.

Hofmann said he had bought the Bible the previous month because it was inscribed by a Samuel Smith, possibly the great-grandfather or great-great-grandfather of Joseph Smith, both of whom lived in the eighteenth century. When he opened the Bible, he said, he discovered the folded sheet of paper bonded between two pages with hard, rubbery glue.

A brief handwritten note was faintly visible on the outside of the folded paper and signed "Joseph Smith Jr." Hofmann said he had cut the paper out of the Bible with a razor blade but couldn't get it open and asked Simmonds for advice on how to do so without harming the fragile, apparently very old document.

Simmonds told Arrington he had compared the handwriting of the note to a sample of Joseph Smith's signature from the university archives and decided they were similar. But he said it was not the possibility that the Mormon Prophet's signature was written on the document that began to make his heart pound: He said he had peeked inside a corner of the folded paper and saw what appeared to be Egyptian hieroglyphics.

Simmonds said he next read the message that was dimly inscribed in faded brown ink on the outside of the paper, and when he did the pounding in his heart grew stronger:

These charactors were diligently coppied by my own hand from the plates of gold and given to Martin Harris who took them to New York City but the learned could not translate it because the Lord would not open it to them in fulfillment of the prophecy of Isaih written in the 29th chapter and 11th verse.

Joseph Smith Jr.

Simmonds, a large and scholarly-looking man with long hair and thick glasses, was not a Mormon. But he had lived in Utah long enough to recognize the significance of those words: It was *possible* he was holding the Anthon Transcript, the sheet of paper on which Joseph Smith in 1828 had copied symbols from the gold plates and which he had given to Martin Harris to show Professors Charles Anthon and Samuel Mitchell.

Using solvent and a scalpel, Simmonds cut away the hard black glue bonding the edges of the sheet of paper and opened it. Fully opened, it measured about eight by eleven inches and was covered by drawings and symbols that meant nothing to Simmonds, although that did not surprise him.

He recalled that in an 1834 affidavit Charles Anthon described the sheet of paper brought to him by Martin Harris, and he found a copy of it. Anthon stated that the paper Harris showed him

consisted "of all kinds of crooked characters disposed in columns;
Greek and Hebrew letters, crosses and flourishes, Roman letters
inverted or placed sideways, were arranged in perpendicular columns and the whole ended in a rude delineation of a circle divided
into various compartments decked with various strange
marks. . . ."

The Reorganized Church of Jesus Christ of Latter-day Saints,
which was founded by Mormons who remained in Nauvoo after
Brigham Young led others to Utah in 1847, owned a document
suspected of being a copy of the Anthon Transcript. But the symbols on it were arranged left to right in parallel lines, not perpendicular as Anthon's affidavit stated, and it did not contain a circle.

Hofmann's piece of paper, Simmonds told him excitedly, appeared to match Anthon's description of it exactly.

Hofmann hurriedly left to show the document to Dan Bachman,
a historian at the church Institute of Religion at Utah State. "Call
me, night or day, whenever you learn anything," Simmonds
shouted as he left. Later, Simmonds would call opening the folded
piece of paper a historian's dream come true, one that had given
him "the same sort of satisfaction that Howard Carter had when
he peered into King Tut's tomb [and said]: 'I see things, wonderful
things.' "

Bachman drove Mark to Salt Lake City the following afternoon
to solicit the opinion of Dean Jessee, the church Historical Department's best-known expert on handwriting and old documents.

After examining the document for several minutes, Jessee broke
into a smile:

The writing on the yellowed sheet of paper, he said, *appeared* to
be that of Joseph Smith, the church prophet.

Jessee cautioned that he would need several days to be sure of
his initial conclusion. Then all agreed to keep the matter a secret
until he made a final decision. Hofmann, however, was unable to
keep his secret from two people. As many Mormons did, he kept a
journal to record the events of his life and on April 21, 1980, he
confided in the journal that he had broken the news of the discovery to Bill and Lucille Hofmann.

They think that it's not a coincidence that the Lord brought it forth in the sesquicentennial year. They, as I, can hardly believe it. They want me to take good care of it now that the Lord has brought it forth.

Hofmann noted that Bachman had also broken his vow of secrecy and told Jan Shipps, an Indiana college professor who was president of the Mormon History Association, about the discovery:

Jan said she was speechless when he told her. She also said that she thought the announcement should be made through scholarly channels and that it was worth lots of money. She said "one with five zeroes behind it."

Hofmann's studies for the medical school entrance examination were forgotten. Three days later he returned to the church headquarters and received a hero's welcome. Dean Jessee signed a statement declaring, "I carefully inspected the document shown to me by Mark Hofmann on April 18, 1980 which begins with the words, 'These characters were diligently copied . . .' and signed 'Joseph Smith Jr.' and conclude that the document is a Joseph Smith holograph."

Then the shy, twenty-five-year-old college senior was ushered into the office of the First Presidency, center of the universe for the world's Mormons. In an ornate room with a simple wooden conference table, he was introduced to the three senior leaders of the church: Prophet, Seer and Revelator Spencer W. Kimball and his counselors, Presidents Nathan Eldon Tanner and Marion G. Romney.

The three men, all in their eighties, ruled the church under a patriarchal system that reserved the highest positions of power for those who lived the longest. They listened as he described his discovery, and Arrington, Bachman, Apostles Gordon B. Hinckley and Boyd K. Packer and other church officials shared what all regarded as a historic moment for the church: The Anthon Transcript had been found.

Hofmann was deferential and timid among the highest officials of his church, and bewildered by the attention suddenly accorded him. He described his mission in England and how it had inspired

him to collect old books from the church's past and how he had
come to possess the unusual document:

He said that because it contained Samuel Smith's signature, he
had bought the Bible the previous month from an acquaintance
who had purchased it in Carthage, Illinois, from a descendant of
Catherine Smith Salisbury, one of Joseph Smith's sisters. Now he
hoped the church would help him determine whether it was authentic or not. If it was genuine, he said it was his hope that the
Anthon Transcript would remain forever in the custody of the
church.

Six days later, the church's Public Communications Department
announced Hofmann's discovery at a press conference that made
the reticent college student an overnight celebrity in the Mormon
world and produced headlines around the world. Excited church
officials said there was little doubt the newly discovered document
was genuine.

"We can see more clearly than ever before what the characters
were like on the gold plates," Dean Jessee said.

"Are you sure it was written by Joseph Smith?" a reporter
asked.

"It is impossible to conclude that anyone other than Joseph
Smith wrote this," Jessee answered.

Comparing the Anthon Transcript's discovery to the discovery
of the Dead Sea Scrolls, Mormon historians predicted modern
computers, linguists and cryptologists would be able to translate
the characters from the gold plates just as Joseph Smith had done
when he transcribed the Book of Mormon using the special stones
loaned to him by the angel Moroni.

"This offers as good a test as we'll ever get of the authenticity of
the Book of Mormon," said Hugh Nibley, a prominent Mormon
scholar. "It can be translated."

Meanwhile, those leaders of the church who had worried that
eager rummaging by historians into the church's past endangered
the faith of Mormons could rejoice: The Anthon Transcript was
faith promoting.

Within a few weeks, there was more good news: A prominent
scholar announced that he had deciphered the Anthon Transcript.

9

There was little doubt, Barry Fell thought as he looked up from a photograph of the Anthon Transcript in his office near Boston. Its characters were encoded in Arabic in a primitive cipher and revealed the existence of an ancient book by an author named Nephi or Nefi. The symbols on the document, he said, had been copied by an illiterate hand in not one but five different archaic North African scripts.

Fell—marine biologist, linguist, professor emeritus at Harvard, director of the National Decipherment Center, president of the Epigraphic Society—had spent much of his professional life trying to decode the writings of ancient peoples. Within a few weeks of its discovery, he said he believed he had translated the Anthon Transcript, and he wrote down the text:

Revelation of Nephi: I have written these things. . . .

I, Nefi, a son born to sagacious parents . . . in series 19 of Ancient Alphabets . . . have transcribed this:
Zedekiah in Judah had just begun his reign
My father, Lehi, was of Salem, the Holy City Most Sacred (The

19th cipher still I write) It happened that a tornado occurred. Brilliant lightning flashed overhead. . . .

In a report sent to linguists at Brigham Young University, Fell said he believed authors of the ancient history employed an obscure cipher that had been used in Baghdad during the ninth century by agents of the Caliph Aabdul Malik bin Manwan. There was also evidence in the document of a cipher used by scholars in ancient Israel to encode sacred books and keep them secret from gentiles. "The decipherment," he concluded, "leads me to believe that there must once have existed, and may yet exist, an ancient book entitled the Revelation of Nefi, dealing at its outset with some events at the beginning of the reign of King Zedekiah in 597-596 B.C., and that an Arabic version of this book, or a fragment of it, was known to exist as late as the 12th or 13th century A.D., when some unidentified scribe cited passages from it. The cited passages somehow served as a model for an illiterate copy that was made in ink on paper, apparently about the year 1828. Somehow this illiterate copy found its way to Logan, Utah."

Barry Fell was a controversial figure in academia. One Harvard colleague, an archaeologist, had once said of him: "He sees mysterious signs everywhere that he deems significant that the rest of us don't." After he completed his analysis of the Anthon Transcript, there was more controversy. Other scholars disagreed with his translation and said they believed the characters on the Anthon Transcript resembled hieroglyphics of the Micmac Indians who once inhabited Nova Scotia.

Although Fell won the support of some researchers, the scholarly dispute continued without resolution, and the meaning of the symbols on the Anthon Transcript would remain as much a mystery as when Charles Anthon saw them in 1828.

On June 27, 1980, two months after enlisting Jeff Simmonds's assistance in opening the document found in the 1668 Bible, Mark Hofmann knocked on the door of a small house in Carthage, Illinois. The home was only a few steps from where Joseph Smith and his brother Hyrum had met their deaths in 1844. Mark's father stood beside him.

The door opened slowly, and Dorothy Dean, a granddaughter of Joseph Smith's sister, Catherine, peered out warily.

Mark told her he was on a treasure hunt in reverse: He had found a treasure and wanted to establish its source. He said he had bought the Bible from a man in Salt Lake City, who said he'd bought it at an antique store in Carthage during the 1950s. "He thought he bought it from a daughter of Catherine Smith Salisbury," Hofmann said.

He handed her the Bible and asked if she recognized it.

Dorothy Dean was a gray-haired woman in her seventies who had seen news reports about the discovery of an untranslated portion of the Book of Mormon in a Bible purchased in Carthage and was anxious to see it.

"It doesn't look familiar," she said after examining it a few moments.

It was true, she said, that her mother, Mary Hancock, a daughter of Catherine Smith Salisbury, had operated an antique store in Carthage during the 1950s.

"But if she had a family Bible, I'm sure she wouldn't have sold it," she added.

Nevertheless, she conceded, it was possible her mother might have sold the Bible unwittingly and offered to look over the store's old records to learn whether she could find anything helpful to him.

The following day, Mrs. Dean called Hofmann's motel and said she had discovered something in her mother's account books that might be of interest to him.

When Mark and Bill Hofmann returned to her home, Mrs. Dean showed them her mother's handwritten ledger from the 1950s. There was an entry for a $6 sale on August 13, 1954, with a notation that the buyer was a "relative to Ansel White from California."

"That must be it," Mark said.

"I suppose it might be," the elderly woman said.

She said her mother had kept lots of old books around the store and might have sold the Bible without opening it and hadn't seen the signature of one of her ancestors, Samuel Smith.

"I'm *sure* she wouldn't have knowingly sold a family Bible," she said, as if apologizing for her dead mother.

* * *

In Salt Lake City several weeks later, church officials said tests had been completed on the Anthon Transcript and they confirmed Dean Jessee's preliminary conclusions that it was genuine.

The former missionary who once scoured the musty bookshops of southwestern England for bibliographic treasures was rewarded handsomely for his find: In trade for the Anthon Transcript, the church gave him a $5 Mormon gold coin minted in 1850, a first edition of the Book of Mormon and several examples of pioneer Mormon currency from its archives that, in all, were worth more than $20,000.

Mark told his parents that the excitement over the Anthon Transcript had changed his life as if God had sent him a message. Because of the publicity surrounding its discovery, he had become a celebrity in Utah and he said he was going to take a gamble and try to convert his fame into a career. He skipped the examination that would have qualified him for acceptance to medical school, dropped out of the university and informed his friends that he was going to try to make his living as a full-time dealer in coins and old documents.

Steve Christensen, meanwhile, had also decided to drop out of college. A few months short of graduation he told his wife, Terri, that he had decided to accept Gary Sheets's offer of a job.

Christensen and Hofmann symbolized the Utah dream: In different parts of Salt Lake Valley, both set out to become millionaires.

10

The twenty-eight-story headquarters of the Church of Jesus Christ of Latter-day Saints is the tallest building in Salt Lake City. Indeed, the skyscraper known to almost everyone in the city simply as the Church Office Building is the tallest building in Utah. From a site beside Temple Square, it towers above the broad boulevards of a community Brigham Young decreed should have streets wide enough for an ox-drawn wagon to turn around on, the copper dome of the state capitol a few blocks away, the piercing spires of the Salt Lake Temple beside it and a smaller but formidable building of classical Greek architecture known as the Church Administration Building. In the latter building, behind a row of marble columns, members of the First Presidency and other General Authorities directed the global operations of the church.

In the months following the Anthon Transcript's discovery, Mark Hofmann became a frequent visitor to this cluster of church buildings that dominated life in Utah.

He often visited Donald T. Schmidt, a balding, tall man in his early sixties who had a pale and gaunt face. Schmidt was an ex-teacher who was virtually the sole survivor of the Historical Department that Leonard Arrington had organized in 1972.

Arrington's independence began to erode in the mid-1970s after conservative General Authorities accused his team of historians of failing to write faith-promoting histories. G. Homer Durham, a General Authority and former president of Arizona State University, was imposed over him as managing director of the Historical Department. Its staff and budget were gradually reduced until it no longer existed, and in 1980, Arrington's band of historians was reassigned to the Brigham Young University faculty in Provo, more than fifty miles from the church archives.

As chief archivist, Schmidt presided over a huge cache of documents that was rich evidence Mormon pioneers had obeyed Joseph Smith's mandate to keep a record of their time on earth. It was Schmidt's job not only to protect the archives from those who would do the church harm but to add important new items as they became available and to dispose of others that were not essential to the collection.

Like many large archives, it contained duplicates and other materials that were expendable. As a result, Schmidt spent a good deal of his time buying, selling and trading Mormon documents.

In the months following the discovery of the Anthon Transcript, Mark Hofmann became not only Schmidt's friend but his most frequent trading partner. Several times a month, he arrived at the Church Office Building to offer an item for sale or inquire if Schmidt had any documents to sell or trade.

Schmidt prided himself on being a shrewd negotiator. It was his style not to show a great deal of interest in a document or book when it was first offered to him by a collector or dealer because, he said, "The price doubles if I show enthusiasm for it."

On February 16, 1981, Hofmann showed Schmidt a photocopy of what appeared to be a faded 1844 document bearing the signature of Joseph Smith, the Prophet. Hofmann said he had acquired it from a descendant of Thomas Bullock, one of Smith's scribes, and asked Schmidt if he wanted to buy it.

Schmidt had recently decided that beneath Hofmann's shyness and scholarly demeanor was the mind of another shrewd trader who, after innocently inviting him to make an offer on a document, often used the offer as a base to negotiate a higher price.

When Mark suggested the document in his hands might be worth $5,000, Schmidt chuckled. He said it wasn't worth it.

There were thousands of patriarchal blessings in the church's archives, he said.

Schmidt suspected that if he waited Hofmann out, he could buy it for a lot less than $5,000.

"When you get the original," Schmidt said, "let me see it."

Hofmann was surprised by his response. He had expected Schmidt to buy the blessing on the spot and *bury* it, and as he left the Church Office Building, he wondered whether Schmidt had even *looked* at the document, which read:

A Blessing, given to Joseph Smith 3rd by his father, Joseph Smith Junr., on Jany. 17, 1844

Blessed of the Lord is my son Joseph who is called the third— for the Lord knows the integrity of his heart and loves him, because of his faith, and righteous desires. And, for this cause, has the Lord raised him up; that the promises made to the fathers might be fulfilled, even that the anointing of the progenitor shall be upon the head of my son, and his seed after him, from generation to generation. For he shall be my successor to the Presidency of the High Priesthood: A Seer, and a Revelator and a Prophet, unto the church, which appointment belongeth to him by blessing, and also by right. . . .

To Hofmann the document appeared to undermine the church's fundamental claim of legitimacy, that it was the church founded by Joseph Smith. He was astonished Schmidt didn't want it.

For more than a century the Reorganized Church of Latter-day Saints in Independence, Missouri, the church that had been formed by Mormons opposed to polygamy and that had remained in Nauvoo after others followed Brigham Young to Utah, had claimed it—not the church led by what it called "the Brighamites" —was Joseph Smith's church.

Before his martyrdom, it said, he had designated his eleven-year-old son, Joseph Smith III, as his successor. In 1860 the younger Smith had become Prophet of the Reorganized Church. Since then, the Missouri church had always been led by one of Joseph Smith's descendants, and it claimed that the direct line of succession leading from Joseph Smith made the Missouri church God's only true church.

Many nineteenth-century Mormons had said they were present when Joseph Smith formally anointed his son as his successor, but the Missouri church had no written proof of this claim of legitimacy: All of the church's records from Nauvoo had been taken to the Salt Lake Valley by the Brighamites, where, it claimed, Brigham Young ordered the evidence of Joseph Smith III's ordination as his father's heir destroyed.

Mark Hofmann now claimed to have the written proof, and Schmidt didn't want it.

If *his* church wasn't interested in owning the Blessing, Hofmann told him a few days later, perhaps the Reorganized Church in Missouri would want it. Perhaps, he hinted, it might exchange the Blessing for a copy of the 1833 Book of Commandments, the rarest of Mormon books, which collectors valued at $40,000.

"If you think you can get a Book of Commandments," Schmidt said, "then you ought to try."

It was a rebuff Schmidt—and the leaders of his church—soon regretted.

In a journal entry dated February 27, 1981, Schmidt recorded that he and other members of the Historical Department had informed Gordon B. Hinckley, one of the church's twelve Apostles, that it was possible a document signed by Joseph Smith designating Joseph Smith III—not Brigham Young—as his successor could fall into the hands of the Reorganized Church.

We discussed it with Elder Hinckley for a considerable time. He in turn called and talked to Elder Boyd Packer and President Nathan Eldon Tanner. After considerable discussion in regards to the matter, it was decided that the church should attempt to obtain the document. President Tanner's words were, "We need it," or something similar to that.

When the meeting was over, a frantic race began for the Blessing of Joseph Smith III.

Schmidt, under orders to prevent the Blessing from falling into the hands of the rival church and to keep its existence a secret, began searching the Salt Lake Valley for Hofmann. To his dismay he could not find him anywhere.

He called the president of Hofmann's stake, then his bishop, then members of his ward. No one had his unlisted telephone number. Schmidt tried everyone he knew in the church who might have the number. No one had it.

Schmidt contacted by telephone one of Hofmann's neighbors, who suggested that he might be at LDS Hospital, where his wife had gone to have a baby. At last, Schmidt found Hofmann. He was in the maternity ward.

It was urgent, he said, that they meet as soon as possible. Hofmann agreed to see him in the morning.

It would be too late, however, for Donald Schmidt to keep the Blessing a secret.

11

At 8 A.M. on an icy Saturday morning on which the Wasatch Front was covered with the kind of soft, powdery snow that lured skiers to its slopes from distant places, Don Schmidt arrived at Hofmann's home in the Salt Lake City suburb of Sandy. Then Hofmann gave him bad news:

After Schmidt had rejected the Blessing for a second time, he had followed his advice and called Richard Howard, the Reorganized Church's historian, and offered to trade it for a Book of Commandments.

Howard, he said, was flying to Salt Lake City on Monday morning to inspect the Blessing and conclude the deal.

Schmidt left and drove to his office in the east wing of the Church Office Building and telephoned G. Homer Durham, the new Church Historian, who was at home. Schmidt said they had been too late: Hofmann was already negotiating to sell the Blessing to the Reorganized Church and, he said, it would be unethical to bid for the document while these negotiations were under way. Schmidt hung up, thinking the matter was closed. But a few minutes later, Durham called him back and said he had just spoken to Gordon Hinckley. It was vital, Durham said, that Schmidt get the

Blessing. Durham ordered the church archivist to make a counter offer to Hofmann before his meeting with Richard Howard on Monday morning.

Schmidt spent most of the next two days trying to find Hofmann. Finally, he reached him at home late Sunday afternoon and appealed to him to let *his* church have the Blessing. Hofmann urged him to calm down and agreed to meet Schmidt and Homer Durham at the Church Office Building at 8 A.M. Monday. It was an hour before he was scheduled to see Howard.

At the meeting, the two church officials came to the point quickly: They wanted the Blessing and were ready to deal for it.

Hofmann, they said, *owed* it to his church to save it from the embarrassment it would cause.

"After discussing the implications of the Reorganized Church obtaining this document," Schmidt later wrote, "he agreed that he did not want it to go to them and that he would refuse their offer and offer it to the Historical Department."

After the meeting with Schmidt and Durham, Hofmann met with Howard, to whom he had previously sent a letter granting him a ten-day option on the document, until March 8.

Hofmann showed Howard the Blessing but revealed that the Utah church also wanted it.

Howard responded that the Reorganized Church was determined to have the Blessing and he was certain they could come to terms if laboratory tests confirmed the document was genuine.

Howard flew home from Salt Lake City with a Xerox copy of the Blessing and Hofmann's promise to come to Independence in a few days with the Blessing so that it could be examined by experts.

But within minutes of Howard's departure, Hofmann returned to Schmidt's office and confirmed that he had decided to let his church have the Blessing.

In trade for the Blessing, Schmidt offered a first edition of the Book of Mormon, an 1860 Mormon gold coin, a pattern used in the minting of the coin, and four pieces of rare Mormon currency —collectively, they were worth more than $20,000.

Hofmann accepted the offer and handed the Blessing to Schmidt. Later, he gave him a notarized affidavit signed by Alan Lee Bullock, a descendant of Thomas Bullock, who lived in the

Utah town of Coalville, in which he declared he was Hofmann's source for the Blessing.

After Hofmann left his office, Schmidt called Homer Durham and revealed they had won the race for the Blessing.

"I just concluded a discussion of yesterday's events with Elder Durham in his office," Schmidt wrote the following day. "He appreciated the fact that we do have the document and had contacted Elder Hinckley who also was quite pleased that it had not gone to the RLDS church."

The race for the Joseph Smith III Blessing was not over yet, however.

After returning to Missouri, Richard Howard contracted with a Kansas City document expert to examine the Blessing to determine if it was authentic, selected a Book of Commandments for the trade and waited for Hofmann to call him with the schedule of his arrival in Independence.

By week's end, Howard had still not heard from Hofmann. When his telephone rang, it was a call from a writer for *Sunstone Review,* who said she had heard rumors about the discovery of a Blessing in which Joseph Smith had named his son as his successor.

The reporter said she had been advised that Howard had a copy of the Blessing and asked him to read it to her. Howard demurred, saying it was inappropriate to comment until he had possession of the original Blessing.

"I'm told that the LDS church acquired it this morning from Mr. Hofmann," the writer said. Spokesmen for the Utah church were refusing to let her see it, she said.

Stunned, Howard called Hofmann in Salt Lake City. When Hofmann confirmed the trade, Howard protested that he still had an option to buy the Blessing. Hofmann replied that Howard's option was going to expire in a few days and it would have been impossible for him to conduct the authentication tests he required before it expired.

Howard said angrily that as far as he was concerned the matter was not closed. He telephoned Donald Schmidt and asked for a certified copy of the Blessing and permission to make it public.

Schmidt told him to put his request in writing, then told Durham about the call.

To church leaders, it was clear that it would be impossible to keep the Blessing secret. There was also a possibility of an embarrassing lawsuit by the Missouri church. A few days later, they offered the Blessing to Howard as a gift.

Howard said it was inappropriate for his church to accept such a gift but suggested if laboratory tests confirmed the Blessing was authentic, he would accept it in exchange for the same copy of the Book of Commandments that Hofmann was to have received for it.

The next day, a story appeared on the front page of *The New York Times* under the headline, "Mormon Document Raises Doubts on Succession of Church's Leaders."

Quoting unidentified sources, it reported the Blessing's discovery and drew exactly the kind of inference that leaders of the Utah church had feared its revelation would bring—the inference that the Missouri church, not the Utah church, was the church founded by Joseph Smith.

With no other choice, the Utah church called a press conference to confirm the discovery and publicly present the Blessing to Howard.

Two weeks later, more than five thousand people filed into the Mormon Tabernacle, a remarkable wooden structure in Salt Lake City with a high, domed roof shaped like the shell of a tortoise. Built by the pioneers who emigrated to Utah during the nineteenth century, the cavernous building was a sturdy monument to their tenacity in creating a gathering place for the Saints.

Twice each year—in April and October—Mormons from around the world met in the Tabernacle to listen to their leaders review the state of the church, reveal new doctrines and to vote to sustain these leaders in office.

On the April morning in 1981, Mormons from more than seventy countries entered the huge hall, many of them wearing kimonos, saris and other native dress, to hear speeches by General Authorities that were translated simultaneously into Cambodian, Danish, Dutch, French, German, Greek, Italian, Mandarin, Navajo, Polish, Spanish, Tongan and almost a dozen other languages.

A succession of men in dark suits reviewed the church's success in taking the Mormon gospel to peoples of the earth: Membership had passed 4.7 million, and a decision was announced to build nine new temples—in Chicago, Dallas, Guatemala City, Seoul, Frankfurt, Stockholm, Manila, Lima and Johannesburg—in addition to the twenty-two then in existence.

The Mormons gathered in the Tabernacle and thousands of others who followed the proceedings via church-sponsored radio and television hookups were admonished to hold themselves to high standards, read the Book of Mormon, live within their means and protect their families from the moral decay inflicting society. Outside Temple Square, several dozen women marched with placards attacking the church for opposing the Equal Rights Amendment and for excommunicating one of its members, Sonia Johnson, for advocating the ERA.

Apostle Gordon B. Hinckley rose and took a position at a lectern overlooking the huge audience where he was silhouetted against a huge, gleaming pipe organ that rose behind him. He said he wanted "to say a few words about the recently discovered transcript of a Blessing, reported to have been given January 17, 1844, by Joseph Smith to his eleven-year-old son. . . .

"We determined that we would give full publicity to the discovery," he said, "even though we were confident that critics, knowing little of the factual history of the church, would seize upon it as suggesting a flaw in our line of authority. . . ."

At seventy, Gordon Hinckley had spent virtually all of his adult life administering the affairs of the church. Within a few weeks he would be named a counselor to the church's seriously ill Prophet, eighty-six-year-old Spencer W. Kimball, becoming the church's first career employee to reach the First Presidency's Office. And soon after that—because of the poor health of his two colleagues—he would become the sole functioning member of the First Presidency's Office, the de facto head of the church.

Distinguished-looking, tall and stocky, with receding gray hair and sensitive eyes that looked out from behind rimless glasses, Hinckley had been called as an Apostle in 1961 after helping to lead the church into the modern age of communications and becoming its premier image-maker. His career in the church bureaucracy had begun shortly after his return from a mission in Depression-era England where he had preached the Mormon gospel at

London's Hyde Park Corner. Later, he adapted modern audio-video technology—movies, filmstrips, radio and television—to serve the church's missionary efforts while developing a sophisticated public-relations apparatus to polish the image it presented to the gentile world and reduce old perceptions that it was eccentric and cultish.

Hinckley told his audience that its enemies would suggest the newly discovered Blessing undermined the Utah church. But he said other documents in its possession revealed that Joseph Smith always intended the line of succession and the presidency to pass through the Council of Twelve Apostles, not bloodlines. He said that Thomas Bullock, the scribe who transcribed the Blessing, had followed Brigham Young to Utah and gone on a mission to England in 1856. That was in itself evidence that he believed Brigham Young was the church's true Prophet, Hinckley said.

"Every President of the church since then has come to that most high and sacred office out of the Council of the Twelve. Each of these men has been blessed with the spirit and power of revelation from on high. There has been an unbroken chain from Joseph Smith, Jr., to Spencer W. Kimball. Of that I bear solemn witness and testimony before you this day."

What Gordon Hinckley did not tell the assembly, however, was that the crisis posed by the Blessing of Joseph Smith III did not end when it appeared to end.

Mark Hofmann told acquaintances that shortly after he traded the Blessing to Donald Schmidt, he asked to meet privately with Hinckley. He said he entered his office and placed a five-paragraph letter on his desk, a letter addressed to Brigham Young from Thomas Bullock. Hinckley did not mention the letter in his speech to the General Conference.

Private

G.S.L. City Jan. 27, 1865

Dear Prest. Brigham Young

My rhemnatism being very much improved to day, I sit down to write you a letter, hoping we may be reconciled. I have attempted to speak with you privately, but on account that you are too busy to chat with me, since my dismissal from the Historian's Office, I resort to paper and ink.

I have only the kindest regards for you, and for brother G.A. Smith. Altho' I must confess that I felt insulted at being turned out, without advance notice, nor warning; and this after nearly 17 years of faithful employment. I have never said that you are not the right man to head the church, and if any man says otherwise, he is a *liar;* I believe that you have never pretended to anything that did not belong to you. Mr. Smith (Young Joseph) has forfeited any claim which he ever had to successorship, but *I do not believe* that this gives you license to destroy every remnant of the blessing which he received from his Father, those promises *must* be fulfilled by some future generation.

I will not, nay I can not, surrender that blessing, knowing what its certain fate will be if I returned, even at the peril of my own livelihood and standing. I regret the necessity of disobeying your instructions, altho' I believe that you understand my feeling of loyalty towards brother Joseph, as well as towards yourself.

You will please to excuse the warmth of my sentiment, my earnest desire is for the good of the Martyre, his heirs, the First Presidency, and all the Saints of God. My conscience is "clear as Rocky Mountain water," I do not want a stink, and trust that you do not want one either.

Dear Brother, when again we meet, may our hands strike in mutual respect and affection, our long friendship unchanged, is the prayer of

Thomas Bullock

P.S. I would write more, but my hand smarts. Can we talk privately?

Hofmann said he had found the letter in the same collection of documents kept by Bullock's family in which he had discovered the Blessing of Joseph Smith III. He told Hinckley he did not want the letter to fall into the hands of the enemy and offered to donate it to the church.

No one, he stressed, knew of its existence, including Richard Howard.

Hinckley accepted the letter as a gift, and it was locked in the First Presidency's Vault.

On May 15, Wallace B. Smith, the president of the Reorganized Church and one of Joseph Smith's great-grandsons, announced that a team of experts had tested the Blessing of Joseph Smith III and had established that it was genuine. The document, Smith said, had merely confirmed what his church had always said: Joseph Smith intended the presidency of his church to pass to his descendants, not to the Utah church led by Brigham Young.

12

If Brent Ashworth had gone on a mission, perhaps things would have been different. When he turned nineteen, it was 1968. The Vietnam War was consuming hundreds of lives a week and the church had agreed that only two Mormon boys a year from each ward would go abroad as draft-deferred ministers of religion. Ashworth was not one of those called from his ward in Provo. Instead, he went to Brigham Young University, got married, attended law school, became a lawyer, had eight children and became the bishop of his ward. It was a life of considerable accomplishment, but Ashworth's inability to serve a mission left a vacuum in his life that would haunt him long after his two friends returned from their missions.

Like Mark Hofmann and Steve Christensen, Ashworth became obsessed as a child with reading about church history and collecting old documents and books. It started with a letter he found in a family trunk written to his grandmother during the 1930s by the church Prophet. The letter introduced him to a world of intimacy with historical figures and launched him on a search for the signatures of other people that he had previously known only through the impersonal pages of history books.

What had been Ashworth's hobby as a child became his passion as an adult. As he prospered as a lawyer, the walls of his home became covered with framed documents bearing the autographs of George Washington, Abraham Lincoln and other legends from American history and the history of his church.

One item conspicuously absent from the collection was a letter in the hand of Joseph Smith. Ashworth was a devout Mormon and thought of such a letter as his crowning prize. After reading about Mark Hofmann's discovery of the Anthon Transcript and his decision to become a full-time dealer in Mormon documents, Ashworth called him and said:

"I'd sure like a letter written by Joseph Smith if you can ever find one."

To Ashworth's surprise and pleasure, Hofmann said he had recently been tipped off about a letter written by Joseph to his wife, Emma, in 1833, regarding the donation of a plow to the poor. It was owned by a family in Texas which, he had been told, was willing to sell it.

A few days later, Ashworth bought the letter from Hofmann for $4,000, plus several autographs of lesser value from his own collection. Smith's letter was exactly as Hofmann had described it, and he hung it proudly on his wall.

At the Church Administration Building, the negative publicity that followed the discovery of Joseph Smith's Blessing of his son acted like kerosene poured on smoldering embers to ignite the fears of General Authorities over the indiscriminate digging by scholars into the church's history. New, tighter restrictions were imposed on access to church archives, and in a series of pronouncements General Authorities assailed the incipient Mormon intellectual movement.

Apostle Boyd K. Packer, employing perhaps the heaviest weapon in the arsenal of an ecclesiastical leader, warned Mormon scholars that their objective research was placing their *salvation* at risk. Speaking to religious instructors at the BYU campus, Packer assailed historians "who want to tell everything whether it is faith promoting or not."

"One who chooses to follow the tenets of his profession—regardless of how they may injure the church or destroy the faith of

those not ready for 'advanced history'—is himself in spiritual jeopardy."

Once out of the bottle, however, vapors of intellectual freedom
were not to be easily contained.

At BYU, an independent student newspaper, *Seventh East Press,*
joined *Dialogue* and *Sunstone Review* in 1981 as a forum in which
Mormons could express thoughts differing from those of the
church hierarchy. And the new restrictions limiting access to historical archives had an effect unanticipated by the hierarchy: It
gave birth to the Mormon Underground.

The rigid limitations put a premium on information about controversial aspects of the church's history that was already available
and made it a challenge to uncover new facts. Information became
a forbidden fruit. Like erotic books circulated surreptitiously in a
boarding school, old diaries, journals, letters and other documents
took on a mystique that energized efforts to possess them. Secretly,
students and instructors at BYU, as well as nonstudents who were
interested in church history, began to photocopy documents and
exchange them like collectors of baseball cards. They referred to
themselves as the Mormon Underground.

In an interview in *Seventh East Press,* one participant in the
Underground was asked:

"How did the Mormon Underground originate?"

"In a way, the L.D.S. Church gave birth to the Underground
and keeps it alive. For example, seminary kids are taught the
importance of gaining religious knowledge, are encouraged to
collect magazine articles and other written information about
the church. . . . Seminary students are taught that some of the
most precious teachings in Mormonism are the secret teachings
of the temple. Thus by the time a young Mormon is missionary
age, he is well indoctrinated with the idea that, one, collecting
and cataloging religious knowledge is useful or important, and,
two, the best knowledge is often secret knowledge. . . ."

"How could the church do away with the Underground?"

"I think everyone in the Underground looks forward, perhaps
with some unrealistic idealism, to the day when there is no need
for an Underground because the Historical Department of the

church is willing to let all responsible interested parties examine all available historical materials. . . ."

As the Mormon Underground grew, so did the assertiveness and courage of a few Mormon scholars.

One of them was Dennis Michael Quinn, a BYU professor and member of Leonard Arrington's team of church historians until he left to earn a doctorate at Yale. Quinn informed his students that he had been born "with a split identity"—seventh-generation Mormon on his mother's side, Roman Catholic on his father's side. But from adolescence onward, he said, he always considered himself a devout Saint.

In the fall of 1981, as conservative church leaders were accelerating their attacks on scholars, Quinn responded to them in a speech to BYU's Student History Association:

"Ezra Taft Benson and Boyd K. Packer," he declared, "want church history to be as elementary as possible and as defensive as possible . . . history for consumption by the weakest of the conceivably weak Saints, for the vilest of the conceivably vile anti-Mormons, and for the most impressionable of the world's sycophants."

But Quinn said it was impossible for responsible historians to ignore that some church leaders led flawed lives. "Mormon historians would be false to their understanding of L.D.S. doctrine, the Sacred History of the Scriptures, the realities of human conduct, and the documentary evidence of Mormonism if they sought to defend the proposition that L.D.S. prophets were infallible in their decisions and statements. . . .

"The tragic reality is that there have been occasions when church leaders, teachers and writers have not told the truth they knew about difficulties of the Mormon past but have offered to the Saints a mixture of platitudes, half-truths, omissions and plausible denials."

His eyes glistening with tears, Quinn continued defiantly:

"Elder Packer and others would justify this because 'we are at war with the adversary' and must also protect any Latter-day Saint whose 'testimony is in seedling stage.' But such a public relations defense of the church is actually a Maginot Line of sandy fortifications which 'the enemy' can easily breach and which has been built up by digging lethal pits in which the Saints will stumble. . . ."

In time, his words would prove to be strangely prophetic.

13

As Steve Christensen approached his twenty-eighth birthday early in 1982, he could have described his life by the name of the tree-shaded community north of Salt Lake City in which he had grown up: *Bountiful.*

His wife, Terri, was about to deliver his third son, Jared. They owned a two-story Cape Cod home in the town of Centerville a few miles from Bountiful. He had been called to serve as the bishop of his ward. He was earning almost $150,000 a year—and he had become a member and financier of the Mormon Underground.

In many ways Gary Sheets and Steve Christensen were an incongruous team: Sheets was an unabashed extrovert—aggressive, confident, optimistic, flamboyant. "Gary is a very simple man," a close relative would say of Sheets. "He's a salesman type of person. He likes people. But he's not a very intuitive person. Some people might call him insensitive but he doesn't mean to be this way; he's a very loving person. I don't think he really understands people. I think he expects everybody to be like him, which is simple."

Steve was more complex—more introverted, more comfortable, as always, with books than people. He had a curious and nimble mind and was interested in other people but he was stingy when it came to letting others into his thoughts. Although they were an odd couple, Gary Sheets and Steve Christensen had strengths that complemented each other and they soon developed a friendship as loving as that between father and son.

The company Sheets had created ten years earlier, Coordinated Financial Services, had become an enormously prosperous financial conglomerate representing almost two thousand wealthy entrepreneurs, professional people, athletes and entertainers, including one of Utah's best-known families, the Osmonds.

The company's message to prospective clients was appealing: Many people with high incomes, it said, are too busy making money to manage it effectively and need professionals not only to make their money earn more money but to reduce taxes. Looking back on the formula that had made him a millionaire several times over, Gary Sheets said the creed of his company was that "total financial affairs should be coordinated—it was an idea that consumed me."

By the early 1980s, C.F.S. was managing more than $150 million in investments and was a corporate umbrella for scores of companies, real estate syndicates and investment partnerships. It had more than two hundred employees, had branched out to California, Nevada and Idaho and was diversifying rapidly. It was investing in geothermal energy projects in California, a gold mine in Oregon, mineral developments in Montana and the purchase and leasing of executive jets to corporate customers.

Initially, Christensen worked as a kind of secretary for Gary Sheets, answering correspondence and dealing with minor errands. But he quickly expanded the parameters of the job by introducing something into Sheets's business life that had been missing before: organization. Christensen planned Sheets's schedule, set up appointments, made sure he had the right promotional materials when he solicited investors and saw to it that he followed up at the right moment to close a deal.

Often sleeping only four or five hours a night, Christensen studied real estate law, insurance and tax regulations and evolved into a tireless all-around support system for Sheets. Sheets had self-confidence, optimism, an ability to make people like him. After a week's trip to Las Vegas, his favorite hunting ground for investors, he often returned to Salt Lake City with hundreds of thousands of dollars in new investments. Christensen helped Sheets do even better. During the first year Steve worked for him, Sheets doubled his personal sales production; by the end of the second year, it had nearly tripled.

Sheets was a generous man and invited Christensen to share in his increased income. He formed a new company, J. Gary Sheets & Associates, to make investments and serve as a recipient for some of his income from C.F.S. and made Steve a partner, increasing his share each year until he owned half of it.

Sheets was proud of his protégé and boasted that he had hired the smartest person he had ever met. Because Christensen was better organized than Sheets and often more knowledgeable about real estate and investment regulations, other C.F.S. employees turned increasingly to him for guidance and before long he was a major influence in the operation of the company.

Most of Sheets's employees, like many of his customers, were Mormons. To those at the top of the company this shared heritage was not of incidental significance: It created not only a personal bond but a divinely mandated responsibility to do the right thing. Years later, one member of the firm tried to explain this sense of obligation: "We felt we were the keepers of the priesthood of God, the chosen ones, and that we had a higher duty—to be more fair, more moral than those who did not hold the priesthood."

For Terri Christensen, life was not only materially bountiful but happier than she ever expected it to be. Since her earliest recollections in the church's Primary classes, she had dreamed only of fulfilling her duty as wife and mother. Now, she was pregnant again and confident that she and Steve would have more children after this one.

It was a happy but not a perfect marriage.

Steve had always had difficulty expressing his feelings, and for Terri that meant a never-ending battle to persuade him to admit her into the shell he had placed around his thoughts. And sometimes it was a lonely marriage. Steve's drive and eagerness to succeed kept him at his office long hours; his duties as bishop took even more time away from her. And even when he was at home, Steve often withdrew from her into his book collection. Still, he always reserved weekends for the family: a Friday or Saturday night out with Terri, the rest of the weekend with the children.

Their problems were no greater than those in most marriages, and for every moment she might feel troubled there were a thousand when Terri Christensen blessed her marriage to a man who not only loved her but believed in practicing honesty, generosity, compassion and other values taught by the church—not only on Sundays but every day.

When Steve was asked to serve as bishop, Terri was only twenty-three and thought to herself: "I'm too young to be the mother of the ward, I don't want all this pressure to be a perfect person."

Then she thought again and found peace in the thought: "Where much is given, much is expected."

As Steve's income increased, so did the tangible evidence of their success: first one expensive BMW automobile, then another, then a Jeep for excursions to the mountains.

Terri loved clothes and jewelry and now she could afford them, while Steve spent much of his share of their rising income on his book collection, which had grown to more than ten thousand volumes. He also invested in the Mormon Underground.

Some conservatives in the church leadership considered anyone who participated in the underground trading of documents subversive. Yet many, perhaps most, of the participants—including Steven Christensen—were faithful members of the church who were simply interested in its history and the saga of its people.

After going to work for Gary Sheets, he had less time to conduct his own research about the Mormon past among the documents he traded and collected as a member of the Underground. But as his income increased he told friends that he felt an obligation to share his good fortune with less affluent amateur researchers and to help support their research. He established a foundation to channel contributions to researchers and donated $30,000 to underwrite the cost of a conference on church history held by the journal *Sunstone Review*.

Some of his friends advised Christensen to distance himself from such groups, saying that it was inappropriate for a bishop of the church to participate in the Underground. But Christensen replied that if he were forced to make a choice, he would rather pursue his love of church history than remain a bishop—and he said he was not consorting with the devil.

Honesty, he said, was a principle Mormon children were taught as soon as they could speak and was one of the touchstones of their faith. As far as he was concerned, the doctrinal foundations of the church were solid enough to withstand any scrutiny of its history, and it was morally wrong for leaders of the church to conceal the truth about its past.

Honesty was a topic that came up often in conversation with Steven Christensen, and there was a phrase he often repeated when the subject was at hand: "Truth is truth," he said. "What's right is right."

"Our history and doctrine," he wrote to one friend, "should be taught in an honest manner. Faithful history should not be dishonesty. Truth is truth. We must admit that we don't know everything theologically."

14

On March 6, 1982, Mark Hofmann telephoned Brent Ashworth and said he had something very important to show him. When he drove up an hour later to Ashworth's home in Payson, a small town south of Provo, he was carrying the most exciting piece of paper Ashworth had ever seen. It was a letter dated January 13, 1873, bearing the signature of Martin Harris, the wealthy farmer who was Joseph Smith's first convert.

The words Ashworth read made his hands tremble. They described the sight of an angel and the voice of God. He had never seen anything like it.

In 1830, Martin Harris and the two other early disciples of the Prophet—Oliver Cowdery and David Whitmer—signed a statement prepared by Joseph Smith in which they attested to having had a vision the year before in which the angel showed them the gold plates of the Book of Mormon and God commanded them to tell others it was genuine. The statement of the three men—who were to be called the Three Witnesses to the Book of Mormon—was to be included as a preface to every copy of the book.

Now, Ashworth held what appeared to be a personal account by

Martin Harris of the vision that revealed, for the first time, what God had said during the vision:

"*. . . and lo, there came a voice from heaven saying, 'I am the Lord,' and that the plates were translated by God and not by men, and also that we should bear record of it to all the world. . . .*"

"This is marvelous . . . incredible!" Ashworth said. "If it's genuine. . . ."

They agreed the letter, which was written in pencil on a lined sheet of paper and addressed to a Walter Conrad, was going to be hard to authenticate. It appeared to be in the handwriting of *two* people: One hand had written the text, another, mysteriously, the signature.

"If we can authenticate it," Ashworth said, "I'll take it."

A deal was struck: If Dean Jessee, the church handwriting expert, determined that it was genuine, Mark could have the pick of virtually anything in Ashworth's autograph collection.

Tentatively, Hofmann selected documents signed by George Washington, Abraham Lincoln and Robert E. Lee valued by Ashworth at $27,000. The documents were three of the jewels in his collection.

Dean Jessee agreed to examine the letter, but he said it would take several months because few examples of Harris's handwriting had survived with which he could compare the script on the letter. The presence of a second handwriting only made the problem more difficult.

Only a few days had passed before Hofmann called Ashworth again. A collection of nineteenth-century letters from the Palmyra area, he said, was coming on the market on the East Coast, mostly letters that had never been delivered because they were misaddressed or were sent to the dead-letter office for other reasons. They had been saved by a collector of postmarks who paid little attention to their contents. Now that the collector had died they were coming on the market, and he had been told one letter was signed by a Lucy Smith, who might be the Prophet's mother or sister.

On July 29, Hofmann showed him the letter. Ashworth said it gave him a spiritual high as thrilling as any he ever expected on this side of the veil.

The letter, dated January 23, 1829, and signed by Lucy Mack

Smith, the mother of Joseph Smith, described graphically the coming forth of the not-yet-published Book of Mormon.

"It is my pleasure," the letter, addressed to a sister-in-law of Lucy Mack Smith, began, "to inform you of a great work which the Lord has wrought in our family, for he has made his paths known as to Joseph in dreams and it pleased God to show him where he could dig to obtain an ancient record engraven upon plates made of pure gold and this he is able to translate. . . ."

Filling almost two pages of tightly written script, the letter recounted the journey of the Israelites to the New World. "On account of negligence translation of the first part of the record was carried off by some unknown person," she said, apparently alluding to the lost 116 pages of the Book of Mormon. Then she gave a few details of the Prophet Lehi's flight from Jerusalem with his family and the family of his wife's brother, Ishmael—details from the lost Book of Lehi never known before.

If Dean Jessee said the letter was genuine, Ashworth said excitedly, Hofmann could select from whatever documents he still wanted in his collection.

Jessee, who was still conducting research on the letter that apparently bore the signature of Martin Harris, said he had no doubt about the letter bearing the name of Lucy Mack Smith.

A few days later, the church called a press conference to announce a discovery that made headlines around the world.

"The handwriting is definitely that of Lucy Mack Smith," Dean Jessee told an audience of reporters packed into an auditorium at the Church Office Building. The letter, he said, was unassailable evidence of the legitimacy of the church.

Once again, he said, a kind of Dead Sea Scroll of Mormonism had been unearthed—contemporary evidence from the nineteenth century that confirmed what the church had been saying for more than 150 years. "It shows that at the beginning—as the curtain goes up on the church in 1829—the Smiths are talking and saying the same thing that they say in their histories later on; it kind of knocks in the head the idea [expressed by church critics of subsequent changes in the story] associated with Joseph Smith's religious experience, that these things evolved as the need for them arose—a so-called need to be placed in a marvelous light."

It was in early October, on the eve of the fall General Conference, that Jessee finished his research on the letter written in two hands that appeared to be an eyewitness account of the words of God.

The *signature,* he said, was in Martin Harris's handwriting. He said he had established this by comparing it with Harris's signature on an 1871 application for a federal pension for his service in the War of 1812 and the 1831 contract when he was forced to sell his farm because he had mortgaged it to finance publication of the Book of Mormon. Jessee said the *text* of the letter was in the hand of his son, Martin Harris, Jr., with whom Harris lived during the final years of his life. The son, he said, had apparently transcribed the letter as his father dictated it.

Church Historian G. Homer Durham led Brent Ashworth into the office of Gordon B. Hinckley and said:

"Gordon, we've got another great letter from Brent."

Hinckley read it aloud while others in the room listened silently. After he had finished, Hinckley said: "Brent, this is a marvelous letter—and it will be great for the church."

The next day the church called another press conference and released its second important faith-promoting document in less than six weeks. Once again, church leaders said, there was contemporary evidence that the Book of Mormon was true and divinely inspired.

Brent Ashworth, like Mark Hofmann before him, became a celebrity in Utah. Senior church officials invited him to their offices. He was featured in newspaper articles and church publications and was soon a sought-after speaker. Ashworth told his wife, Charlene, that he had not sought personal publicity, but the experience had taught him something—at last, he might have found a way to serve a mission.

Still haunted by a lack of fulfillment rooted in his inability to serve a mission at nineteen, he said he thought God might have now called him to serve a different kind of mission: ferreting out faith-promoting documents and taking them to the world to advance the work of the church.

Although Ashworth received much of the notoriety following the letters' discovery, Mark Hofmann managed to make sure that reporters knew *he* had actually found them.

As reports spread about his prowess as a hunter of old documents, friends and others in the church began to compare him with Indiana Jones, the fictional hero of a hit movie, *Raiders of the Lost Ark,* who scoured the world in search of the biblical lost Ark of the Covenant.

As his business grew, Hofmann encouraged such comparisons while enjoying a privilege rare for a member of his faith, direct access to members of the First Presidency.

Three weeks after the General Conference, he telephoned Gordon Hinckley to offer him still another faith-promoting document—an 1873 letter written by David Whitmer, another of the Three Witnesses to the Book of Mormon.

Whitmer had broken from Joseph Smith in 1838 and never returned to the church. But in this letter apparently written in his old age, Whitmer, as had Martin Harris, said his testimony as one of the Three Witnesses had always remained steadfast. "Anyone who is without prejudice," he said, "can easily learn the Book of Mormon is the word of God if he will earnestly seek the truth."

After Hinckley agreed to meet his asking price of $15,000 for the letter, Hofmann said he was embarrassed to take so much money from the church and accepted $10,000 instead.

In press interviews, Hofmann began to reveal guardedly the techniques he used to find lost documents. The principal reason for his success, he explained, was that no one before him had tried to mine in a systematic way the wealth of old documents Mormon families had accumulated for generations in compliance with Joseph Smith's mandate to make a record of their lives. He also attributed his success to simple hard work—particularly, tracing the genealogy of early Mormons and tracking down their modern descendants. Hofmann hinted that he had developed a network of tipsters and dealers who helped him in his searches and, to a few collectors, he confided that among the most productive veins he had mined were collections of nineteenth-century stampless covers.

Used before envelopes came into use in midcentury, stampless covers were rectangular sheets of stationery containing a message on one side and an address on the other. After writing a message, a correspondent folded the sheet twice, secured it with a wax seal and wrote an address on the outside of the fold. A postmaster dated the letter with a hand stamp and noted the amount of postage near the postmark.

Over the years, hundreds of people had collected stampless covers, Hofmann said, but most paid little attention to their contents because they were collectors of old postmarks. He said he had discovered hundreds of stampless covers mailed from the small towns in western New York during the years when Mormonism was emerging and they were a treasure trove for those interested in the early years of the church.

"Although I do have fun," he told *Sunstone Review*, "it's really not as romantic as it sounds. It seems you always have people who hate you or are mad at you. There is a pretty close-knit group of collectors. I have only 240 collectors on my mailing list. If I find something and sell it to someone and then word gets around to a collector who also collects in the same field, this guy wonders why I won't sell to him." Some historians, he added, were also unhappy with him because the publicity over his discoveries had created a high-priced and competitive marketplace that kept important documents in private hands, out of the reach of scholars. "But," he said, "I'm in this for the money."

His greatest ambition, Hofmann added, as if he were referring to the Holy Grail, was to find the 116 pages of the Book of Mormon lost by Martin Harris.

Only to Ashworth and a few friends did he confide that he was also searching for a "bombshell" that he called the McLellin Collection.

15

It is not clear precisely when Mark Hofmann decided to blackmail his church. Perhaps it was during the tumultuous week when he was courted and pursued by rival religious camps frantically seeking the Joseph Smith III Blessing; perhaps it was when he watched the eyes of a church Apostle flicker as he read Thomas Bullock's secret letter to Brigham Young that challenged for a second time the church's claim to wear the mantle of Joseph Smith; or, perhaps, the idea had taken root long before that, when Hofmann first began to have doubts about his faith in the church.

Blackmail, like beauty, is a characteristic best defined by the eyes of the beholder. Whether leaders of the Church of Jesus Christ of Latter-day Saints submitted to blackmail by Mark Hofmann—or whether, as they would say, they were only trying to comply with Joseph Smith's mandate to keep a record of church history—would be blurred by conflicting interpretations of motives and events and left to the judgment of history.

Mark Hofmann's secret commerce in documents with the church began during the first week of January 1983, when he called G. Homer Durham, the church historian, and confided that he had discovered a letter the church should see.

It was to be one of many times that Hofmann would bypass the conventional channels by which the church acquired historic documents—through the office of Donald Schmidt—and deal directly and privately with high-ranking leaders of the church.

Durham read the letter shown to him by Hofmann and then called President Gordon B. Hinckley. A few moments later, Durham escorted Hofmann into Hinckley's office in the Church Administration Building.

At seventy-two, Hinckley had begun filling the role that would increasingly dominate his life, his role as de facto president of the church. Spencer Kimball, the church's eighty-seven-year-old Prophet who had presided over its greatest period of growth, was frail and nearly blind. His first counselor, Marion G. Romney, was eighty-five and growing feeble, leaving Hinckley to oversee the day-to-day operations of the First Presidency.

The letter Hofmann presented to Hinckley was dated 1825 and bore the signature of Joseph Smith, Jr. It was addressed to Josiah Stowell, a farmer who briefly employed the Prophet as a young man. To someone unversed in the controversies surrounding the church's origins, the letter might have seemed a historical curiosity, but not one capable of threatening harm to a large and wealthy institution with millions of faithful members around the world. Nor did it seem on the face of it threatening enough to compel the leaders of the church, as they would do, to exact a pledge of secrecy from Hofmann regarding its existence. But as innocuous as it might seem, the letter raised an old and tender issue for the Mormon church: the possibility that Joseph Smith, the founder of the church, dabbled in black magic.

Canandaigua   June 18th, 1825

Dear Sir:

Your father has shown me your letter informing him and me of your success in locating the mine as you suppose, but we are of the oppinion that as you cannot ascertain any particulars, you should not dig more untill you first discover if any valluables remain. You know the treasure must be guarded by some clever spirit, and if such is discovered, so also is the treasure. So do this. Take a hazel stick one yard long, being new cut and cleave it just in the middle and lay it asunder on the mine so that both

inner parts of the stick may look one right against the other one
inch distant and if there is a treasure after a while you shall see
them draw and join together again of themselves. Let me know
how it is. Since you were here I have almost decided to accept
your offer and if you can make it convenient to come this way I
shall be ready to accompany you if nothing happens more than I
know of. I am,

Respectfully yours,

Joseph Smith Jr.

Among the topics being probed by scholars participating in what
had come to be called "the new Mormon history" in the late 1970s
and early 1980s was the possibility that Mormonism, along with a
number of other American religions that sprouted briefly in the
early nineteenth century, may have budded in a topsoil of the occult.

Along the frontier, interest in folk magic was endemic during
the early years of the new nation, as were hopes of finding buried
treasure with the assistance of magical appliances such as "seer
stones" and divining rods. The terrain was littered with earthen
burial mounds of ancient Indians, and each, like the pyramids of
Egypt, was suspected of hiding a treasure. The frontier was pocked
with empty holes that were monuments to the unfulfilled dreams of
treasure hunters. Despite so many disappointments, however, the
search went on. Newspapers carried endless reports of "money
diggers" and "glass lookers" and other sorcerers who claimed a
power to make the earth transparent and discover buried gold and
silver. Among those money diggers and soothsayers was Joseph
Smith, Jr.

According to court records, in 1826, three years after he was to
later say he was visited by the angel Moroni, and a year before he
said the angel had given him the gold plates of the Book of Mormon, he was arrested and tried in Bainbridge, New York, on the
complaint of a neighbor that he was a "disorderly person and an
imposter" who fraudulently claimed the ability to tell fortunes and
find underground treasures. Smith was convicted but allowed to
remain free. In 1830, he was tried again on a similar charge, and
according to witnesses, indicated he had used the same "seer

stone" with which he had told fortunes and searched for buried money to find the gold plates of the Book of Mormon.

By the time the Mormon church began its postwar period of expansion, claims that Joseph Smith had been a money digger and sorcerer had been all but washed away by the passage of time and the church's lionizing of him as a prophet chosen by God to restore His church to earth. Officially, church leaders denied suggestions that he had been involved in folk magic and sympathetic Mormon historians dismissed the court records as forgeries.

The letter held by Gordon Hinckley and addressed to Josiah Stowell resurrected the old stories about money digging. Worse, it indicated that Smith believed in magical sticks and buried treasure guarded by a "clever spirit" at the same time he said he was meeting annually with the angel Moroni. Indeed, the account in the letter was uncomfortably close to the story Smith told of being led by Moroni to the gold plates from which he translated the Book of Mormon.

Hofmann told Hinckley he had brought the letter to him because he was afraid that it might fall into the wrong hands.

"Does anybody else in the church besides Elder Durham know about it?" Hofmann was asked.

He said only his wife and an East Coast document collector from whom he had obtained the letter knew it existed.

Hofmann asked $16,000 for the letter, then lowered the price to $15,000. The church officials accepted the terms if the letter's authenticity could be established. They said, however, that they did not want any of the church's document examiners or other historians to see it; outside of Durham and Hinckley's secretary, only the twelve church Apostles and members of the First Presidency were to know it existed.

Hofmann said he knew someone in New York City who could determine if the letter was genuine, and the deal was struck.

Five days later—on January 10, 1983—Hofmann boarded American Airlines Flight 484 in Salt Lake City and after changing planes at the Dallas/Fort Worth International Airport, flew to La Guardia Airport in New York City. From there he took a taxi to the Hotel Empire at Sixty-third Street and Broadway. The following afternoon he was greeted like an old friend by Charles Hamilton, the city's foremost autograph dealer, at his gallery on West Fifty-seventh Street.

In the nearly three years since he had become a full-time dealer, Hofmann had diversified widely from his initial dealings exclusively in Mormon documents. He now traded in documents bearing the signatures of a pantheon of famous names—Lincoln, Beethoven, Daniel Boone, Miles Standish, Emily Dickinson, Billy the Kid, Edgar Allan Poe and many others. And he had become a familiar face in the tight, gossipy world of major-league document dealers largely centered on a handful of bookstores, galleries and auction houses in New York City.

Charles Hamilton was the dean of American autograph dealers. His Manhattan gallery, opened in 1963, was the nation's first devoted solely to the sale of autographs, and it became the setting for many of the highest-priced autograph sales in history, as well as a magnet for affluent collectors around the world.

Hamilton, in his early seventies, was known to his best clients as Bud. White-haired, garrulous, outspoken, controversial, he was something of a detective as well as a document dealer. He frequently traveled around the country and to Europe to testify at trials in which the authenticity of a will, a contract or other documents were in dispute and had helped put in jail more than a dozen professional forgers. When detectives or prosecutors wanted to understand the minds of gifted forgers or learn the tricks of their trade, they often turned to a book he had written, *Great Forgers and Famous Fakes.* Some of his competitors viewed Hamilton with less than awe. They considered him egotistical, arrogant and dogmatic—too ready to shoot from the hip, willing, for example, to look at a three-hundred-year-old signature and decide in a few seconds whether it was genuine or a fake. Nevertheless, even many of his detractors considered him America's most gifted detector of fraudulent documents.

Hofmann had first visited Hamilton's gallery the previous year dressed in the dark suit of a Mormon missionary and so unsure of himself that Hamilton quickly decided he was a bumpkin beyond his depth in Manhattan's high-voltage world of document trading. Although Hofmann never got over the shy, reluctant manner of his first visit, Hamilton's respect for him grew: He decided that Hofmann was highly intelligent and discovered that his interest in documents, like his own, was eclectic and informed, not limited to a few famous names or a single era—as were the interests of many collectors—but embraced all of history, from Napoleon to the trappers and mountain men who explored the American West. Moreover, unlike many dealers, he had a good grasp of the historical significance of the documents he bought and sold.

After realizing Hofmann was not the green novice he first appeared to be, Hamilton sized him up as a reticent and scholarly young man who, like himself, enjoyed digging into the refuse bins of history and uncovering cast-off diamonds that could become prisms through which the past could be examined from a new perspective.

During his visit to Hamilton's gallery in January 1983, Hofmann opened his briefcase and showed him the same letter signed by Joseph Smith that he had shown a few days earlier to Gordon Hinckley.

Joseph Smith was one of thousands of people whose signatures Hamilton had come to know over the preceding five decades. When he saw the signature on Hofmann's letter, he said:

"Mark, I'm sorry, that's not the Prophet's handwriting."

It was one of the instant decisions for which Hamilton was famous and controversial.

"How can you tell? You didn't even read it."

"I don't have to read it. The spelling's too good and the handwriting is stiff and labored—like a man walking, strutting with his chest out. Smith's handwriting is bent over like a man running and leaning forward."

Hofmann looked disappointed.

"Mark, there were enough Joseph Smiths in upstate New York to outfit a regiment; you've just got the wrong man. Where'd you get this?"

As he put the letter into his briefcase Hofmann said he bought it for $15 from a stamp dealer.

"Would you look at it once more?" he asked.

"All right," Hamilton replied condescendingly.

During his second inspection of the letter, Hamilton noticed it was dated in 1825, ten years earlier than the oldest document in the hand of Smith that he had previously examined.

As he read the text of the letter he recognized a characteristic he had seen before in the writings of Smith: several words were misspelled using double consonants, such as two p's in the word oppinion. He recognized other similarities.

"You know," Hamilton said, "he was only a nineteen-year-old kid then. It's possible his writing could have changed.

"Maybe this could be in Smith's hand," he said as he read further.

"Jumpin' Jehoshaphat," Hamilton shouted when he came to the sentence about a "clever spirit." Then he read the passage aloud.

"You know, Mark, I think this *is* the Prophet. This was Joseph Smith's handwriting when he was a very young man."

"What do you think it might be worth?" Mark asked.

"On the open market, maybe $10,000. But the church would probably pay $25,000 for it, just so it could burn it. This shows Joseph Smith was a treasure hunter, not a God seeker."

Hamilton meant the remark as a joke—and Mark did not tell him that he had already approached the church with extortion in mind.

After Hofmann returned to Salt Lake City with a note signed by Hamilton attesting that the letter was in the hand of Joseph Smith, he met alone with President Hinckley at the Church Administration Building on January 14. Hinckley gave him a check for $15,000. Mark gave him the letter, along with his word that no one else had a copy of the letter. Hofmann said he was glad to have been able to help the church, and then the letter was locked in the First Presidency's Vault.

16

Standing almost six feet four inches tall, with broad shoulders and muscular arms, Brent Lee Metcalfe had the beefy body of a football linebacker. Because of his size, it was not surprising that when he returned to Salt Lake City in 1979 from his mission, the church's Security Department hired him as a guard at the church headquarters, where his father supervised operations for its worldwide network of temples.

At East High School in Salt Lake City, his teachers had called Metcalfe smart but lazy. He studied too little and played too much and his high school grades reflected his habits: When he returned from his mission, he lacked the academic credentials needed to enroll in college.

While seeking converts for the church in London, Metcalfe for the first time in his life encountered organized resistance to Mormonism. He was given anti-Mormon tracts that ridiculed Joseph Smith's story of the gold plates and his 1842 revelation that he had translated hieroglyphics found with an Egyptian museum mummy into an important Mormon scripture called the Book of Abraham. The tracts contended modern Egyptologists had studied portions of the papyri and concluded that they were simply ordinary Egyptian funereal documents known as the Book of the Dead and were identical to papyri packed with thousands of mummies in ancient Egypt for the purpose of helping them fare well in the afterlife.

Other anti-Mormon literature Metcalfe encountered contended the church believed that Adam was the *father* of Jesus Christ. Determined to prove them wrong, Metcalfe discovered to his surprise that in 1852 Brigham Young had in fact proclaimed Adam and God the Father were one and the same—and that Jesus was Adam's son. But the doctrine had split the Saints and it was quietly dropped from church liturgy in the twentieth century except by Mormon fundamentalists.

Metcalfe believed that most of what he read in the anti-Mormon literature was lies or distortions, and when his mission was over, he decided to launch a counterattack and undertake what he called "anti-anti-Mormon" research.

In Salt Lake City, he began to haunt libraries and in his spare time search for evidence challenging the anti-Mormon propaganda. Although untrained as a scholar, he plunged into his work with the commitment of a zealot as well as with a talent for research and writing, and before long he was being invited to contribute to publications such as *Sunstone Review* and *Seventh East Press,* the independent newspaper at BYU.

Metcalfe had made a good impression with his superiors in the church's Security Department and in 1981, after several lesser assignments, he was promoted to work in a communications center that served as the command post for its operations. The Department's mission ranged from guarding Temple Square to the monitoring by undercover agents of meetings of polygamist groups, Mormon homosexual organizations and groups that supported the Equal Rights Amendment. One of Metcalfe's jobs was to take calls from church intelligence agents in which they reported the license numbers of vehicles parked near such meetings; Metcalfe then called the Salt Lake City Police Department, which ran a check of the license plates and identified the people attending the meetings.

On February 11, 1983, Metcalfe was summoned by his superiors to a meeting and accused of being subversive by associating with the publishers of *Sunstone* and *B.Y.U. Studies,* a journal that carried articles by members of the nascent Mormon intellectual movement and other scholars.

Surprised, Metcalfe said he had been trying to have research work published that *supported* the church.

After a fatherly talk, he was ordered to sever his connections with the publications, placed on probation and warned he would be fired if he continued to associate with antichurch elements. Following orders, Metcalfe dutifully advised the suspect publications that he could no longer write for them.

Almost eight weeks later, Metcalfe was summoned again by his superiors for a meeting that Metcalfe would later denounce as a religious inquisition. It began with an explanation by a senior official of the Personnel Department:

"We have reason to believe you have violated your probation and have associated with antichurch elements.

"Do you give your research to anti-Mormons?"

"No," Metcalfe said. *"I do research because of my love for the church, not because I'm rejecting it."*

Then came a volley of questions spoken so rapidly Metcalfe felt he was a target in a shooting gallery.

"What kind of research do you do?"

"Who are your friends?"

"Whom do you give your information to?"

"Do you deal with *Dialogue*?"

"They wouldn't know me from Adam," Metcalfe said.

"They wouldn't even know *Adam* with all the way-out theories they have," a security official said sarcastically.

"What books have you been reading?"

"I've been reading a number of books . . ."

"Have you been reading any *old* books?"

"Yes."

Metcalfe conceded that he had recently checked out of the church library a biography of Elias Smith, a Vermont preacher and contemporary of Joseph Smith. In the book, Metcalfe had noticed, a reader before him had made a note citing parallels between Joseph Smith's story of a divine vision and a similar experience claimed by Elias Smith.

The men in the room glanced at each other.

It was the answer they had been waiting for. That was why the meeting was called.

An informant in the Correlation Department had seen Metcalfe return the book to the library, had looked it over and had then reported to a church Apostle that Brent Metcalfe had read a subversive book.

Metcalfe said he hadn't written the note in the book. It was there before he read it, he said.

A senior personnel administrator of the church looked at him with scorn:

"Your research is delving into the mysteries."

"I didn't know researching church history was considered a crime."

"The Brethren feel it's harmful to the church," the administrator said.

"Do you have a Temple Recommend?"

"Yes," Metcalfe said.

"When you associate with apostate groups, how could you have answered the questions from your bishop truthfully that you support the General Authorities?"

"I sustain the General Authorities. I don't consider the people at *Sunstone* apostates."

Metcalfe was dismissed by the four men who had summoned him to the meeting. Nine days later, he was fired by the church, then allowed to submit his resignation.

Several weeks later, Brent Metcalfe received a telephone call from a Salt Lake City businessman who said he shared his interest in historical research. The caller said he didn't have enough time anymore to conduct his own research and inquired if Metcalfe was interested in a job as a researcher for him.

Metcalfe agreed to take the job. His new employer was Steven Christensen.

In the months following the secret acquisition of the letter about a "clever spirit" purportedly written by Joseph Smith to Josiah Stowell, conservatives in the church hierarchy further intensified their efforts to restrain the growing assertion of independence by

Mormon scholars. The catalyst for the new crackdown was an interview published January 11—the same day Mark Hofmann took the letter to Charles Hamilton—in *Seventh East Press.*

Sterling M. McMurrin, a professor of philosophy at the University of Utah who had served as United States Commissioner of Education under President Kennedy, revealed in the interview that since childhood he had found it impossible to accept the Book of Mormon as the literal truth. Still, he said he regarded himself a faithful Mormon who loved his church.

"You don't get books from angels and translate them by miracles," he said.

"But the church is more than a book . . . the church is the people who constitute it and their relationships to one another, their hopes and aspirations, their mutual love, their joys and tragedies; there is so much good in Mormonism as a religion and moral culture, and so much basic strength in Mormon theology, and so much goodness in the Mormon people. . . .

"We are going through a stage of indoctrination in the church that robs the individual of intellectual freedom," he said, and it had produced a "reprehensible and odious" attempt to distort history.

McMurrin contended that church leaders such as Apostle Boyd K. Packer "regard genuinely honest church history as dangerous to the faith."

Possibly, he added, they had good reason for doing so.

"To a remarkable degree," the philosopher continued, "the church has concealed much of its history from its people, while at the same time causing them to tie their religious faith to its own controlled interpretation of its history." That the church had sought to control access to the truth was not unusual or surprising, he said. "Honesty is not a particularly common virtue of churches or of any other organization.

"There is nothing new about churches perverting history. This has been done ever since we have had churches and I suppose it will continue as long as churches persist. Most institutions—including churches, governments and government agencies—look out for themselves and often find it advantageous to ignore historical facts and do a little reconstructing here and there on their own history; if the church is interested in controlling its history to make it look better than it actually is or as a means of achieving a measure of thought control over its people, Apostle Packer's advice and instruction would seem to be quite in order. His task is to pursue the purposes of the church as a defender of the faith."

Shortly after the article was published, the administration at BYU banned the sale of *Seventh East Press* at the university, and the resulting loss of sales forced the student newspaper to cease publication.

In the weeks that followed, Brent Metcalfe was not the only member of the church who was summoned before informal tribunals. A committee of churchmen led by former leaders of the Correlation Department had compiled a list of church members who had written for *Dialogue, Sunstone Review,* and similar publications or otherwise raised questions about the church's official version of its origins and dogma and forwarded the offenders' names to their bishops or stake presidents, who were advised that they had been involved in propagating information that was not faith promoting.

At least a dozen researchers were warned such work was placing them in spiritual jeopardy. If they persisted in asserting claims of academic freedom, they were told, they could lose their Temple Recommend and thus be barred from doing the sacred work that the church maintained was essential to ensure their own salvation and the salvation of their ancestors.

17

As he drove home from his office, Brent Ashworth was puzzled by a radio news report about an auction at Charles Hamilton's gallery in New York City at which an autographed photo of Al Capone had sold for $4,200.

"... *The seller of the rare photograph was Mark William Hofmann of Sandy, Utah, who bought it at a garage sale for $50. ... Hofmann, a collector of autographs since he was twelve, said he had been buying and selling documents professionally for three years and was now earning enough to support a wife and son and to recently buy a house. ... Hofmann said he had sold thousands of autographs but this was his biggest thrill. He said he had expected the gangster's photograph to bring only about $300 at auction. ...*"

When the story was repeated that night by Dan Rather on *The CBS Evening News,* Ashworth was even more puzzled: The Al Capone picture had come from *his* collection and he had traded it to Mark for Mormon documents worth $2,000.

The next time they met, Ashworth asked him how the news reporters had gotten their facts so confused. Hofmann responded with a blank stare, as if to say he had no idea what Brent was talking about.

It was not the first time Ashworth had seen that look, or the last.

Mark was becoming increasingly secretive about himself and his document dealings, and it troubled Ashworth. He was also troubled by some of the people who were gravitating around Hofmann, a group of Mormon youths who said they were helping him find rare documents. Hofmann seldom volunteered information about his business and increasingly concealed his thoughts behind the vacant, stoic glance with which he responded to the question about Al Capone's photograph.

Hofmann sometimes dropped out of sight for days at a time, and when he reappeared he wouldn't tell Ashworth where he had been. In the document business, he said, dealers had to keep their sources secret because they didn't want others to go to the same trough. If Hofmann didn't like a question he was asked, he responded with that stare—or, sometimes, as Ashworth began to discover, he lied. And when he did talk about his business, it was usually to boast about his success.

None of Hofmann's disagreeable habits mattered to Ashworth, however, because he had become a man possessed.

Buying the letters written by Martin Harris and Lucy Mack Smith had changed his life: It had filled it with the sense of purpose that had been absent since he was nineteen.

He took the letters to sacrament meetings and firesides all around the country and, holding them up as if they were scripture, offered them as evidence God had seen fit to bring forth in the twentieth century to confirm the divine origin of the Book of Mormon. At some of these meetings Ashworth felt the presence of God. He was on his mission at last.

By making him a celebrity, the church had provided him with a platform that he could use to further the Lord's work. He went to his office; he performed his duties as bishop; he enjoyed the love of his wife and children. But, he joked, he was a fanatic as obsessed with finding more faith-promoting documents as a drug addict in need of a fix.

Periodically, Hofmann satisfied his appetite by selling him more documents—none as dramatic or as uplifting as these two letters, but he bought dozens of letters and documents of lesser importance that filled in new details about the history of the church.

Although Ashworth had a successful career as general counsel for Nature's Sunshine Products, a manufacturer of vitamins and herbs, he and his wife, Charlene, were not wealthy. But they decided to invest whatever they could in his collection; it was to be an annuity, one that would first provide spiritual sustenance and later be a source of income for their retirement. Stock options in his company had brought them $200,000 from Wall Street; they invested this windfall, along with much of their savings, to buy more documents.

Each Wednesday, Ashworth drove from Provo to Salt Lake City for a business meeting. En route, he stopped at Mark's home or met him outside a bookstore at the Crossroads Mall in Salt Lake City to exchange gossip about their mutual preoccupation with rare documents. Ashworth sometimes went away from their meetings with a bitter taste: Whatever story Ashworth told, Hofmann topped it; when he mentioned that President Kimball had hugged him when he had shown the Lucy Mack Smith letter to him, Mark said that when he had been in Kimball's office, the Prophet had taken his head in his hands and *blessed* him. Mark bragged that he had been allowed to enter the First Presidency's Vault and that he had had secret dealings with the Brethren.

"I just sold a letter to President Hinckley that's a bombshell," he confided at one meeting.

"What was it?"

He said he had promised Hinckley not to tell anyone about it or to make any copies. But he said he had a copy and offered to show it to Ashworth.

"Want to see it?"

"Well, no, Mark, I don't if you promised President Hinckley not to show it to anybody; remember, I'm a bishop in the church.

"If you told him you weren't going to make a copy of it," Ashworth added, "why did you?"

"It's a letter written by Joseph and it's a bombshell," Hofmann said without answering the question.

"I sure would have loved that," Ashworth said after hearing the name of Joseph Smith.

"I don't think you would, Brent—you wouldn't have wanted

this letter: It mixes Joseph Smith up in black magic between the time of his first visit by Moroni and the time he got the gold plates."

Seldom if ever in Ashworth's thirty-four years had he doubted the divine origin of the Book of Mormon. But after leaving Hofmann, he sought out his father, a Provo architect, and told him what he had just heard. He said it had shaken his faith in the church.

"Don't let it shake your testimony," his father counseled. "We all have questions we'll have to answer someday; I'd just put it on the shelf and forget it."

Although the words of his father helped, they did not end the depression that had descended upon Ashworth.

Several weeks later, while he was on a business trip to Missouri, he visited the archives of the Reorganized Church of Jesus Christ of Latter-day Saints in Independence where he was permitted to inspect one of the most precious artifacts in Mormondom: a letter written by Joseph Smith to his wife, Emma, from the Carthage Jail shortly before his murder that concluded: "I am very much resigned to my lot. . . ."

After returning to Utah, he told Hofmann of his excitement at holding the letter and a second the Prophet had written shortly before his martyrdom. Hofmann replied that he had heard rumors about the existence of another letter written by Joseph from the jail, one in which he had summoned the commander of his militia —General Jonathan Dunham—to rescue him. According to the rumors, Dunham ignored the appeal. After the letter was found discarded on the street in Nauvoo, Dunham was murdered by grieving Mormons. Then the letter vanished.

"Mark, if you ever hear anything about that letter, I'd love to buy it; it would be tremendous—a dream."

Hofmann recalled reading that General Dunham had in fact died violently and promised to begin a search for it. Someone, he said, had told him it was owned by a Mormon family named Huntington.

A few weeks later, Hofmann said he thought he had located the letter. Ashworth won his promise to offer it to him first, before other collectors.

"It may cost $30,000," Hofmann said.

"I don't care," Ashworth said. "I'll sell more stock."

"Okay, you've got the right of first refusal," Hofmann said.

Ashworth's obsession—his life's work—now focused on a single prize: Joseph Smith's final message before his death.

But when Hofmann telephoned him shortly before Christmas Day in 1983, he offered Ashworth a different prize.

It was a letter, Ashworth responded, that should be buried.

18

Hofmann handed Ashworth a typed letter dated October 23, 1830, and said it was the text of a stampless cover recently discovered by one of his document scouts in New York.

If he wanted the original, Mark said, the price was $50,000.

Ashworth wore thick eyeglasses set in heavy plastic frames that, when he was surprised or excited, gave him the look of a curious owl. His eyes grew larger as they scanned the typescript for evidence to support the huge price Hofmann was asking for the letter.

As always, Ashworth felt a spiritual tingle as he read a newly unearthed document from the church's past.

Then his eyes came to an abrupt stop at two words: *white salamander.*

"Mark, I don't want this. You can't let anybody except the church have this," he said.

"I don't think *any* collector should have it. No collector should have to *explain* something like this."

Hofmann said no other Martin Harris letter like it would ever come on the market.

"Brent, it's going to make *Time* magazine."

"I don't care, I don't want it. I think it's a forgery; it sounds like a forgery from the 1830s by some anti-Mormon group."

"Dean Jessee has already seen it," Hofmann said, "and he said it's Martin Harris's handwriting."

Ashworth looked at the typewritten letter a second time.

"I just don't want it," he repeated. "This should go to the church."

The letter addressed to William Wines Phelps, a newspaper editor and early Mormon convert, contained a description of the coming forth of the Book of Mormon remote from the glorious accounts taught to Mormon children beginning in nursery school and repeated thousands of times a day by Mormon missionaries around the world:

Palmyra Oct. 23d, 1830

Dear Sir:

Your letter of yesterday is received & I hasten to answer as fully as I can—Joseph Smith Jr. first come to my notice in the year 1824. In the summer of that year I contracted with his father to build a fence on my property. In the corse of that work I approach Joseph & ask how it is in a half day you put up what requires your father & 2 brothers a full day working together? He says I have not been with out assistance but can not say more only you better find out. The next day I take the older Smith by the arm & he says Joseph can see any thing he wishes by looking at a stone. Joseph often sees Spirits here with great kettles of coin money. It was Spirits who brought up rock because Joseph made no attempt on their money. I latter dream I converse with spirits which let me count their money. When I awake I have in my hand a dollar coin which I take for a sign. Joseph describes what I seen in every particular, says he, the spirits are grieved, so I through back the dollar. In the fall of the year 1827 I hear Joseph found a gold bible. I take Joseph aside & he says it is true. I found it 4 years ago with my stone but only just got it because of the enchantment. The old spirit come to me 3 times in the same dream and says dig up the gold, but when I take it up the next morning the spirit transfigured himself from a white salamander in the bottom of the hole & struck me 3 times & held the treasure & would not let me have it because I lay it down to cover over the hole when the spirit says do not lay it down. Joseph says when can I have it? The spirit says bring your brother Alvin. Joseph says he is dead, shall I bring what remains? but the spirit is gone. Joseph goes to get the gold bible but the spirit says you did not bring your brother—you can not have it—look to the stone. Joseph looks but can not see who to bring. The spirit says I tricked you again—look to the stone. Joseph looks and sees his wife. On the 22d day of Sept. 1827 they got the gold bible—I give Joseph $50 to move him down to Pa. Joseph says when you visit me I will give you a sign. He gives me some hiroglyphics. I take them to Utica Albany & New York. In the last place Dr. Mitchel gives me a introduction to Professor Anthon. Says he, they are short hand Egyptian the same way was used in ancient times. Bring me the old book & I will translate, says I, it is made of precious gold & is sealed from view. Says he, I can not read a sealed book—Joseph found some giant silver specticles from the plates. He puts them in a old hat & and in the darkness reads the words & in this way it is all translated & written down—about the middle of June 1829 Joseph takes me together with Oliver Cowdrey & David Whitmer to have a view of the plates. Our names are appended to the book of Mormon which I had printed with my own money—space & time both prevent me from writing more at presant. If there is any thing further you wish to inquire I shall attend to it.

Yours respectfully
Martin Harris

Although he did not acknowledge it to Ashworth, Hofmann had already offered the letter to the church.

He had been reluctant to take the letter to Gordon Hinckley himself—anyone who carried *that* letter into the First Presidency's Office would be looked on as an extortionist—so he had asked a surrogate to do it for him.

But it had been a mistake. He had sent the wrong man.

Lyn Richard Jacobs, who was the son of an electrical engineer employed at the Church Office Building, had once listed his occupations this way: *pianist, artist, taxidermist and tailor.* Most of all, however, he was a student.

Now six months short of his twenty-ninth birthday, Jacobs had been considered precocious since early childhood. Born in Provo and reared in Salt Lake City in a devout Mormon family, he had been ordained, like most of his male classmates, a deacon, teacher, priest and Elder in the church. Following his graduation from high school, where he usually got straight A's, he enrolled at the University of Utah and helped meet his expenses by working at a church-owned company that manufactured the special undergarments many Mormons wear. Later, he worked as a clerk in the church Genealogical Department, a vast repository of information about births and deaths and other records used by church members while preparing for what they called "temple work"—serving as stand-ins for the dead during vicarious baptisms and marriages.

At nineteen, Jacobs interrupted his studies for two years to serve a mission in Quebec, then returned to Salt Lake City and was graduated from the University of Utah in 1978 with two bachelor's degrees, in philosophy and French literature. Meanwhile, he had become conversant in French, German, Latin, Greek and Coptic.

Hofmann and Jacobs met in 1980 while they were shopping at a bookstore. When Jacobs left two years later to study at the Harvard Divinity School, he agreed to be a document scout for Hofmann on the East Coast.

They were, on the surface, an incongruous pair of friends: Hofmann, quiet, soft-spoken and deferential, blended easily into the conservative terrain of the church. Jacobs, by contrast, was a flamboyant personality in Salt Lake City. After completing his mission, he grew a Vandyke beard and began wearing a gold earring, acquired a reputation for arrogance to those he regarded as intellectual inferiors and sent signals that he was preparing to pursue a lifestyle different from that advocated by his church.

When Jacobs's Harvard classes recessed for the Christmas holidays in 1983, he flew home to Salt Lake City and made an appointment with Gordon Hinckley, identifying himself as a returned missionary who had an important document to show him.

Hinckley read the letter, said it was interesting and waited for Jacobs to name a price.

Jacobs offered to trade the letter for a $10 Mormon gold coin, one of the rarest coins ever minted in America. The few in existence were valued at more than $100,000.

Hinckley for a few moments sat silently rereading the letter, Jacobs later reported. Then he said he thought the asking price was too high.

Jacobs lowered his price: a copy of the Book of Commandments, which was worth about $40,000.

Hinckley became lost in thought again for a few moments and then said he didn't know if the church really wanted the letter. The price of documents was getting too high. Then the church president bade goodbye to the bearded former missionary with the gold earring.

After Jacobs had told him how much he intended to ask for Martin Harris's letter, Mark Hofmann had expected him to be dismissed by the First Presidency.

But he had not stopped Jacobs; Hofmann, as always, had been curious to learn how the church would respond to the offer. If Hofmann enjoyed anything, it was watching leaders of his church squirm.

After Ashworth also rejected the letter, Hofmann contacted the Church Archivist Donald Schmidt and revealed that he thought he could buy it from Jacobs for $20,000, and Schmidt said he would take the matter up with his superiors in the Historical Department. When Schmidt later indicated that church officials were leery that Jacobs might tell others the church had purchased an embarrassing letter, Hofmann suggested an alternative plan: Perhaps a wealthy church member could be found to buy it, keep its existence a secret and then donate it to the church.

Hofmann later explained to Jacobs that the Brethren preferred to encourage members to donate potentially embarrassing documents in lieu of their tithing. This enabled church leaders to deny having purchased the documents if their existence later became known.

After initially notifying Hofmann that the church wanted to buy the letter directly, Schmidt said his superiors had decided it should be acquired by a middleman, a faithful member who would look out for the church's best interests.

"Do you know anybody who would buy it and donate it?" Jacobs asked.

Hofmann recalled a telephone call that he had received from a friend, Brent Metcalfe. Metcalfe had told him that he had recently gone to work for a Mormon bishop. The bishop was a history buff who had expressed interest in looking at any interesting documents Hofmann uncovered.

Mark told Jacobs he would call Metcalfe and ask if his new boss was interested in the letter. His employer's name, Hofmann said, was Steven Christensen.

19

Shortly after Christmas, Church Historian G. Homer Durham telephoned Steve Christensen to confirm what Hofmann had already told him: The church would be pleased to have Martin Harris's letter in the hands of a faithful member and be grateful if he acquired it and eventually donated it to the church. On January 6, 1984—three days before his thirtieth birthday—Christensen purchased Martin Harris's letter to W. W. Phelps, a letter that was soon referred to in whispers and gossip as "the salamander letter."

Hofmann asked $50,000 for the letter but accepted an offer from Christensen of $40,000 payable over eighteen months: $1,000 down, $9,000 in two weeks, the balance in increments of $10,000 at six-month intervals.

For Steve Christensen and Gary Sheets, running C.F.S. was no longer as simple or as easy as it had been during the hyperinflated real estate boom of the late seventies and early eighties, when the value of the apartment houses and other properties it bought for investors soared overnight.

In some cities where C.F.S. had invested heavily—particularly Houston, where the energy boom of the previous two decades was collapsing under the weight of a sharp drop in world oil prices—real estate values were falling. Moreover, some of the company's other investments were doing poorly as well. Steve responded to the bearish new investment climate by working harder. He appeared at the C.F.S. Building in downtown Salt Lake City earlier, worked later and reached an agreement with Terri: He could work as long as he wanted, but was to be home every night for dinner and to say goodnight to the children. Then he could go back to work.

There was plenty of wealth in the life of Steve and Terri Christensen to help compensate for the longer hours. Steve was earning almost $200,000 a year and was *almost* a millionaire: In a financial statement prepared a week before Brent Metcalfe mentioned the telephone call he'd received from Mark Hofmann about the availability of an important letter by Martin Harris, Christensen had added up his net worth. The total was $980,000. There was plenty of money for Terri to buy jewelry and new clothes and they consulted an architect who sketched out plans for their dream house in the Wasatch foothills near Bountiful. The home's design focused on a huge two-story library for Steve's collection of books, now approaching thirteen thousand volumes.

After Homer Durham told him the church would be grateful if he bought the Martin Harris letter from Hofmann, Christensen plumbed his expertise as a financial planner for rich clients and devised a plan that made it feasible: He would buy the letter, eventually transfer its ownership to J. Gary Sheets & Associates, finance research to determine its authenticity and historical significance and then, after one year, donate it to the church at an inflated value. For a Mormon, such a ploy served two purposes: It was not only an income-tax write-off but it reduced the amount of cash required to comply with the church's mandate to donate ten percent of his income to the church. Although Gary Sheets had no previous interest in historical documents, he agreed to underwrite seventy percent of the research costs.

Christensen told Metcalfe he wanted to finance a research project that would not only determine whether the letter was genuine but, before it was made public, place it in proper historical context and anticipate the kind of criticism anti-Mormons almost surely would level against it. Although some leaders of the church wanted him to, it was not his intention to hide the letter. It was true, he said, that in the wrong hands the letter could hurt the church. But suppressing it would do more violence to the values of the church because it would be dishonest. In a letter to Homer Durham he detailed his plans:

My intentions are as follows:

1. To spend a reasonable amount of time having the historical issues presented in the document researched. I am not a professional historian myself. However, it is my intention to retain one or two competent and faithful historians to do the work for me.

2. After the research is completed it is my desire to have the document and annotated commentary published. I would also like to have quality photographs of the document published with the text.

3. At such point in time as the research and printing is completed, it is my intention and desire to donate the document to the Church of Jesus Christ of Latter-day Saints.

I am sensitive to the fact that this is the only letter currently known to exist in the handwriting of Martin Harris. I am also aware that if the document were to be published that a careful commentary should accompany its introduction to the public. It is most exciting to have in writing Martin Harris' testimony that he saw the gold plates as well as his role with the "hierophyphics" and Professor Anthon. . . .

Christensen had decided to stretch out payments for the letter over eighteen months for two purposes: to provide time for his research project and to discourage Hofmann and Jacobs from prematurely disclosing its existence to anyone.

He drafted a sales contract acknowledging that Hofmann and the church could keep their copies of the letter but requiring Hofmann and Jacobs to pledge not to reveal what they knew about it until either the church or Christensen authorized them to do so.

"You can't talk about this to anyone," Christensen said. "We don't want anybody to know about it until we're ready."

"If anybody asks me about it," Hofmann replied, "I'll deny knowing anything about it."

"Are you sure no one else knows about it, that you haven't told anyone besides the church?"

"Yes," Hofmann assured him.

It was a lie.

Hofmann had already informed members of the Mormon Underground who were among the most hostile to the church about the letter.

In late January, Hofmann told Christensen he was experiencing a cash-flow problem. Because a document he had sold at auction in New York fetched a lower price than he had anticipated, he needed immediate cash to consummate another transaction. He asked Christensen if he would advance him, in addition to the $9,000 initial payment that was due on the letter, $5,000 of the amount scheduled to be paid six months later. In return, Hofmann offered Christensen a bonus: the transcript of a contract dated November 1, 1825, in which Joseph Smith's father, Josiah Stowell and several partners agreed on the division of proceeds from a money-digging enterprise they had organized to find buried treasure. Hofmann said two elderly sisters owned the original of the contract, and he was negotiating to buy it. He suggested Christensen might want to have it because it complemented the letter from Martin Harris by adding new details about the Prophet's money-digging ventures. Christensen advanced him the money in exchange for a copy of the text and the right to buy the original for $15,000 if and when Hofmann acquired it.

Then, Christensen acted quickly to establish and finance a secret research team to evaluate the letter. Leonard Arrington agreed to loan two of his senior researchers at BYU—Dean Jessee and Professor Ronald Walker—to conduct a professional study of the letter with the help of Brent Metcalfe and to write a book about it when they were finished.

In a letter to the researchers, Christensen wrote:

I have tremendous respect for historians such as yourself who are faithful, honest and eager to make significant contributions to the scholarship of Mormon history and theology. . . . I believe that the work that you brethren do will have significance to Mormon scholarship in the years to come, that this can and will

become a standard cited reference, and that the church will be
blessed as a result of the honest, accurate, historical foundation
which the three of you men will provide to the study of early
Mormon origins. I would also have you know that I do not
intend on getting in the way. I am excited and interested to
participate financially and support this project. . . . I am eager
that this work reach such a high standard that it would be extremely difficult for anyone coming from an anti-Mormon point
of view to discredit the research and the standard which has
been reached. . . . Naturally I desire to participate in any way
possible, but preferably at your request. I look forward to our
association during the coming months.

While the research team was getting organized, Brent Ashworth
was relaxing at his home in Provo on a Sunday evening when his
mother-in-law called from Phoenix and read him the text of a letter
she had just read:

Carthage Jail June 27, 1844
Major General Dunham

Dear Sir
    You are hereby ordered to resign the defense of the City of
Nauvoo to Captain Singleton and proceed to this place without
delay with what ever numbers of the Nauvoo Legion as may
safely and immediately come. Let this be done quietly and or-
derly but with great hast we are in the hands of our sworn
enemies.

Joseph Smith

Ashworth's mother-in-law said the letter had been quoted in an
article published that morning in the newspaper that served
Arizona's Saints community. It reported that Richard Marks, a
Phoenix dentist whom Ashworth knew as a rival collector, had
purchased the last letter written by Joseph Smith before his martyrdom in the Carthage Jail. The seller was Mark Hofmann of Salt
Lake City.

For a moment, Ashworth was speechless after his mother-in-law
finished reading the letter.

It was *his* letter. It had been promised to him. It was his *dream* to own that letter.

Stunned, he sprinted to his car, steered it onto Interstate 15 and drove as fast as he dared in heavy Sunday evening traffic toward Salt Lake City. When he arrived an hour later outside Mark Hofmann's home it was after 10 o'clock and the house was dark.

He ran to the door and pounded on it. When he didn't get a response, he ran back to his car and pressed the horn again and again until he saw a light go on in the living room and Hofmann, wearing a bathrobe, appeared at the front door.

Ashworth shouted:

"What are you doing selling my letter to Dick Marks?"

Mark stared at him without expression.

"Did you or did you not sell *my letter* to Dick Marks? Did you not promise me that letter? Did we or did we not have a deal for $30,000?"

Hofmann shrugged his shoulders and opened the front door, silently inviting him to enter.

"Mark, that's *my* letter. You made a deal. You promised it to me."

Hofmann said nothing until Ashworth started to leave.

"Brent," he said, "come on back here and sit down. Get it off your chest, you'll feel a lot better."

"Mark, I just got it off my chest and I feel a whole lot worse."

Ashworth slammed the door, got in his car and drove to Provo, promising himself never again to deal with Mark Hofmann.

But a few months later, they were again meeting each Wednesday at the Crossroads Mall and negotiating another transaction. He'd have dealt with the devil himself if necessary in order to carry on the Lord's work.

20

Perhaps only Utah in the last half of the twentieth century could have produced someone like Michael Marquardt or Jerald Tanner. Through 150 years of persecution, travail and growth, the Mormon church had had many enemies, from frontier newspaper editors and federal marshals to homicidal bigots and disillusioned apostates. Marquardt was a mailman for the United States Postal Service whose hobby was wading through the ocean of paper left behind by generations of Mormons and writing research reports that almost always contradicted the church's version of its history and origins.

Tanner was a machinist turned publisher whose historical research, probably more than that of anyone else except Fawn Brodie, had given birth to what was called "the new Mormon history."

By the broadest definition, they were members of the Mormon Underground, the unorganized collection of history buffs who traded copies of old documents like members of a spy ring passing secrets. But while many participants in the Underground, such as Steve Christensen, were fiercely loyal to the church and convinced its doctrines could survive candid scrutiny of its history, Michael Marquardt and Jerald Tanner were thoroughly committed to the premise that much of what the church taught was false and manipulative.

Marquardt was dark-haired, thin and fragile in appearance and, at forty-two, he spoke so slowly that his voice reminded some people of a slow train trying to climb a hill. He had converted to Mormonism as a teenager, moved to Salt Lake City, immersed himself in the study of church history as a hobby, then become disenchanted with Mormonism and resigned fifteen years after joining the church. Although he left the church in 1976 he continued to study its history with the passion of a missionary, searching libraries and archives for evidence to repudiate the church hierarchy. One of the people with whom he shared information was Mark Hofmann.

Jerald Tanner, a fifth-generation Mormon, was born in Provo in 1938. As a teenage seminary student he read a statement attributed to David Whitmer, one of the Three Witnesses to the Book of Mormon, denouncing Joseph Smith for revising the wording of revelations that he said had come from God. Tanner's teachers told him to ignore the claim, but he set out to prove it wrong. Instead of refuting it, he found evidence in nineteenth-century books that not only proved Whitmer right but conflicted with other lessons from the seminary.

At twenty, Tanner, a large and husky man with a thick head of black hair, fell in love with Sandra McGee, a great-great-granddaughter of Brigham Young.

Like her future husband, she had stood before members of her ward as a child and offered her testimony of belief that Joseph Smith was a prophet of God, that his story of the bringing forth of the Book of Mormon was true and that her church was the only true church on the face of the earth. But, like Jerald, she had an inquisitive and skeptical mind and sometimes questioned her religious instructors. They told her not to analyze the church's teachings, just obey them.

An unusual courtship developed between the two young Mormons: Their dates became a forum of religious inquiry in which they compared books and scripture from the nineteenth century with modern publications of the church. They discovered what they regarded as inconsistencies, implausibilities, errors and attempts to conceal embarrassing historical facts about the church.

Some scripture revealed by early prophets, such as the Adam-God Theory, had been excised by the modern church as if it had never existed, and there were multiple, conflicting versions of other important doctrines.

Although Brigham Young had been revered as a saint in Sandra McGee's family, Jerald showed her copies of sermons in which he promulgated a doctrine called blood atonement, a belief that some sins—ranging from adultery and murder to sexual relations with a Negro—were so grievous that the crucifixion of Jesus could not redeem the sinners, who could only reach the Celestial Kingdom if they were killed and "their blood spilt on the ground as a smoking incense to the almighty." Tanner unearthed early Mormon writings indicating that the doctrine had on occasion been practiced to assassinate Mormons who dissented from their leaders.

Two years after their marriage in 1959, Jerald and Sandra Tanner decided to leave the church. They explained the decision in letters to relatives to which they attached copies of some of the historical documents that troubled them. Soon, the letters were in heavy demand by other Mormons who were considering resigning from the church and from Protestant ministers seeking ammunition to stem the defection of their parishioners to Mormonism. In 1964, Jerald Tanner quit his machinist's job and he and Sandra began writing a book based on their research. From those beginnings would spring an extraordinary mom-and-pop temple of anti-Mormonism in the heart of Mormondom, the Utah Lighthouse Ministry. From a Victorian home in a middle-class Salt Lake City neighborhood, they began turning out a torrent of books and reproductions of early church documents—often passed to them by participants in the Mormon Underground—that had a singular purpose: to discredit and embarrass the church's claims of divine origin and its insistence that the Book of Mormon and Joseph Smith's account of receiving it from an angel were literally true.

A month before Hofmann sold the Martin Harris-to-W. W. Phelps letter to Steve Christensen, he invited Michael Marquardt to dinner at his home. During the visit, he showed him the text of the salamander letter. Hofmann said he did not own the original but expected to acquire it soon from a source in the East he did not identify, and he asked Marquardt for advice on how to make it public. They discussed approaching *Time, Newsweek,* or *The New York Times,* but did not reach a decision. Two days later, Hofmann called Marquardt and said he didn't want to make the letter public after all. He said he was trying to sell it and asked Marquardt to keep it a secret.

It was too late, however.

Marquardt had already told a half-dozen anti-Mormon researchers around the country about the salamander letter, including Jerald Tanner, and as the new year began, Tanner was wondering how to make the best use of the information. Meanwhile, passages from the letter, sent anonymously, began arriving at newsrooms and scholars' offices around the country, often accompanied by allegations that Gordon Hinckley had seen the letter and was trying to cover it up. Several reporters tracked rumors about the salamander letter to Steve Christensen, but he refused to acknowledge it existed. After an editor of *Time* called, read a portion of the text and said he was about to publish an article about it, Christensen vowed to sue the magazine if it did. He retained a lawyer to investigate seeking a court injunction to prevent the publication, but, citing the First Amendment, the lawyer said there was little that could be done to stop the magazine.

In late February, Christensen called Gordon Hinckley and told him he was having difficulty keeping the letter secret and might have to acknowledge that he owned it in a publication such as *Sunstone Review.*

Responding to an inquiry from *Time,* Jerry Cahill, the church's director of public affairs, released a statement to the magazine in which Hinckley acknowledged that he had seen the letter but had elected to withhold public comment about it until it had been "thoroughly researched in the context of the time and the environment in which it was written . . . I would think that no reputable individual or journal would issue a speculative story until such had been done."

Along with Hinckley's statement, Cahill delivered a letter to *Time* declaring there was little reason to be surprised at Martin Harris's use of the word *salamander.* The dictionary, he wrote, defined a salamander as "A lizard-like animal supposed to *live in or to be able to endure fire,*" a term that applied equally to persons or spirits who lived in fire. Cahill cited biblical quotations that associated miraculous events with a pillar of flame, including Exodus 3:2: "And the angel of the Lord appeared unto him in a flame of fire out of the midst of a bush and he looked, and, behold, the bush burned with fire, and the bush was not consumed." "In summary," the church official wrote, "it seems clear that fire is frequently the symbol of God's or His messenger's presence, revealed either in mercy or in judgment, or to demonstrate glory, or holiness, or protection or guidance, or punishment of the wicked; or the Holy Ghost as a purifying agent, or tongues of fire as on the day of Pentecost."

The church had confronted the white salamander for the first time and it had established its line of defense.

Two days later, Steve Christensen—and the church—lost the battle to keep the letter's existence a secret. The disclosure was not in *Time* but in Jerald Tanner's *Salt Lake Messenger*. Beneath a bold headline, "Moroni or Salamander?" Tanner quoted lengthy passages from the letter and wrote: "If the letter is authentic, it is one of the greatest evidences against the divine origin of the Book of Mormon" and added weight to the argument long denied by the church that Joseph Smith had dabbled in the occult.

There was probably no one in the Salt Lake Valley who was more anxious to believe the letter was genuine than Tanner. He had done more research than anyone else trying to link Joseph Smith to magic, money digging and the occult. The letter supported his contention that rank-and-file Mormons had been deluded by a fraudulent account of the coming forth of the Book of Mormon. But Tanner told his readers he had reservations about it because some passages reminded him of other nineteenth-century documents he had studied while researching Joseph Smith's involvement in magic.

"While we would really like to believe the letter attributed to Harris is authentic," he wrote, "we do not feel that we can endorse it until further evidence comes forth." One way to solve the mystery, he suggested, was to turn the letter over to reputable handwriting experts for an examination and to make a thorough investigation of its origin.

After Tanner's article appeared, Christensen was forced to issue a press release affirming that he owned a letter written by Martin

Harris to W. W. Phelps, but he said he would not permit its contents to be published until the work of authenticating it was complete. Then Christensen set out to do what Jerald Tanner had suggested: determine with scientific tests whether the salamander letter was genuine.

21

Members of the Church of Jesus Christ of Latter-day Saints from around the world filed into the Mormon Tabernacle in early April for their spring General Conference. The great humpbacked hall grew silent as they prayed for their Prophet, Spencer W. Kimball, who was missing from the tableau of gray-haired, dark-suited General Authorities seated together at the front of the Tabernacle. Then came a moment for celebration and congratulations: President Gordon B. Hinckley announced that the church's membership was approaching 5.5 million and that because of its continuing rapid growth, new temples were to be built in Toronto; Portland, Oregon; Las Vegas; San Diego; and Bogotá, Colombia, bringing the total around the world to forty-seven. To bring new talent into the church hierarchy, he said that henceforth appointments to the First Quorum of the Seventy—the seventy men who headed the church's operating bureaucracy—would be for three to five years, not for life.

When the afternoon session began, Spencer W. Kimball walked haltingly into the Tabernacle and took his place as the head of the church, delighting the audience. Now almost totally blind, Kimball slept most of the time and for those who dared to speculate about such things, anticipation was growing over what changes the man who was in line to succeed him, Ezra Taft Benson—considered the most conservative of Mormon leaders—would bring to their lives.

No major publications had picked up the Tanners' report, published in March, about the salamander letter, and fears of a journalistic storm over Joseph Smith's interest in magic that had threatened to engulf the church began to ease in the Church Administration Building.

Meanwhile, under a blanket of secrecy appropriate for a clandestine military project, Brent Metcalfe, Dean Jessee and Ronald Walker attacked the job of establishing the history and authenticity of the salamander letter from three directions: First, there had to be a rigorous physical examination to determine if the paper the letter was written on, its ink and its other physical properties were what they should be. Next, the provenance, or history, of the letter had to be traced as far back as possible to establish its origin and a credible chain of ownership. Finally, the text of the letter had to be evaluated critically to determine if the contents were historically consistent with its time.

For the physical examination, they turned to Kenneth Rendell, a document dealer, appraiser and examiner in Newton, Massachusetts. Along with Charles Hamilton—a professional rival with whom he sometimes quarreled—Rendell had helped determine that the "Hitler diaries" were forgeries and was frequently consulted by the FBI and prestigious libraries and archivists when the authenticity of an old document was in doubt.

Hofmann told Rendell that Steven Christensen wanted the most exhaustive examination possible of the salamander letter because when it was made public it would almost certainly come under attack from critics in the church uncomfortable over its contents. Rendell agreed to take on the assignment, but said it would take months: The scarcity of handwriting samples by Martin Harris would make the task difficult.

Hofmann said it didn't matter how long it took. It was important to remove all doubts about the letter. He said he did not care whether Rendell proved the letter was genuine or a fake: The goal was to conduct the most thorough and competent examination possible.

While Rendell launched a search for experts to analyze the letter's ink and paper, detective work by Dean Jessee identified the source of the mysterious letter as an obscure dealer in rare postmarks in New Hampshire. Lyn Jacobs said he had purchased the letter from William Thoman, the owner of Cortland Covers, a dealer in stampless covers in Cortland, New York. Jessee determined that Thoman had acquired it from Elwyn Doubleday, a dealer in postal memorabilia in Alton Bay, New Hampshire. Doubleday confirmed he had sold Thoman a large selection of early nineteenth-century stampless covers from the Palmyra region and the salamander letter was probably among them. Although it was a lucky find, he told Jessee, it was not surprising: Collectors of stampless covers were usually interested only in their postmarks and paid little attention to contents of a letter, and unless they were Mormons they probably would not have recognized the significance of a letter signed by a Martin Harris.

The final element of the research project focused on the issue of whether the salamander letter was consistent historically with its time and apparent circumstances. It led Walker, Jessee and Metcalfe down a road that for the most part had been taboo for Mormon scholars in the past, the study of Joseph Smith's involvement in the occult and money digging. During months of research, they found an abundance of material, ranging from court records of his trials in Bainbridge, New York, to obscure writings by early disciples. This information indicated that during the same period of time Smith claimed to have been led to a buried cache of gold plates by the angel Moroni, he was trying to make his living with claims of supernatural powers which enabled him to locate buried treasures of gold and silver with a seer stone and other superstitious occult practices.

Late in August, almost eight hundred people gathered in a Salt Lake City hotel for the annual *Sunstone* Theological Symposium. Even before the conference formally opened, the hotel lobby was abuzz with speculation about the secret salamander letter and reports of *another* secret letter that purportedly linked Joseph Smith to folk magic. The letter had supposedly been sent by the Prophet in 1825 to Josiah Stowell and, according to the rumors, had been purchased and hidden by the church in the First Presidency's Vault.

As the church history buffs filed into the meeting, Sandra Tanner stood in the lobby of the hotel handing out a pamphlet headlined, "The Money Digging Letters," in which her husband expressed strong reservations about the Martin Harris letter.

"We have recently been given a complete transcript of the salamander letter," he wrote. "The more we examine the letter attributed to Harris, the more questions we have about its authenticity."

The next morning, Mark Hofmann rang the doorbell of the two-story wooden house that served as the Tanners' home and headquarters of the Utah Lighthouse Ministry.

Sandra Tanner, who had known Hofmann for years, had never seen him so upset.

"Why you, of all people?"

Mark acted, she thought, as if he had been betrayed by a friend.

"Mark, we *want* to believe it's genuine. But you won't say where it came from or give any evidence that it's authentic."

Hofmann said Steve Christensen wouldn't let him discuss anything about the letter but insisted that in a short time, when his research project was finished, everything would be made public about the letter and Jerald's doubts would be satisfied.

"I'm sworn not to release it," he said. "When I sell a document, that's the condition you make: The buyer has the option to publish it or not. My hands are tied. I could understand the church questioning it, but you? This basically shows that what Jerald has been saying is right."

The paper and ink, Hofmann continued, had been analyzed and experts said it was genuine.

"It passed all the tests."

"Where did Lyn Jacobs get it?"

Hofmann said it was a violation of the unwritten rules of document dealing to reveal a seller's identity. He couldn't do so unless Christensen gave his approval. But he confided that the source was a major dealer in New York. "There's only three or four major dealers in New York. It should be easy for you guys to figure it out; check 'em out."

Hofmann said he had given buyers a bona fide provenance for

every document he had ever sold. When the church bought the Blessing of Joseph Smith III, he gave it an affidavit showing that the Blessing was part of a collection of old documents saved by the family of Thomas Bullock.

Lowering his voice while he made certain no one else was in the foyer of the Tanners' house—the Utah Lighthouse Ministry's bookstore—he said that the Bullock Collection was likely to produce more gems soon, including letters implicating her ancestor, Brigham Young, in misusing his position with the church to become a multimillionaire.

He was also on the trail of an even bigger bombshell, the papers of William E. McLellin, an early Apostle of Joseph Smith who broke with the Prophet in 1838 and became a dedicated anti-Mormon.

According to church lore, McLellin kept a journal critical of the Prophet and took a cache of incriminating documents with him when he left the church. Hofmann said he knew the McLellin Collection was someplace in Texas and, among other things, it contained a long-lost piece of Egyptian papyrus referred to as Facsimile Number Two that Joseph Smith claimed to have translated into the Book of Abraham and modern scholars could examine to learn if his translation was a fabrication or not.

Hofmann's revelations excited Sandra Tanner and she urged him to show her the material as soon as he found it. That evening she told her husband she was now convinced the salamander letter was genuine and proved Joseph Smith's involvement in magic and money digging. She advised Jerald to be cautious about what he wrote about the letter. Otherwise, they might get sued for libel. Tanner said he would await the scientific testing before coming to a final decision about the letter.

22

When the Sunstone Conference ended, the *Los Angeles Times* revealed the salamander letter's existence in a long article published August 25, 1984, that began: *"A letter purportedly written in 1830 by Mormonism's first convert is now threatening to alter the idealized portrait of church founder Joseph Smith."*

Within days, newspapers and magazines, radio and television stations around the world repeated the story. Although no journalists had yet seen the letter, it did not deter many from employing the language of doomsday to characterize its potential impact on the church. "It threatens to shake the Mormon church at its foundations" was one of the most commonly used phrases.

The church issued a statement calling the term *white salamander* completely consistent with Joseph Smith's description of receiving the gold plates of the Book of Mormon from an angel.

Rhett James, a Mormon historian who was a specialist on Martin Harris, said that the letter strengthened the foundations of the Prophet's story of his discovery of the gold plates and that it sounded very much like Harris, a man who "had the ability to talk to farmers like a farmer and to poets like a poet."

Steve Christensen told *The Deseret News,* the daily newspaper in

Salt Lake City published by the church, that if tests proved the letter was authentic, it would be made public within a year and serve as the nucleus of a book reexamining the roots of Mormonism. Christensen predicted the letter would "fit comfortably into the overall account of the coming forth of the Book of Mormon."

BYU professor Ronald Walker told reporters the letter was taking scholars into exciting and unexplored crannies at a time in history when religion and folk magic were closely intertwined. In the past, he said, historians had focused too much on "institutional religion. Now we are finding strains of religion we have not studied before. Some of them are very old, extending back before American history. Activities in which Joseph Smith was engaged were not unusual for his time."

While the journalistic storm continued, Mark Hofmann took a flight in early September to New York City and checked in at the Empire Hotel. Hofmann was now a frequent guest at the hotel near Lincoln Center, which was across the street from New York City's Mormon Visitors Center, the principal beachhead for communicating the church's message on the East Coast. It was also a short walk from most of the city's major midtown autograph dealers.

He called on Charles Hamilton, then Harmer Rooke, an autograph dealer on East Fifty-seventh Street to whom he and Lyn Jacobs, who was stopping in New York before resuming his classes at Harvard, sold autographs by Nathaniel Hawthorne, Mark Twain, Paul Revere and Orville Wright. Then Hofmann went to the Schiller-Wapner Galleries on East Sixty-first Street, where he had introduced himself the preceding April as a Salt Lake City dealer in rare coins and bullion who was anxious to start a collection of rare children's books for his wife.

Since then, he had become a frequent visitor to the prestigious gallery, where he was welcomed as a tasteful and discerning collector who spent upwards of $10,000 a month on first-edition books by authors such as Lewis Carroll, J. R. R. Tolkien, Hans Christian Andersen and Beatrix Potter. "He wants only the best," Justin Schiller told his partner, Raymond Wapner, after one visit.

Hofmann returned to Salt Lake City on September 26, just in time to learn from Kenneth Rendell that William G. Krueger, an Appleton, Wisconsin, consultant who was regarded as the nation's foremost forensic examiner of paper, had concluded there were no indications of forgery in the salamander letter. Krueger said the paper on which it was written was typical of the kind available in western New York in 1830. Now, Rendell said, he had to find an equally competent expert to evaluate the ink.

Like Steve Christensen, Hofmann was enjoying the financial fruits of success. The news of his discoveries and high prices being commanded by old letters and autographs had produced a curious new kind of investment business—speculation in historical documents. Friends, relatives and strangers began to press money into Hofmann's hands with a request to invest it in old documents. He responded by forming syndicates to acquire documents in much the same way that Gary Sheets's company, Coordinated Financial Services, pooled the money of wealthy investors to buy apartment houses.

When reports circulated that some investors had made profits of as much as thirty percent in a month, the mystique surrounding Hofmann grew and still more people lined up to invest with him, despite some unusual work habits:

He was seldom on time for appointments and sometimes arranged for investors to meet him late at night to discuss the acquisition of a century-old document, then disappeared into the darkness; his checks often bounced, at least temporarily; he said he suspected the church or the IRS was tapping his telephone; he often let days pass before returning a phone call, and when he did it was often from a telephone in his car. The once prim ex-missionary began to dress sloppily, prompting one friend to call him "Gomer Pyle" and accuse him of buying his clothes at K mart. When investors dropped in unexpectedly at his home, Dorie Hofmann sometimes said he was gone even though they could see his car parked in the driveway. At other times she said he was at work in his basement office and couldn't be disturbed.

Clients tolerated his eccentricities because he was the best in the business, and some began referring to him as a genius.

Socially, the focus of Dorie and Mark Hofmann's life was, as always, the church, where he carried on his priesthood duties and she worked as a volunteer in the Relief Society. The five-foot-nine-inch-tall document dealer enjoyed food—enjoyed it too much, perhaps. As he grew older his body began to thicken and his face became round.

On weekends Mark and Dorie Hofmann often invited friends from the ward to their home for a party, and over ice cream and punch he held them spellbound with tales of his Indiana Jones adventures as a hunter of what he called "paper antiquities."

Some of his most exciting stories focused on his unsuccessful searches. He said he had made several trips to Texas to find the McLellin Collection, but so far had come up empty-handed. And he said his greatest, most elusive and most frustrating target remained the lost 116 pages of the Book of Mormon.

If he could find this Holy Grail of Mormondom, he said, it would be worth millions.

The parties often ended with the Hofmanns and their guests piling into the couple's hot tub or with the playing of games such as Celestial Pursuit, a trivia game about Mormon history that Hofmann invariably won. Among the couple's most frequent guests were Mark's parents. To his friends, Bill Hofmann sometimes confided that his son spoke often with President Hinckley and that he was one of the few people in Salt Lake City outside the Quorum of the Twelve Apostles who had his private telephone number. Now, more than ever, his parents were certain that Mark was destined for elevation to the highest rungs of the church hierarchy.

23

At the fall general conference of the church in early October, Apostle Bruce R. McConkie leveled a blistering attack in the Mormon Tabernacle on church members who conducted—or supported—historical research threatening to the faith of other Saints. Three days later, Steve Christensen called Brent Metcalfe to his office, told him he was fired and said the research project to study the salamander letter and its historical implications was being abandoned.

Metcalfe was stunned.

Christensen told him that Gary Sheets had been underwriting seventy percent of the research. Someone in the church had told Sheets that Metcalfe was losing his testimony because of the salamander letter, and he had decided to withdraw his financial support of the project.

As he listened to Christensen, who seemed distraught and embarrassed by his own words, Metcalfe recalled Bruce McConkie's speech. Then he remembered another incident that had happened on the same weekend. He had given a report to teachers at the LDS Institute of Religion at the University of Utah on the progress of the research team's work on the salamander letter. Christensen was originally scheduled to make the speech, but at the last minute he had asked Metcalfe to pinch-hit for him.

Metcalfe gave the teachers an overview of the work, including a review of some of the parallels that were being found between historical accounts of nineteenth-century money-digging ventures with seer stones and Joseph Smith's story of how he had found the gold plates of the Book of Mormon. Afterward, one of the teachers confronted Metcalfe and demanded that he repeat his testimony regarding belief in the book's divine origin.

Metcalfe refused, saying he was visiting the institute as a historical researcher, not to discuss his personal life. The answer did not satisfy the religion instructor and a shouting match ensued. The teacher continued to insist that Metcalfe repeat his testimony on the spot. Other teachers watched the confrontation in embarrassed silence. Finally, several came to Metcalfe's defense, and he was allowed to leave without having to affirm his belief in the Book of Mormon. The instructor, a friend of Ezra Taft Benson's, departed angrily.

"*Have* you lost your faith?" Christensen asked him.

Metcalfe's mind raged with doubts about the church, but he said:

"No. If my faith has weakened at all, it's because my own quest to find God has failed me. The Martin Harris letter has had no impact on my faith whatsoever."

Christensen said he had spent two days wrestling with his conscience over a decision.

He said he believed in pursuing historical truth wherever it led, but he did not want to undermine any man's faith.

"Is honesty really the most important thing, even if it means someone's faith will be destroyed?"

Christensen did not attempt to answer his question and neither did Metcalfe.

Steve was a man, Metcalfe thought, who was in pain.

Christensen said that Metcalfe's salary would continue for three months and he would receive half of his salary for three months after that. After Metcalfe left, Christensen sent a letter marked "personal and confidential" to Gordon Hinckley that informed him of the decision to suspend research on the letter and drop plans to publish a book about it:

The authentication work on the letter has been completed and the letter should be back in my hands by the end of the month. (It is authentic, by the way.) . . .

The foregoing commentary leads up to the events of this past week. Last Thursday, I had the unpleasant experience of terminating the working relationship with Brent Metcalfe. The main reason is that Gary Sheets and myself became uncomfortable with some of Brent's personal opinions relative to Church History and Doctrine. More important, we did not want to financially underwrite a book relating to the early origins of the church and the coming forth of the Book of Mormon if the work had the potential of doing more harm than good. While I am certain that Brothers Walker and Jessee would have had final editorial say on the book, I did not feel comfortable supporting Brent's continued involvement. It was almost the feeling of paying someone to lose his testimony. . . .

I was extremely impressed with your Conference talk, Sunday, October 7th. I am concerned that some of Brent Metcalfe's research, as interpreted by himself and perhaps others, would challenge some of the basic concepts to three out of four of the "foundations of the church" addressed in your talk. Most likely we will always be learning new things historically from our past; however, I believe that the church has more pressing work to accomplish than to be consumed by questions and contradictions from the past. While it is better that we lead forth in historical inquiry rather than leaving the task to our enemies, those so engaged must have sufficient faith that the day will come when all is revealed and then the pieces will all fit together.

I am still not eager to thrust the document in the hands of the media. Personally, I would like to stay as low profile as is possible. My current intention is to probably sit on the letter and release it to *The Deseret News* (if they are so desirous). . . . A second alternative which I have is to sell the document back to Mark Hofmann. He is anxious to buy it back for $50,000. (I originally paid $40,000 over time for the letter.) Mr. Hofmann has been approached by a representative of Yale University who would like to seriously consider having the Yale Library purchase the document were it to become available. My original intention was to donate the document, in a quiet fashion, to the church. The tax deduction which I would receive would serve as sufficient compensation for my expenditures. What I would appreciate knowing is whether or not the church feels strongly about owning the letter. If it would be more of a thorn than a rose I would gladly let Mr. Hofmann sell it to Yale or some other institution which would pay his "highway robbery" prices. If the church would like it, it is yours for the asking.

I am sorry to trouble you with the above; however, I judged it to be better to let you know rather than pass up the opportunity. I would have you know that I receive great joy (mixed with a lot of learning experiences) from my calling as a Bishop. I would never want my actions to blemish this sacred office. . . .

The next day, Christensen encountered Hinckley at a charity luncheon in Salt Lake City. The church President acknowledged that he had received the letter and said that he was still anxious for Christensen to donate the letter to the church.

Christensen replied that it would be an honor to do so. But within a few weeks, he asked Hinckley to let him back out of the deal. The reason: The money-making machine created by Gary Sheets had suddenly gone into a tailspin.

The company had purchased more than 2,100 apartments in Texas during the peak of the oil boom. Now much of the Texas economy was in ruins because of plunging oil prices and nearly half were vacant. Troubled real estate investments were only part of the problem: A charter airline organized by Coordinated Financial Services to operate expensive corporate jets bought with investors' money seldom had any passengers other than Sheets and other C.F.S. executives, because airline deregulation had stimulated fare cutting that drastically undercut the cost of charters. Lower oil prices had jeopardized huge investments by C.F.S. in alternative energy projects. A gold mine in Oregon that had cost millions was yielding little gold. The water slide project in Colorado was a bust. The cost of remodeling a Salt Lake City office building the company had bought as its corporate headquarters was going through the stratosphere. Everywhere they looked C.F.S. investments were in trouble.

Robbing Peter to pay Paul failed to solve the problems.

To pay its mounting debts, the company shifted money from

profitable syndications to money-losing projects. But that only sent
the profitable ventures into the red, forcing C.F.S. to liquidate
some of its properties at a fraction of their original cost.

To meet its bills, the company borrowed heavily from banks and
other lenders that required Sheets, Christensen and other senior
officers of the company to sign personal guarantees that the loans
would be repaid.

Gary Sheets asked Christensen to take over as chief operating
officer of the company and find a way to pull it out of the tailspin,
and his protégé said he would try.

After rumors began to circulate that C.F.S. was in financial trouble, Sheets optimistically reassured investors that things would
work out well for everybody: No one who ever invested with him
had ever lost money, he said, and none would now.

Sheets was a living example of the fact that the Mormon dream
could come true, and he was not going to let his dream die.

On February 15, Christensen received a report from Albert H.
Lyter, a forensic chemist in Raleigh, North Carolina. Lyter said he
had examined the ink on the salamander letter and determined it
was an "iron gall" variety used widely in the early nineteenth century and concluded: "There is no evidence that the examined document was prepared at other than during the stated time period."

Eleven days later, Christensen wrote another letter to Hinckley
and it was delivered by hand to the Church Administration Building:

Once again I have received recent opportunities to sell the Martin Harris letter. In the past I have always turned these offers
down since I had no financial need to satisfy and as a result, I
offered to provide the letter to the Church. At the current time
of these most recent offers, my situation has changed to where
the funds offered would be most welcome in assisting me with
the reduction of some extremely heavy short term debt. Sources
which were previously thought to be available to me have not
proven out. I am however willing to trust in the Lord to assist
me in my financial affairs should it be your opinion that the
letter really belongs with the Church. I have no desire to sell the
letter to the Church to ease my monetary needs. If you want the

letter I would prefer to make good on my original commitment and donate the letter to you . . . if you feel that the Church's possession of the letter is not that essential then I will sell the letter. . . .

Three days later, Christensen was told the church would not let him off the hook. He wrote in his journal:

President Hinckley called. Confirmed church wanted letter.

On the same day, Gary Sheets informed his wife, Kathy, that he had something sad and important to tell her, and afterward she wrote in her journal:

Gary layed the Co. problems out tonight. Very scary and upsetting. Oh, I pray things turn out okay. I am really scared. He always pulls things off; but this is scary.

While a shadow had fallen over the lives of Gary Sheets and Steven Christensen, Mark Hofmann's business was prospering as never before. He told friends he was earning hundreds of thousands of dollars a year and revealed that he and Dorie were shopping for a half-million-dollar house in the Wasatch foothills, a place where many achievers of the Salt Lake Valley aspired to live. It had been less than eighteen months since they had bought his parents' ranch house in a suburban subdivision where Mark had been raised, but Dorie said it was too small: There were already two children in the household, another on the way, and they wanted several more children.

Once or twice a month Mark flew to New York to attend an auction at Sotheby's or Christie's, to meet with Charles Hamilton and other autograph dealers and to add to the collection of rare books he was buying for Dorie. He paid $22,500 for a first edition, including its unsoiled dust cover, of *The Adventures of Sherlock Holmes;* $7,475 for an 1866 second edition of *Alice's Adventures in Wonderland;* $3,500 for a 1768 first edition of *Famous Tommy Thumb's Little Story Book;* and $10,000 for a first edition of Carlo Lorenzini's *Le avventure de Pinocchio.* If he was unable to attend an important auction, Justin Schiller or Raymond Wapner bid in his place.

As his business grew, Hofmann recruited more agents and document scouts: In addition to Lyn Jacobs there was Rick Grunder, the thirty-six-year-old son of an Idaho farmer who had served a mission in France, graduated from BYU and become an autograph dealer; Shannon Flynn, a college dropout who had served his mission in Brazil and shared Hofmann's interest in church history as well as a new interest he had developed in firearms; and, several months after his discharge by Steve Christensen and Gary Sheets, Brent Metcalfe.

Whenever he needed capital, he had access to a widening circle of investors. One was Alvin Rust, a shrewd, portly businessman who operated a coin shop on Main Street in Salt Lake City. Another was Kenneth Woolley, a cousin of Dorie Hofmann's and a personification of the Mormon dream that held prosperity befell members of the Lord's Elect who worked hard, led a worthy life and believed in the restored gospel. Starting with little capital after earning a doctorate at Stanford's graduate school of business, Woolley had become a millionaire in his thirties through investments in real estate and several businesses.

During a family get-together, Hofmann told Woolley about a collection of eighteen land surveys and other documents signed by Daniel Boone that he could buy for $70,000 from one of Boone's descendants, an elderly woman who lived in North Carolina. With any luck, he said, he could probably sell the items individually for $200,000 or more.

Woolley invested $50,000 to buy the Boone collection. A few weeks later, Hofmann gave him a check for $25,000 as his share of the proceeds from the sale of several of the land surveys and said he expected the biggest prize in the collection to bring as much as $100,000 by itself at auction. It was a letter from Daniel Boone to his partner, Richard Henderson, dated April 1, 1775, describing a perilous trip Boone had just completed through the Cumberland Gap, fighting Indians and blazing what became known as the Wilderness Road. Although its text had been published in the 1830s and helped establish the legend of Boone as a fearless frontiersman, the letter had been lost until now.

Hofmann also told Woolley he had found two pages of the original 1830 manuscript of the Book of Mormon that they could buy from the University of Chicago Library for $50,000. Woolley agreed to underwrite half the purchase. A week later Hofmann called and said he had sold the two pages to a private collector for $90,000, netting each a profit of $20,000. Two weeks later, he invited Woolley to roll over the profit into what was potentially an even more lucrative investment: A Dutch collector named Oppenheimer had died and some of the finest books in his collection—including a 1643 portfolio of Shakespeare's plays and books by Charles Darwin, Daniel Defoe, Sir Isaac Newton and other writers—were available for $238,000. Woolley gave him $74,000. Together with his profits from the previous sales, that made Woolley an equal partner with Hofmann in the transaction. Within a few days, Mark announced he had sold all of the books and when all were paid for, their total return on the investment would be $430,000, a profit of almost $100,000 for each of the two partners.

For Woolley, it was like a very profitable roller coaster ride.

In the spring of 1985, Hofmann confided to Woolley and a few other friends that he may have made his greatest discovery of all. He said he believed he had found the most sought-after lost document in American history.

24

Stephen Daye, a locksmith, landed in Boston in September 1638 aboard the ship *John of London*. His employer, the Reverend Josse Glover, Rector of Sutton in Surrey, had died during the eight-week crossing, leaving Daye to assemble a printing press Glover had purchased in London. During the months that followed, on Crooked Lane in Cambridge, Daye and his brother, Matthew, established the first printery in the Massachusetts Bay Colony and produced the first printed document in the British colonies.

It was called the Oath of a Freeman. Not much larger than a postcard, it was an oath taken by freemen over twenty who had met their debts and other obligations to the Massachusetts Bay Company and had become legal citizens of the colony. It began:

I . . . being by God's providence an inhabitant and freeman within the jurisdiction of this commonwealth, do freely acknowledge myself to be subject to the government thereof. . . .

Conspicuously missing from the oath, however, was a vow of allegiance to the British sovereign, Charles I, which was contained in similar oaths required of members of other London-chartered companies. And it contained the slightest assertion of independence by the Puritan colonists:

> . . . I do solemnly bind myself, in the sight of God, that when I shall be called to give my voice touching any such matter of this state in which freemen are to deal, I will give my vote and suffrage as I shall judge in my own conscience may best conduce and tend to the public weal of the body, without respect of persons or favor of any man. . . .

Twenty-five years later, upon the demands of Charles II, a pledge of allegiance to the crown was added to the freemen's oath in the Massachusetts colony. But the spirit of the original Oath of a Freeman—the first written expression of the American vision that people should control their own destiny—survived and more than a century later it was incorporated into the Declaration of Independence. The fifty or so copies of the oath itself, however, were lost.

On the afternoon of March 11, 1985, Mark Hofmann boarded a Continental Airlines jetliner in Salt Lake City, and after a change of planes in Denver, landed shortly before midnight in New York. He attended an auction the following day at Sotheby's, where Justin Schiller, acting as his agent, bought a first edition of *Uncle Tom's Cabin* for $13,200.

Several days later Hofmann, after returning to Salt Lake City, telephoned Schiller and said that following the auction he had visited the Argosy Book Store on East Fifty-ninth Street and bought several old English broadsides. He said he was curious about one of them, which he had seen referred to in a 1647 pamphlet offered for sale in a Sotheby's catalogue.

"Do you know anything about the Oath of a Freeman?" he asked.

Schiller said he had never heard of it; his specialty was children's books.

"Why don't you make a photocopy and send it to me and I'll find someone who knows something about it."

A few days later, on the eve of another Sotheby's auction, Hof-

THE OATH OF A FREEMAN.

I·AB· being (by Gods providence) an Inhabitant, and Freeman, within the iurisdictiõ of this Common-wealth, doe freely acknowledge my selfe to bee subject to the governement thereof; and therefore doe heere sweare, by the great & dreadfull name of the Everliving-God, that I will be true & faithfull to the same, & will accordingly yield assistance & support therunto, with my person & estate, as in equity I am bound: and will also truely indeavour to maintaine and preserve all the libertyes & privilidges thereof, submitting my selfe to the wholesome lawes, & ordres made & stablished by the same; and further, that I will not plot, nor practice any evill against it, nor consent to any that shall soe do, butt will timely discover, & reveall the same to lawefull authoritee nowe here stablished, for the speedie preventing thereof. Moreover, I doe solemnly binde my selfe, in the sight of God, that when I shalbe called, to give my voyce touching any such matter of this state, (in which freemen are to deale) I will give my vote & suffrage as I shall judge in myne owne conscience may best conduce & tend to the publick weale of the body, without respect of personnes, or favour of any man. Soe help mee God in the Lord Iesus Christ.

mann arrived in New York and showed Schiller a receipt for
$51.42 for five items he had purchased at Argosy March 13. One
item, listed at $25, was the "Oath of a Free Man." He handed
Schiller a small, yellowed piece of paper with ragged edges on
which "THE OATH OF A FREEMAN" was printed at the top. He said
he had found it in a bin of miscellaneous eighteenth-century English pamphlets and broadsides at Argosy.

When he returned to Salt Lake City, he said he had gone to a
library and discovered that the Oath of a Freeman had played an
important role in American history but that all copies had been
lost; he suggested the broadside he had purchased might be a facsimile of the original oath that was subsequently printed in England, although he found it tantalizing that the floretlike ornamentation that surrounded the text was very similar to that on a
hymnal Stephen Daye himself had printed in 1640, *The Bay Psalm
Book*.

Schiller agreed. A plump man with a fleshy rounded face and
curly black hair, he suggested that they consult an expert, and he
called Michael Zinman, a businessman who lived in suburban
Westchester County and was one of the country's leading collectors
of seventeenth-century American printed items. When Zinman answered, he said:

"I have a client here who may have found the Oath of a Freeman."

"You're a week early for April Fool's," Zinman, a friend of
Schiller's, replied with a laugh.

"I think this may be serious," Schiller said. His voice was flat.

Schiller's earnestness impressed Zinman and he offered to leave
his office early that afternoon and drive to New York City with
several reference books about Daye and the Cambridge Press.

When Zinman looked at the document, he said he was skeptical.
It looked too good to be real.

"How come it's so white?" he asked.

Hofmann explained that it had been glued to a piece of old
cardboard when he bought it, and he had separated the two pieces
by soaking them in water; perhaps the water had bleached the
paper slightly, he suggested.

Zinman, a short, bearded man in his forties with inquisitive eyes,
looked at the earnest young man wearing steel-rimmed glasses who

was standing next to Schiller's desk. He was shy and unsure of himself and let Schiller do most of the talking.

An hour, then a second hour passed while they examined the small, fragile sheet of paper. Again and again, they compared the printing and border ornamentation on it to a reproduction of *The Bay Psalm Book* and agreed that they looked similar. Zinman had brought a book containing the text of the original Oath of a Freeman, which had been preserved in the archives of Massachusetts; the text was almost identical to the language in Hofmann's document. They held his document—which measured about four by six inches—up to a light and saw what appeared to be threadlike lines in the fiber of the paper; they looked like the chain lines that were left during the manufacturing and drying of paper made prior to the mid-nineteenth century.

Zinman said he was still dubious but his enthusiasm seemed to be growing. It was possible, he said, Hofmann had found the Oath of a Freeman. They walked to Oliver's, a restaurant on Fifty-seventh Street near Lexington Avenue, to have dinner, and the curious document continued to be the principal topic of conversation.

"How much do you think it might be worth?" Schiller asked Zinman.

While Zinman was en route to Manhattan, Hofmann suggested that if the document were genuine it might be worth $18,000 or $20,000. Schiller had said he thought the sole surviving example of the first document printed in America might bring as much as $500,000.

Zinman replied:

"The Bay Psalm Book, if anybody would sell one, is worth about a million, a million-two. The Freeman's Oath would be worth at least as much, probably more. But it's going to be hard to authenticate."

Shortly after 8 A.M. the following morning, Justin Schiller arrived at the great columned building on Fifth Avenue that houses the New York Public Library. The library was having a special exhibition of its rarest treasures, including one of the twelve surviving copies of *The Bay Psalm Book,* and through the intercession of a friend, Schiller had arranged to be admitted to the exhibition before it was opened to the public.

A security alarm was deactivated, the hymnal was removed

from a locked glass case and, as his friend watched, Schiller examined the floretlike embellishments with which Stephen Daye had ornamented the borders of the pages of the hymnal, then believed to be the oldest surviving printed document in English America. The ornamentation on the pages of the hymn book was virtually identical to that on the broadside. The typeface was almost identical, too. Slowly, he began to turn the pages of the 350-year-old hymnal and compared the chain lines in the paper to those of the Oath. At first, he was disappointed; the chain lines on several pages were spaced wider apart than on the Oath. Then he turned another page, laid the Oath of a Freeman beside it and saw that the chain marks were exactly parallel. He turned another page, and once again the chain lines matched perfectly. It was likely, he thought, that the paper used to print the Oath and the hymnal had come from the same batch of paper brought to the colony from England.

Never in his life had Justin Schiller been as excited as he was when he strode down the broad steps of the library onto Fifth Avenue. As he passed the concrete lions that stood guard like sentries in front of the library, he wondered to whom he should offer the Oath, then realized there was really only one choice: the Library of Congress.

The following day, James Gilreath, a specialist in American historical documents at the Library, flew to New York City with a fluoroscope. Beneath its eerie light he could find no erasures, overprintings, scratches or other obvious evidence of forgery.

The document was indeed interesting, Gilreath said, and he suggested it be brought to Washington for testing by the Library's technical experts. One week later, in an operation mounted with great secrecy in order to keep the discovery from reaching the gossipy world of document dealers, William Matheson, chief of the Rare Book and Special Collections Division of the Library of Congress, accepted the broadside and said it would be subjected to a battery of tests measuring it against the Library's copy of *The Bay Psalm Book.*

Schiller sent a copy of the Oath to Katherine F. Pantzer, an antiquarian book specialist at Harvard University's Houghton Library. "On the whole," she wrote after she had evaluated it, "my impression from the Xerox and knowing practically nothing about

Stephen Daye, is that the Oath looks genuine. Now more expert study needs to be done than I can supply."

Gilreath said that the document examiners at the Library of Congress had said it would take them about a month to reach a decision about the Oath.

25

Among Mormon historians who had examined the salamander letter during the spring of 1985, there had never been much doubt about its authenticity. And, just as the Library of Congress began its study of the Oath of a Freeman, their confidence was vindicated when Kenneth Rendell, the Massachusetts document expert who had helped prove that the Hitler diaries were forgeries, sent his final report on the letter to Mark Hofmann and Steve Christensen:

He said he had examined the letter under ultraviolet light and "the ink fluoresced in accordance with other inks of this period. The paper itself had a fluorescence consistent with the period." The type of paper upon which the letter was written, he said, was in common use in New York during the early nineteenth century, and the postmark appeared identical to that on another letter mailed from Palmyra during the same period of time.

The signature on the letter is consistent with three other known examples of Harris's signature. The original was examined very closely under a microscope for any signs of tracing, and no signs were found. It is my conclusion, based upon all the evidence, as well as the ink and paper tests undertaken independently of me, that there is no indication that this letter is a forgery.

"I've got a real tax problem," Mark Hofmann told his wife's cousin, Ken Woolley, several days after the Library of Congress took custody of the Freeman's Oath.

The faded old broadside he had bought for $25 in New York, he said, might be worth as much as $2 million. If that were true, Woolley agreed, Mark would indeed face huge capital-gains taxes on his profit.

Hofmann said he might represent himself to the Library of Congress as a foreign citizen, which would allow the payment to be deposited in an overseas account, and he would avoid the tax.

"Mark, you can't do that," Woolley, a devout member of the church, said. "Just get a tax adviser to help you."

Subsequently, Hofmann confided to other friends that he was proceeding with the plan; he told them he rarely paid taxes. It was one reason why he didn't keep written records of his transactions.

Mark told Dorie Hofmann it would probably take a while for the Library of Congress's examiners to authenticate the Oath of a Freeman, but when the examination was finished, they would be able to buy the new house she wanted in the Wasatch foothills.

Hofmann's expected giant windfall did not deter him from undertaking less glamorous transactions in partnership with lawyers, dentists, businessmen and other people who had heard rumors of the huge profits his investors were reaping. When Thomas Wilding, his insurance man, who had been a friend and classmate at Utah State, said he represented a group of investors who were interested in getting in on one of his deals, Hofmann said he had taken an option on eighteen rare books available for $40,000 through New York dealer Justin Schiller. If Wilding's group put up $22,500, he said he would finance the balance. The market for books was so strong, he said, that they might be able to double their money in a few months. Wilding called his brother-in-law, Harold Vincent, a logger who had lost his hand in an Idaho sawmill accident. He had received an insurance settlement for the accident that he wanted to invest.

Wilding knew as much about rare books as he did about *The*

Theory of Relativity, the title of one of the books in which Hofmann offered to invest. But the potential payoff was appealing and they decided to gamble. Within a month, the gamble paid off beyond their expectations: Hofmann said he had already sold several of the books and doubled their money. After he returned their $22,500 investment to them, plus a profit of $10,000, Wilding and Vincent decided to invest the balance of their profit on another deal: Hofmann's purchase of the manuscript of a book by Charles Dickens, *The Haunted Man and the Ghost's Bargain.* The price was $300,000, plus a $30,000 commission for Schiller. Hofmann said the market for such literary rarities was booming more than ever and he predicted a net profit on the deal of at least fifty percent.

Wilding and his investment group quickly raised $160,000 to buy a half-interest in the manuscript.

As the snow-covered slopes of the Wasatch range turned emerald in the spring of 1985, Steve Christensen and Gary Sheets battled to end the losses at C.F.S. and placate increasingly restive investors, some of whom had begun to accuse them of fraud. Meanwhile, Kathy Sheets recorded in her journal the daily joys and tribulations of her life: her battle to lose weight *("I hate being so fat!");* her enjoyment of church activities, tennis, movies and accompanying Gary on his business trips; helping her married daughters find their first homes; the fun of overnight trips to Park City; the sadness of her elderly mother's illness; and, above all, the pleasures given her by her grandchildren.

But the mounting problems at C.F.S. were seldom far from her pen, and like a meteorologist reporting vagaries of the weather, she recorded the daily fluctuations in her husband's mood as he tried to save the company: "Gary feeling low again," she wrote one night. "I worry about him." Another day, she wrote: "Gary in much better mood—nothing new in business—he's just more up. Hurrah!!!" A few days later: "Gary depressed again."

On another day, as she worried about the whirlpool she knew her life was being drawn into, she wrote: "Tended all kids tonight. They are so darling—but a hand full. Slept in. It was nice. Gary and I had a good talk. Wish we were more companionable—did more together. I feel left alone a lot."

* * *

On April 18, 1985, the members of the First Presidency—Spencer W. Kimball, Marion G. Romney and Gordon B. Hinckley—in a letter to Steven Christensen marked "confidential," accepted the salamander letter and thanked him for donating it to the church.

As new rumors about the still unpublished letter spread over the Salt Lake Valley, church officials, pressed by reporters to release its text, braced for what they knew would be a new rush of Mormon-bashing.

A few days before Christensen had formally donated the letter to the church, Mark Hofmann visited Alvin Rust, the Main Street coin dealer who had invested profitably in many of his document deals.

"This has got to be secret," he said while Rust and his twenty-five-year-old son, Gaylen, listened.

"I've got a chance to buy something in New York that's probably twenty times more important than anything we've ever bought before."

Hofmann said he had found the McLellin Collection.

For months now he had spoken—usually in whispers—about his search for the papers of William McLellin, the one-time confidant of Joseph Smith who was reputed to have taken a large cache of secret documents with him when he broke with the church in 1838.

The only thing Al Rust remembered about William McLellin was that he was an early Apostle of the church who was later excommunicated.

"Are they controversial-type documents embarrassing to the church?" he asked. Hofmann knew that Rust, a devout Mormon and former bishop, wanted nothing to do with anything embarrassing to the church.

"No," he said. He explained that the collection contained rare materials valuable to the church and collectors for their historical content—letters written by Joseph Smith, McLellin's personal journals, a copy of the Egyptian papyrus he had translated to write the Book of Abraham—in all, at least twenty items of major importance, plus miscellaneous papers that filled three cardboard boxes.

"It's by far the most important Mormon collection I've ever heard of," he said.

The owner, he said, wanted $185,000 for the entire collection. Hofmann said that he had $35,000 and invited Rust to invest the balance of $150,000. He estimated they could get at least $300,000 for the documents by selling some to the church and the rest to private collectors on a piecemeal basis.

Rust was a successful businessman, but not one with $150,000 lying idle in the bank. Nevertheless, the proposition appealed to him, and he said he would borrow $150,000 from his bank on one condition: Because so much money was involved, he wanted his son to accompany Mark when he went to New York to collect the documents; afterwards, they could hand-carry the most important items to Salt Lake City and those of lesser importance could be mailed to Rust's store, where he would offer them for sale.

Hofmann warned that when the time came they would have to act quickly because if they did not, others might get to the documents first.

A few days later, early on the morning of April 23, Hofmann arrived at the coin shop and told Gaylen Rust that they had to leave for New York in a few hours. "It's ready," he said.

At his father's bank, Rust collected a $150,000 cashier's check and gave it to Hofmann. Then they flew to New York and checked in at the Sheraton Centre Hotel at Fifty-third Street and Seventh Avenue and Rust prepared himself for an adventure in a new and exciting world. It was the eve of the spring antiquarian book fair in New York City. Collectors and rare book dealers were arriving from around the country for an intensive bout of deal-making. Following the book fair, Rust and Hofmann and their wives, who were following them to New York by one day, were to attend an auction at Sotheby's where several documents in which his father had invested with Hofmann, including a letter signed by Vincent Van Gogh, were to be sold.

The morning after their arrival, Hofmann briefed Gaylen on the scenario for the McLellin Collection transaction, which he said had to be carried out in absolute secrecy: While he met with the owner of the documents, Rust was to wait in the hotel for a phone call; after his phone call, they would rendezvous at a bank where the documents were being held in safe-deposit boxes; then they would remove the twenty most important items, package the rest for shipment home and give the seller his money.

As planned, Mark left the hotel at 10 A.M.

After he left, Rust, preparing for the arrival of their wives that evening, booked a second room in the hotel, then waited for Mark's call.

At 4 o'clock he was still awaiting the call and he decided to leave the room briefly for a late lunch. In the lobby he spotted Hofmann, who said that the seller had been unable to break another commitment and they had to delay the transaction one day.

The next day, Gaylen Rust waited again in the hotel room for a call from Hofmann, but the phone never rang.

Late in the afternoon, Hofmann knocked on his door and said he had completed the deal and they now owned the McLellin Collection. He said the seller had been in such a hurry to conclude the sale—and so paranoid about being observed—that Mark had had to meet him alone at the bank and conclude the exchange. Hofmann said he had sent the whole collection to Salt Lake City and showed him postal receipts for three cartons shipped to his home insured for a total of $210,000. It was safer, he said, to send the documents insured through the mails rather than risk having them stolen in New York while they waited for the auction at Sotheby's.

Over the next several days, Hofmann showed his friends from Salt Lake City the other world in which he lived, a glamorous world of Manhattan restaurants, auction houses, galleries and eccentric document dealers who, Rust noted, showed the dark-suited Utahan deference and respect. When they arrived at the Salt Lake City airport the following Monday, Rust was starry-eyed, and Hofmann promised to bring the McLellin Collection to the coin shop in the morning.

When he did not keep the appointment, Al Rust was not surprised. He was accustomed to Hofmann's unpredictability; he knew he seldom kept appointments. Nor was he troubled after several days had passed and he had still not heard from him. He had known Mark for six years and trusted him.

At the end of the week, Rust's patience was vindicated: Hofmann called and said he had sold the complete McLellin Collection to President Hinckley for $300,000. But he cautioned Rust not to mention the sale—or even acknowledge the McLellin Collection existed—to anyone. The church wanted absolute secrecy about it. Only two or three General Authorities in addition to President Hinckley, he said, were to know about it and the church planned to keep several of the documents in the collection secret. Rust wondered fleetingly if Mark had lied to him regarding whether the documents would embarrass the church. Whatever the circumstances, he liked the mathematics of the transaction. Hofmann said payment for the collection, including a profit of almost $120,000 for them to share, would be made shortly by the church.

After several weeks, Rust got impatient for the money. He tried again and again to reach Hofmann, but couldn't find him. Even the church, Rust told his wife, should pay its bills, and he wrote a letter to President Hinckley asking for payment.

Gordon Hinckley, however, never responded to the letter.

26

On the Sunday that Mark Hofmann, Gaylen Rust and their wives were enjoying their final night in Manhattan, church officials announced in Salt Lake City that Steven Christensen had donated the salamander letter to the First Presidency and they made public the text of the letter. "No one, of course, can be certain that Martin Harris wrote the document," President Hinckley said. "However, at this point we accept the judgment of the examiner that there is no indication that it is a forgery. This does not preclude the possibility that it may have been forged at a time when the church had many enemies. It is, however, an interesting document of the times. Actually, the letter has nothing to do with the authenticity of the church. The real test of the faith which both Martin Harris and W. W. Phelps had in Joseph Smith and his work is found in their lives, in the sacrifices they made for their membership in the church, and in the testimonies which they bore to the end of their lives. . . ."

The church knew the letter was to be made public in any case within a few days at the meeting of the Mormon History Association in Kansas City. At the meeting, BYU professors Ronald Walker and Dean Jessee reviewed the process by which the letter had been tested during the previous year and said its examination left no doubt it was genuine. Jerald Tanner said he was still unconvinced, and Rhett James, the scholar who once vouched for the salamander letter, said he had compared its syntax with samples of Harris's writing and now believed it was not written by him. The dissents, however, were expressed against a chorus of approval. Jessee and Walker said the letter's authenticity had been established by the most intensive scrutiny ever given a document in the history of the church.

The day after the church released the letter, *The Salt Lake Tribune* published a story asserting that the church was concealing a *second* letter that also raised questions about Joseph Smith's story of receiving the gold plates from an angel. The church denied the assertion.

"The church doesn't have the letter," Jerry Cahill, the director of public communications, said. "It's not in the church archives or the First Presidency's Vault."

The denial merely added fuel to a rapidly spreading fire.

The release of the salamander letter had ignited a blaze of journalistic interest in the church, and the denial that it was concealing a second embarrassing letter connecting Joseph Smith to black magic was met with disbelief by reporters who had previously been informed by prominent Mormon historians—based on information from Hofmann—that a second letter existed.

Under the headline "Challenging Mormonism's Roots," *Time* published the report that it had begun preparing a year before. It said the letters were causing discomfort for church leaders and persuading Mormons to defect from the church. "It's an incredible crisis of faith for me," said one Mormon quoted by the magazine. "It means our historical foundation becomes a nice story that has no connection to reality."

Anti-Mormon groups fired even more savage attacks on the church: One suggested statues of salamanders should be cast to replace the gilded likenesses of Moroni that graced the tops of Mormon temples around the world.

A week after denying the church possessed a second embarrassing letter, Cahill told reporters that he had made a mistake. In fact, he said, it did exist. Church officials, he said, had initially informed him no such letter existed. But after the *Tribune* published its article, he said President Hinckley advised him such a letter was in the First Presidency's Vault. Then, Cahill made public Joseph Smith's 1825 letter to Josiah Stowell describing buried treasure guarded by a "clever spirit," the letter purchased almost two and a half years before by Gordon Hinckley and hidden in the First Presidency's Vault.

"The enemies of the Church seem to be having a great time," Hinckley said in a letter to Steve Christensen. "Their efforts will fade while the work goes forward."

To counter the storm of negative publicity, the church went on the offensive. A team was assigned to prepare research material documenting the fact that angels could be described as salamanders. The researchers pointed out that salamanders had appeared often in scripture and that God had even showed Moses a salamander in the fire on Mount Sinai. "To people in 1830," John M. Welch, president of the church's Foundation for Ancient Research and Mormon Studies, said, "no image or description would better fit the appearance of a brilliant white spiritual being than the salamander.

"Moroni should be flattered."

The church's Historical Department assigned an emissary to urge Elwyn Doubleday, the New Hampshire stampless-cover dealer who admitted being the source of the salamander letter, to sell important documents directly to the church rather than to Hofmann in the future. "We would much rather deal with you and your associates than go through a middleman," a representative of the department wrote in a letter to Doubleday. "Those people are considerably more costly and generally lack historical sensitivity. We feel that we can establish a very pleasant working relationship with you and those to whom you are willing to introduce me, rather than going through someone who wants our flesh and blood, too."

In early May, Brent Ashworth was recuperating from the flu at his home a few blocks away from the Provo Temple when he received a telephone call from a deputy to a General Authority in Salt Lake City. The Brethren, he said, had a report that Hofmann had found the missing 116 pages of the Book of Mormon and that

Jerald and Sandra Tanner had managed to get a copy and were preparing to publish it. Church leaders were worried, he said, because it was said to contain embarrassing material.

"There's supposed to be a lot of stuff in it about money digging and magic," the church official told Ashworth. "The Brethren want to find out what's in it so they can be ready to defend against it.

"Can you help us?"

The following day, Ashworth arrived at Hofmann's home on a secret mission on behalf of the church.

Without disclosing the reason for his visit and trying to seem as casual as he could, he said he had heard rumors that Mark's long search for the Book of Lehi had finally been successful.

Hofmann replied that in Bakersfield, California, he had seen samples of a document someone claimed was the 116 pages, but he suspected it was a forgery.

"How much do they want for it?" Ashworth asked.

Hofmann estimated the owner might sell it for $5,000.

Deciding the church would want to keep even an embarrassing *forgery* of the Book of Mormon out of circulation, Ashworth said:

"Okay, Mark, if you can get it, I'll give you $10,000."

A few days later, Hofmann told Ashworth the owner of the manuscript had told him he was unwilling to part with the document, which Hofmann remained convinced was a forgery. Ashworth could now advise his contact at the Church Office Building that Hofmann had not yet found the lost 116 pages, but Hofmann was not yet out of surprises for the church.

In early June, Brent Metcalfe invited a reporter for the *Los Angeles Times* to Salt Lake City. Over a meal, Hofmann told him that he had seen a 150-year-old handwritten diary by Oliver Cowdery, one of the Three Witnesses to the Book of Mormon, in the First Presidency's Vault that gave an account of the birth of the church that was fundamentally different from the one taught to Mormons: In the diary, Cowdery, the church's first historian, disclosed that it had not been Joseph Smith who was given the gold plates by Moroni, but his older brother.

Smith's brother Alvin, who died at the age of twenty-five in 1823, had long been an enigmatic figure in the history of Mormonism.

Their mother, Lucy Mack Smith, said that Alvin had been a prophet of God *before* Joseph. And several months after Alvin's death—blamed by his mother on an overdose of patent medicine and by others on eating too many green turnips—her husband placed a notice in a local newspaper, the *Wayne Sentinel,* complaining that unknown people had spread rumors that Alvin had vanished from his grave.

In the advertisement, Joseph Smith, Sr., sought to set the community straight: "I, with some of my neighbors this morning repaired to the grave, and removing the earth, found the body, which had not been disturbed."

When he returned to Los Angeles, the reporter wrote a long article about the secret Oliver Cowdery diary. He said his source "insisted on anonymity in order to preserve his standing in the church" but wanted to reveal what he had seen in the vault because it provided "corroboration for the salamander references in the Harris letter, which some Mormons are claiming is a forgery." The article further intensified a dispute dividing the family of Jerald and Sandra Tanner.

Sandra Tanner was fully convinced the salamander letter was genuine, and she said so in a special edition of *The Salt Lake City Messenger.* In the same issue her husband said he *wanted* to believe it was genuine because it supported "the thesis I had worked for years to prove—i.e., that Joseph Smith was deeply involved in magic and money-digging and that the Book of Mormon was a product of that involvement." But he said he was troubled by what he considered similarities to other nineteenth-century writings. "At the present time," he wrote, "I feel almost alone; while I do believe in miracles, I cannot help wondering if this is not just too good to be true."

As the storm he had started continued to swirl around the church, Mark Hofmann received good news from Schiller and Wapner: The Library of Congress said it wanted to buy the Oath of a Freeman.

27

"It is difficult to 'authenticate' a document of this kind, even as a result of tests as sophisticated as those undertaken by the Library," John G. Broderick, the Assistant Librarian for Research Services, said in a letter to Schiller.

"Nevertheless, in the language of the attached summary: 'No evidence has been revealed that would contravene a mid-seventeenth-century date for the broadside.' There are additional tests that might be performed to reduce uncertainties still further, although they may never be entirely eliminated. Further tests, however, can be performed only within the context of an opportunity to add this document to the collections of the Library of Congress. . . ."

Accompanying the letter was an abstract of a ninety-one-page analysis of the Oath of a Freeman by the Conservation and Research and Testing Offices of the Library of Congress. Weighing almost two pounds with its accompanying computer printouts and x-ray, infrared and color photographs, it summarized the tests conducted by a team of scientists and technicians who dissected the Oath physically and chemically and made more than two hundred photographs of it. "It may never be possible to prove that the

broadside was printed by a given individual, in a particular printing house at a specific date," the report declared. But it said the
testing had established that the ink, paper and type used to produce the Oath of a Freeman appeared to be identical to those of
Stephen Daye's *Bay Psalm Book*. Additional tests were needed before a final conclusion could be drawn, but the available evidence
pointed to its being printed during the same period of time as the
hymnal.

"I invite you therefore," Broderick told Schiller, "to offer the
broadside for purchase by the Library . . . I hope that you will
make such an offer to the Library, for the broadside, if genuine,
could certainly be one of the most significant American acquisitions of recent years for the national collections."

It was a letter Justin Schiller and Raymond Wapner had expected.

During their lifetimes, they had sold millions of dollars' worth of
fine art and rare books, including many one-of-a-kind treasures.
But the Oath of a Freeman was exquisite in a way different from
anything else they had ever sold. They were playing a part in history, the rediscovery of a three-centuries-old document that
reached to the very roots of American democracy.

In their reply to the Library of Congress, they said the price for
the Oath of a Freeman was $1.5 million.

Weary of waiting for his money, coin dealer Al Rust drove to
Hofmann's house in late June, and when Dorie Hofmann said he
wasn't home Rust pointed to their van and a Japanese-built sports
car Mark had recently purchased and accused her angrily of lying
to him.

The next day Hofmann arrived at Rust's home in a Salt Lake
City suburb and for two hours listened to Rust scold him like an
angry parent. Mark owed him not only the proceeds from the sale
of the McLellin Collection but almost $90,000 from previous trans-
actions. He accused Hofmann of being too anxious to expand his
business, of using other people's money to finance the expansion, of
buying new documents before he had sold those already in his
inventory and of being obsessed with becoming a document dealer
of national reputation.

"You're going in too many directions at once, starting new things

before you've finished old ones. You're going like a wild man. You're like a chicken with his head cut off, robbing Peter to pay Paul."

Hofmann looked at him with a blank stare, rarely allowing his eyes to acknowledge Rust's presence.

When Rust went home that night, he said to his wife:

"It was the most peculiar experience. I've never been so harsh on anybody in my life and I got no reaction at all. He didn't deny it, get mad or apologize or *anything*. He just sat there like it didn't mean anything."

Douglas Fullmer was a real estate broker who had known Mark Hofmann most of his life. They had gone to Evergreen Junior High School together, camped and water-skied together, shared the same locker at Olympus High and now lived in the same ward two blocks from each other.

He had sold Dorie and Mark Hofmann their first house almost three years earlier in Sandy for $56,000 and had advised them when they later purchased Mark's parents' home. Thus, it was not surprising that they turned to Fullmer when they were ready to buy their dream house.

Fullmer, like many of Mark's childhood acquaintances, regarded Hofmann as a classic Utah success story: an entrepreneur who had started with nothing, had filled a need no one had exploited before and through drive and hard work had become wealthy. Mark said his earnings were now in the six-figure range and climbing. Although finding Mormon documents had been good to him, he said, he now regarded the market as too confining and limited for his ambitions, and he was expanding rapidly into what he called "national documents"; already, rare documents from American history accounted for eighty percent of his business.

In June, Hofmann told Fullmer that he expected to close a large deal soon and that he and Dorie wanted to buy or build a home in one of the nicer areas along the Wasatch Front.

One area that interested them was The Cove, a plateau nestled like the cove of a lake in the Wasatch foothills that was the setting for some of the Valley's grandest homes. Another possibility was Emigration Canyon, the rugged rocky corridor above the Valley through which Brigham Young brought his followers to the promised land in 1847.

Money was no object, Hofmann said. They wanted something in the $500,000 range and would pay for it over three years.

While waiting for the Library of Congress to respond to their letter, Justin Schiller and Raymond Wapner concluded negotiations to buy for Mark Hofmann the sixty-nine-page handwritten manuscript of *The Haunted Man and the Ghost's Bargain,* one of Charles Dickens's five stories about Christmas, from New York City's Pforzheimer Library collection of rare books for $330,000.

On June 5, Mark and Shannon Flynn flew to Phoenix, rented a car and drove to Mesa, a suburb of cactus and palm trees that was spreading across the Arizona desert like an urban tidal wave. Their destination was the office of Wilford Alan Cardon, a multimillionaire whose holdings ranged from oil and convenience stores to shopping centers and housing developments. During Flynn's mission in Brazil eight years earlier, Cardon had been mission president, a task assigned to mature members of the church whose duty it was to look after the welfare of young missionaries placed in their charge. Cardon and Flynn remained in touch after their return from Brazil, and the previous year, Cardon, at Flynn's suggestion, had invested $12,000 with Hofmann to purchase part ownership of a letter signed by Betsy Ross, the woman who, according to legend, designed the first American flag.

The purpose of their trip was to offer Cardon a new investment opportunity that Hofmann said promised a payoff of fifty percent within a few months: one-third interest in the Dickens manuscript. Cardon accepted the proposition. The following day, his company wired $110,000 to the Carl and Lily Pforzheimer Foundation in New York.

When it came time to close the deal, however, Hofmann said he was short of cash, and asked Schiller and Wapner to delay the closing a week or two. Embarrassed by having to break a commitment after a deal had been agreed to, the dealers borrowed $170,000 from their bank temporarily to consummate the purchase on schedule. Meanwhile, they awaited a reply from the Library of Congress to their offer to sell the Oath of a Freeman for $1.5 million.

Nine days after they mailed their offer, Robert C. Sullivan, Director of Acquisitions and Overseas Operations for the Library of

Congress, responded to it: He said it was his preliminary reaction that the asking price was too high, but the Library of Congress wanted to negotiate further if the Schiller-Wapner Galleries were prepared to warrant that the Oath was authentic and provide the documentation necessary to establish the chain of ownership of the document.

Schiller replied with a promise to refund the purchase price if subsequent testing established within a year that the Oath was not printed by Stephen Daye. But he made clear the asking price was firm:

"In the full belief that the document could find a willing purchaser at a price in excess of that quoted to L.C., but taking into account the belief of our clients that L.C. would be a preferred repository, we affirm our offer to sell the document to L.C. at 1.5 million dollars."

The negotiations continued.

Five days later, Sullivan thanked the dealers for the promise of a one-year warranty, but said, "The Library of Congress is not prepared to purchase this document at the quoted price of $1.5 million." In what appeared to be an invitation to submit a lower offer, Sullivan added that he hoped that they could still come to terms.

Schiller and Wapner had other options in mind, however. They had already passed the news of the document's discovery and its successful examination by experts at the Library of Congress to document dealers, foundations, libraries and other institutions that they believed could afford to buy the Oath of a Freeman. Rumors were rocketing through the rare book trade that the document might bring $2 million at auction, with millionaires Malcolm Forbes and H. Ross Perot the most often cited prospective buyers. Schiller assured Hofmann there was no shortage of potential buyers; their job was to find someone who was willing to pay as much for the Oath as it was worth.

On the same day in June that negotiations broke down with the Library of Congress, Schiller opened negotiations to sell the Oath to the American Antiquarian Society, whose collection of early American books and historical materials in Worcester, Massachusetts, was considered the country's finest outside the Library of Congress. The asking price of $1.5 million, he told the society, was a bargain for the one-of-a-kind historical treasure.

28

President Gordon B. Hinckley would later deny that he ever asked Mark Hofmann to prevent the McLellin Collection from falling into the hands of the enemy. Hofmann would tell a different story. Thus, doubt would remain over precisely what occurred when Hofmann met secretly with Hinckley in the Church Administration Building during June of 1985.

Hofmann asked for an appointment with Hinckley after discovering that the payment he expected for the Oath of a Freeman would be delayed. When they met, Hofmann said, he told the church President the following story:

After years of searching for it, he had found the McLellin Collection. It was in Texas and contained documents that, if published, would be devastating to the church.

President Hinckley—who could read articles almost daily in the newspapers questioning the church and its doctrines and accusing it of supressing documents—indicated he did not want to know about the McLellin Collection.

At this stage of their relationship, Hofmann said, he and the church President had begun to play a word game: Hofmann would hint at something that could be damaging to the church, then he would hesitate, extending to Hinckley the option to ask for more information—or not to do so, enabling him later to deny truthfully that he knew of certain events or documents.

Hofmann said he was involved in a race to prevent the McLellin Collection from falling into the hands of the enemy, which also knew of the documents' existence. He said he had borrowed money from a Salt Lake City businessman, Al Rust, to buy the collection in the belief that he would sell an extremely rare document to the Library of Congress—the first printed document in America—for over a million dollars. Once he received the payment for the document, his intent was to donate the McLellin Collection to the church in lieu of the ten percent share of his income that he would owe the church as a tithing. But the sale had been delayed and Rust—who Hofmann knew had written a letter of complaint to Hinckley—was pressing him for either the money or the documents.

If Rust wasn't paid, Hofmann warned that he might break his pledge of silence and go public with the secrets contained in the documents.

Hofmann said he was hopeful that he could find a faithful member of the church who would advance him the cash in order to prevent this from happening, but if that proved impossible, Hofmann asked, would the church give him the $185,000 he needed to pay Rust?

Because of the conflicts over what transpired at the meetings, it would be impossible to resolve how Hinckley answered Hofmann's question. When Hofmann left the Church Administration Building after their final meeting on the topic, he told friends that the church President had directed him to do whatever he could to keep the documents from the enemy and, if things became desperate, he was to call Hinckley for help.

The following day, Hofmann flew to Phoenix with Shannon Flynn for another meeting with Wilford Cardon. Hofmann told Cardon that President Hinckley had deputized him to keep an embarrassing collection of documents from falling into the hands of the church's enemies and asked if Cardon would provide $185,000 to deal with the crisis. They had little time to avert disaster.

Cardon was puzzled by the proposal: It was not the way the

General Authorities did business. If President Hinckley wanted him to buy the documents, he said, Hinckley should ask him to do so; if he did, he would be glad to donate the documents to the church.

Hofmann immediately proposed that they call President Hinckley. But Hinckley's secretary said he was in Freiberg, East Germany, dedicating the church's first temple behind the Iron Curtain.

The secretary said it was impossible to reach Hinckley by telephone because he was in East Germany, but she said she would tell Hinckley to call Cardon if he telephoned the office.

Two days later, Hofmann telephoned Cardon and said the crisis had passed. He said he had found the cash elsewhere needed to avert publication of the embarrassing documents.

He did not reveal to Cardon that the person he had turned to for help—as he had when a buyer was needed for the salamander letter —was Steve Christensen.

In what he marked as a "confidential" entry in his journal on June 28, 1985, Christensen wrote that Mark Hofmann had called and requested to see him the following morning to discuss a matter of great urgency. When they met, Hofmann disclosed that his search for the papers of Dr. William McLellin had been successful.

He said he intended to donate the McLellin documents to the church as soon as the sale of an expensive document to the Library of Congress was consummated. Although he had expected the deal to close in June it had been delayed until about August 15 and he had to raise $185,000 before June 30 in order to prevent the McLellin Collection from being acquired by critics of the church such as Jerald and Sandra Tanner; Wesley Walters, a Presbyterian minister in Marissa, Illinois, who often wrote about Mormon history in ways the church did not like; or George Smith, the publisher of Signature Books, whom Christensen referred to as a "humanist, intellectual, anti-Mormon and semi–financially independent businessman."

Hofmann explained that the McLellin Collection was an arsenal of anti-Mormon material including a portion of the Egyptian papyrus that Joseph Smith said he had translated into the Book of Abraham that was referred to as Facsimile Number Two in an important Mormon scripture, the Pearl of Great Price.

"Some people delight in pointing out," Christensen wrote, "that the originals of facsimiles one and three were altered before there [sic] inclusion in the PofGP—two may contain similar alterations upon comparison. A further argument is that the facsimiles have nothing to do with our PofGP scripture, but rather that they are documents more appropriately associated with ancient funerals of Egypt."

Also in the collection, Christensen wrote in his journal, were documents showing that Joseph Smith tried to sell the copyright of the Book of Mormon to a Canadian businessman, supporting critics' claims that he had written it all along to make a profit; an affidavit by Joseph Smith's wife, Emma, contradicting his account of being visited by God three years before encountering Moroni, a meeting hallowed in Mormon dogma as the "First Vision"; and personal diaries and letters of McLellin that included an entry supporting a disputed claim by McLellin that he had surprised Joseph Smith while he was having sexual relations with a servant girl.

If there was a single cache of documents waiting to embarrass the church, Hofmann said it was the McLellin Collection.

Christensen noted in the journal that after Hofmann received payment for his pending transaction, he planned to donate the documents to the church:

It then follows that the Church's representatives could say that they were never purchased. With any luck no one will ever ask Mark if he donated the material. Though this form of dialogue walks the fine line of "honest intent" behind a question and the pure reading of the question and reciprocal answer, it perhaps saves the Church for the time being from having to offer an explanation on why they won't release the material and/or be under the necessity of mounting a public relations move to counter the contents of the collection.

Christensen did not inform Hofmann of C.F.S.'s financial problems, but admitted he was not in a position to provide the money Hofmann needed to buy the documents. He suggested, however, that they call Hugh Pinnock, a member of the First Quorum of the Seventy. Pinnock was a friend of Steve Christensen and an even closer friend of his father and Gary Sheets. Pinnock and Sheets had been Sigma Chi fraternity brothers at the University of Utah and they had worked at the same insurance company early in their respective careers.

At fifty-one, Hugh Pinnock was a genial and articulate man with close-cropped dark hair who was noted for having a good head for business. Called as a bishop at twenty-nine, a mission president at thirty-nine, and a General Authority at forty-three, he was considered a comer in the church hierarchy. Christensen wrote in his journal that while Hofmann waited, he telephoned Pinnock and advised him of the threat facing the church because of the McLellin Collection. Pinnock, he noted, replied that he "could arrange for the funds within one hour and that Mark and I should come over to his office as soon as possible."

After receiving Christensen's call, Pinnock walked to the office of Apostle Dallin H. Oaks, a former justice of the Utah Supreme Court, ex-president of Brigham Young University and former chairman of the board of the Public Broadcasting System. Oaks was the man in the church hierarchy to whom Pinnock reported.

He described the telephone call from Christensen and suggested that the church make a loan of $185,000 to Hofmann so that he could acquire the documents. Oaks said President Hinckley was out of the country and only he could approve buying the documents or lending money to Hofmann.

The two church leaders agreed, however, to help Hofmann obtain a loan from someone else so he could obtain the documents. Then, if that *someone* wanted to donate them to the church, it would be glad to accept them.

Christensen recalled in his journal the next link in the day's chain of events:

Upon reaching Elder Pinnock's office we were welcomed most graciously. It was remarkable to both Mark and myself that Elder Pinnock was willing to assist to his fullest extent possible with only a brief explanation. It was as though he sensed completely the potential damage which this material would cause in the hands of the enemies of the Church. Within minutes he was able to arrange for Mark to receive $185,000 in the form of a cashier's check. The check followed a signature promissory note executed by Mark in the favor of First Interstate Bank.

Pinnock, a director of the First Interstate Bank, had simply called a senior vice-president at its main office and arranged for the loan. It had taken only a few minutes.

The unsecured loan was to be issued on Hofmann's signature at an interest rate of one percent above the prime rate.

Before they left his office, Christensen noted in his journal, Pinnock told Hofmann he would like to talk to him sometime about retaining his services to track down two other items, including the lost 116 pages of the Book of Mormon. Hofmann assured him that he was already in pursuit of the missing Book of Lehi. Christensen wrote:

> Elder Pinnock was not in a position to reveal the second item, though he indicated that Elders Petersen and Durham were most interested in it prior to their deaths. He further indicated that they had some etching of it and that the Smithsonian had a file on it, pending a donation of the item which never went through. Mark and I believe that he was referring to the Gold Plates from which we have the Book of Mormon. I personally believe that the Church already has them in its possession (unknown to perhaps the majority of the Twelve and other General Authorities).

Christensen said Pinnock offered to arrange for a plane or armored car to carry the McLellin Collection back to Salt Lake City, but Hofmann said it wasn't necessary.

> Elder Pinnock left with Mark four phone numbers with which to reach him. The extent of his helpful precautions included his having ready $185,000 in cash should the owner try to break the deal since a cashier's check may not be deemed "legal tender" on a Sunday without the ability to convert it to cash. He also offered to make available a propjet and/or an armored car for the transportation of the documents; however, Mark dissuaded him. Though I also am concerned with the risk, Mark will be sending the material home via registered mail, insured for $195,000.

Hofmann promised to leave as soon as possible for Texas, pick up the documents, and then lock them in a safe-deposit box until he received the payment from the Library of Congress. Then he would donate the documents to the church.

> Elder Pinnock's personal actions not only preserved Mark Hofmann's ability to purchase the collection [Christensen wrote], but equally as important, he has saved the Church countless time and money and effort in countering what would have been an avalanche of negative publicity should the collection have fallen into the wrong hands.

Two weeks later, Hofmann visited Hugh Pinnock at the church headquarters and assured him the documents were secure. Then he handed him a wrinkled sheet of yellowed paper.

It was a sample, he said, of the McLellin Collection.

The sheet of paper Hofmann gave Pinnock was a contract of sale dated January 19, 1822, for a parcel of land in Connecticut sold for twenty-one shillings. The principals in the transaction were identified as Sidney Rigdon and Solomon Spaulding.

In this document there were no references to salamanders, clever spirits or Joseph Smith. But it touched an ancient sore in the Mormon church that was perhaps even more sensitive than the legends surrounding Joseph Smith's magical stones and divining rods.

Following the publication of the Book of Mormon, anti-Mormons contended that Joseph Smith was too simple a youth to have fabricated the Book of Mormon and suggested that he had had the assistance of an early convert, an educated Campbellite preacher named Sidney Rigdon.

According to the critics' theory, Rigdon had lifted the elements of the Book of Mormon from an unpublished history of the American Indians that had been written by an impecunious former preacher, Solomon Spaulding. Spaulding's book traced the Indians' ancestry to the Jews of ancient Israel. The theory had largely been disregarded by modern historians, however, because there was no evidence Rigdon and Spaulding had ever met.

The document Hofmann showed Pinnock appeared to establish a direct link between the two men. He permitted Pinnock to copy the contract but asked him to keep its contents a secret.

It was a request, Hofmann later told friends sarcastically, that was probably unnecessary.

29

     Fulfilling Dorie Hofmann's desire for a new home did not prove to be easy for either Mark or his real estate broker. Still, Douglas Fullmer was accustomed to husbands and wives disagreeing over the choice of a new home—it was an emotional time for most couples—and he knew they would eventually agree on a house they both liked. He showed the Hofmanns an acre in the foothills above the city that was priced at $300,000, and they met with an architect to discuss building a home on the site. But construction would have taken almost a year, and they were anxious to move into a larger home sooner than that. After they inspected dozens of houses in The Cove and the canyons above the Valley, the search narrowed to a choice between two special homes: Mark liked an isolated, rambling home perched on a shallow bluff in Emigration Canyon. Dorie wanted an even larger house on Cottonwood Lane in Holladay with five bedrooms, a swimming pool, a tennis court, a guest house, a security system and a satellite dish for receiving television broadcasts. Her wealthy cousin, Ken Woolley, had bought a home not far away. In early August, they submitted an offer of $550,000 for the home Dorie liked and it was accepted. Sealing the contract with a $5,000 down payment, they agreed to pay $200,000 when they moved in on October 1 and pay off the balance with annual payments over the next three years.

While Dorie and Mark Hofmann were approaching the realization of one of their dreams, the dream life of Terri and Steve Christensen was becoming a nightmare.

In late July, Steve drove to a condominium in Park City where Terri had taken the children to escape the Salt Lake Valley's scorching summer heat. After dinner, they put the children to bed and Terri sat on a sofa in the living room and waited for Steve to speak. For weeks she had had a sense of foreboding, but Steve had not wanted to discuss the problems at the company and she had waited for him to decide when the time was right.

C.F.S., he said, was going to have to declare bankruptcy.

"There's no way we're going to be able to pull it out," he said.

"Gary thinks we still can save it, but it's impossible; he's not being realistic."

Honesty was one of the values Christensen cherished most, and now, he said, he had to be honest with himself.

He said he had done everything he could think of to keep C.F.S. solvent, but it simply owed too much money. The company would have to declare bankruptcy, and when that happened he and Terri would have to declare their personal bankruptcy.

When the losses began, he said, he and Gary and three other directors of C.F.S. had borrowed money for the company against their own credit. As a result, everything they owned was mortgaged as collateral for the loans to C.F.S.

"We're going to lose everything," he said: the house, her jewelry, the cars, the building site in Bountiful.

"How about your books?"

"I have to sell them."

Steve did not admit that he had already begun trying to sell the thirteen thousand volumes that they had once imagined lining the walls of a two-story library in a house that would never be built now.

Nothing in the world, except his family, Terri thought, meant as much to her husband as his book collection.

The realization that he would have to sell the books made her burst into tears and she couldn't stop.

Steve, who had always found it so hard to express his emotions, cried for a moment, too.

"Can't you keep the books?"

"No.

"We're going to have to sell everything. But we'll be all right. We'll get a new start. We'll get a three-bedroom apartment and just start over. I can handle everything.

"Don't worry," he said. "We'll be all right." And then he kissed Terri.

She looked at him and suddenly felt comfort. She knew he was right: He *would* start over and she knew he would succeed. He never stopped working until he succeeded.

For Kathy Sheets, much of the life she had known was also crumbling, but, as ever, her inherent optimism battled fiercely against the forces aligned against it.

In her journal she recorded loving descriptions of visits by her grandchildren, the sadness of visits to her ailing mother, expressions of love for her children and reports of the whirl of social events centering on the church and Gary's job as bishop, along with an occasional confession ("I get sick of church," she wrote after returning home one Sunday evening).

"Feel a little better," she noted in late July. "Gary says we will do all we can. *How can this happen to such nice men?* Very depressing."

A few days later, she wrote: "Gary and I went to a movie. It was fun. He is feeling up and confident. Hope it continues. I really love him and I know he will take care of me. I worked hard today on laundry, etc. . . ."

"My friends had a surprise 50 yrs. birthday party for me," she wrote in the journal August 2. "It was hilarious. They all dressed up like old ladies. Jane Forsgren wore knee length garments, had them hanging. . . . Great fun." A day later, she wrote: "Lazy day . . . I am very down. House is a mess. I am fat. Business is bad. I am depressed."

On August 3, Steve Christensen submitted his resignation to Gary Sheets. For weeks he had been working into the late hours reviewing the books of C.F.S. in search of a route to divert it from calamity. He headed a committee established to find a way out of the morass. But the company's investments, he realized, had been so highly leveraged any economic hiccup menaced the whole empire. It had invested $12 million in apartments in Houston alone that were now as empty as if they had been abandoned during a tornado. In a rush to grow, it had diversified into businesses for which it had no management skills. The decision to buy and rehabilitate the office building in downtown Salt Lake City as a grand corporate headquarters for C.F.S. had been a financial disaster. Too much money had been shifted from profitable limited partnerships to losers. Then, in late spring, an adverse auditor's report had made the precarious dominoes start to fall: The auditors concluded that the company owed more than it was worth, that it had a *negative* net worth of $5 million. This meant it could no longer legally syndicate properties or accept money from investors.

In effect, C.F.S. was out of business. Even worse, Christensen realized there was a possibility investors could lose more than $100 million.

The company's salesmen (C.F.S. didn't use this term but called its salesmen "consultants") were having to tell clients, many of them personal friends who had invested their entire savings—money for retirement or a child's education—that their entire investment could be lost. More than 1,200 people were investors in C.F.S. Some were threatening lawsuits, others more direct—even violent—action. One investor said he was setting aside $25,000 to put the company's executives in jail. Some Las Vegas investors, hinting organized crime had invested heavily in C.F.S., suggested that the Mafia did not look kindly on people who lost—or stole—its money.

After completing his analysis of the company's prospects, Christensen told Sheets the only future he saw for the company was its liquidation and distribution of its few remaining assets to investors.

Sheets said Christensen was being too negative.

He had built the company out of nothing. It had survived hard times before. He had led a charmed life. God had rewarded him. He didn't—couldn't—believe God would abandon him now.

The two of them could pull it out, Sheets insisted.

"I love Steve like a brother," he told another executive in the company. "But he's not positive enough. We got to make this go—not let the ship sink."

The executive responded:

"How could this happen, with two bishops and a stake president on the board of directors?"

When Christensen and Sheets met for the last time as business associates on August 4, 1985, several senior executives had already resigned from the company and others were thinking of going.

Sheets knew that most of the remaining employees looked up to Steve as their leader, and he asked him to tell them the company was not doomed.

"Steve, can you just say we *might* have a chance?"

Christensen said he had to be honest with people.

"Can you just say it will be a good fight?"

"No."

Sheets, however, was unable to accept his protégé's pessimism, and they agreed that it was probably best that Steve leave the company.

The next day, Christensen consulted an attorney who was regarded as one of Salt Lake City's leading legal specialists on white-collar crime, and told him that he was resigning from C.F.S. and preparing to lose everything he owned. But he said he was less worried about his own problems than he was about the huge losses facing good people who had invested all their money in C.F.S. And he said he was troubled by activities at C.F.S. that could lead to a criminal investigation.

Christensen said he did not believe anyone had consciously committed fraud, but investors' funds had been shifted from project to project and used in some cases to pay operating expenses at C.F.S. Although their contracts specified C.F.S. could shift their money from one investment to another, he said it was unlikely that most investors realized the implications of this clause and that they would not have risked their money if they had.

The lawyer said that from what Christensen had explained to him, it was unlikely he was personally culpable for any crimes but it was possible criminal charges could be brought against the company and some of its executives.

If the police or FBI instituted an investigation of C.F.S., Christensen said he would be a witness before a grand jury and would tell the truth.

The lawyer was troubled that Christensen had been so forthright in speaking up about his concerns to other people at C.F.S.

It was inviting trouble, he said.

Christensen said he didn't care, he just wanted to protect his own reputation and that of his family.

"What's right is right, what's wrong is wrong," he said.

Before leaving the lawyer's office, Christensen said he had decided to open his own investment business and make a new start. He said he expected to meet any legal expenses resulting from the investigation of C.F.S. by selling his collection of rare books.

It was the only thing of value he still owned, he said.

30

As the summer of 1985 drifted by, Mark Hofmann and his agents, Justin Schiller and Raymond Wapner, began to accept the reality that selling the Oath of a Freeman would take longer than they had expected. Officers of the American Antiquarian Society said they wanted to buy the Oath if it was authentic but said they needed more time to examine it before making a decision. Schiller predicted a deal would be struck, but said they might have to lower their price to $1,250,000. Deducting the dealers' commission, that would leave $1 million for Hofmann.

After receiving the $185,000 bank loan arranged by Hugh Pinnock, Hofmann gave Al Rust, his original investor in the McLellin Collection, $165,000. Rust pointed out that Hofmann still owed him $132,000, a figure that included Rust's share of the profit from the sale of the McLellin Collection to the church.

Mark then confided that the church did not buy the McLellin Collection after all; shortly after the trip to New York City, he said the Brethren became worried that the acquisition might be discovered by the press. Instead, Hofmann said he intended to donate the collection to the church.

Rust protested.

"What do you mean? *Donate* it? I can't afford to donate it to the church."

Rust didn't have to surrender his share of the profits, Mark said. Then he told him about his discovery of the Oath of a Freeman in New York and his expectations of receiving at least $1 million for it by September 1. When he received the money, he promised, Rust would be paid in full—the same amount as if the church had paid $300,000 for the McLellin Collection. Then, Hofmann said, he would donate the collection to the church.

Now that Hofmann had placated Al Rust, he moved to pacify another restless customer, and he did so in a curious way.

Brent Ashworth had never forgotten, or forgiven, Hofmann's sale of Joseph Smith's last letter from the Carthage Jail—his poignant appeal for help to General Jonathan Dunham—to rival collector Richard Marks after promising it to him.

Although he still frequently bought autographs and other items for his collection from Hofmann, Ashworth had embraced a new mission in life: telling fellow collectors that Mark Hofmann could not be trusted.

Nothing in the document business was more vital to the success of a dealer than his reputation, and Hofmann acted to subdue Ashworth's criticism in an expensive fashion.

In early July, he visited—as he often did—Curt Bench, manager of the Fine Arts and Rare Books Department in the Deseret Book Store located across from the Hotel Utah a block from Temple Square.

Like the Hotel Utah across the street, the cavernous bookstore with soaring glass walls was owned by the church—so many things were in Salt Lake City. Bench, after serving his mission in the American South, had graduated from BYU, gone to work for the bookstore as a trainee in a suburban branch and worked up to a senior management position in the company's flagship store. Tall and slender, Bench at thirty-three had the same fresh, boyish looks of a returned missionary that made many young men in Utah seem younger than they were.

Because his department stocked thousands of old books on the history of Mormonism and the American West, it was a gathering place for many young Mormons who took up the study of church history as a hobby during their missions or when they returned home. Many dropped in the store to buy, sell and trade books with Bench.

When he and Hofmann had met in 1980 at the suburban branch where he first worked, Bench was impressed by Hofmann's seriousness and scholarly knowledge of church history as well as his unaggressive, almost meek, personality, and soon they were social as well as business friends. During the ensuing five years their transactions totaled hundreds of thousands of dollars.

"Greetings," Mark said as he approached Bench's cubicle during his visit in early July. It was the way he always opened a visit to Bench.

He said that if Richard Marks could part with it, he wanted to buy back Joseph Smith's letter to General Dunham from the Carthage Jail. Bench agreed to approach Marks with an inquiry.

Marks, who had paid $20,000 for the letter less than two years before, told Bench that, yes, he was willing to sell it—for $100,000. When Bench asked if he would take $90,000, Marks accepted the proposition.

The figure amazed Bench, and he was just as amazed when Hofmann agreed to pay it. The price of documents was rising so fast, he said, that nothing would surprise him.

In all, Hofmann agreed to pay $116,000 to Deseret Book Store on September 1: $90,000 for Marks, a $20,000 commission for the store and $6,000 in sales taxes.

When the deal was closed, Hofmann called Brent Ashworth and said:

"Brent, I think I can get you the General Dunham letter for $60,000, but you have to have cash."

"Mark, you've got a lot of gall.

"That's *my* letter—you stole it from me; you promised it to me for $30,000 and then sold it to Dick Marks. Now you want twice as much. Forget it."

But before a week had passed, Ashworth found it impossible to contain his obsessive hunger for the letter. He told Hofmann he did not have $60,000 in cash but was willing to deal. After an hour of bargaining they reached an agreement: In exchange for $19,000 in cash and documents he valued at $41,000, Ashworth finally owned Joseph Smith's last letter. He took it home and placed it beside Lucy Mack Smith's letter and the letter with Martin Harris's description of an angel and the voice of God. It was the crowning jewel in his collection.

The sale and resale of the Smith-Dunham letter was a curious transaction. It resulted in a loss to Hofmann of at least $56,000. But he had mollified Ashworth and, temporarily at least, quieted Ashworth's public denunciations at a time when he could ill afford a tarnished reputation. And he could afford it: Schiller told him to expect a million dollars soon.

A few days later, Hofmann called the Newton, Massachusetts, office of dealer Kenneth Rendell to whom he had turned for testing of the salamander letter. He said he wanted to buy a page from the Egyptian Book of the Dead written in hieratic script during the first century A.D.

For Rendell, who sold more papyrus than any dealer in the world, it was an unusual request. The most widely recognized Egyptian hieroglyphics—the kind most in demand by collectors— were pictures and symbols, the type, Rendell once said, "Bloomingdale's puts on pillows." Hieratic writing was a rounded curved script used by Egypt's priestly class beginning in the third century B.C. The request for papyrus from the first century A.D. was also unusual. It was a time when the glory of Egypt was fading, Cleopatra was being romanced by Julius Caesar and Egypt was becoming as much Roman as Egyptian. It was not a golden age for hieroglyphics. Still, one of Rendell's assistants said she would attempt to satisfy Hofmann's needs.

The summer of 1985 had been a long and troubled season for leaders of the Church of Latter-day Saints. The skeptical news reports and sniping by anti-Mormon groups precipitated by publication of the salamander letter and Joseph Smith's letter to Josiah Stowell had refused to subside. Rumors were relentless that still more embarrassing documents—some even mentioned a mysterious McLellin Collection—were about to become public. Hofmann and Christensen reassured senior General Authorities that the McLellin Collection was safe from unfriendly eyes, but rumors of its existence continued to sweep over the Salt Lake Valley.

Spokesmen for the church told inquiring reporters that the First Presidency's Vault had been searched thoroughly and no trace had been found of a diary written by Oliver Cowdery containing a reference to a salamander. But the church's previous denial—and subsequent admission—that it had suppressed Joseph Smith's letter to Stowell had exacted a toll on its credibility, and many journalists and historians remained convinced that the church was hiding more explosive secrets.

The situation was not helped by a new willingness—an eagerness, even—by many Mormon intellectuals to climb aboard the scholarly bandwagon of folk magic. After a century in which the topic was taboo, the church's publication of the two letters had made it respectable for historians to acknowledge that Joseph Smith dabbled in the occult and had hired himself out as a sorcerer. And as their research continued, it often seemed to link his work as a sorcerer closer and closer to his story of an angel giving him the gold plates of the Book of Mormon.

Church leaders struggled to hold back the tide of research and regain control over the past. When an employee of the church's Translation Division wrote a scholarly paper which concluded that Joseph Smith had copied faulty translations of an 1829 King James version of the Bible and included these same errors in the Book of Mormon, he was forced to resign. Two Mormon scholars who had written a biography of Joseph Smith's wife, Emma, that described some of his polygamous affairs were banned from speaking at firesides or other church meetings. And then the tempest over publication of the letters was intensified by the University of Illinois Press's publication of a previously secret sixty-year-old study by Brigham H. Roberts, a legendary Mormon leader and historian. His study concluded that the Book of Mormon was a figment of Joseph Smith's imagination.

Roberts, the Church Historian from 1901 until his death in 1933, had sent the report to church leaders in the 1920s with an appeal to help him resolve what he called "problems" with the Mormon scripture. The report pointed out similarities and identical language in the Book of Mormon and *View of the Hebrews,* a book written in 1823 by a Christian minister, Ethan Smith, and suggested the parallels were too numerous to be coincidental. Roberts said he was bewildered by the Book of Mormon's reference to ancient Hebrews' use of steel and domestic animals that were known in nineteenth-century America but unknown in biblical times. On page after page, Roberts cited examples of what he considered discrepancies, implausibilities and contradictions in the Book of Mormon, and concluded, "The evidence I sorrowfully submit points to Joseph Smith as their creator."

Roberts, who later in his life defended the Book of Mormon, was perhaps the church's first intellectual to be torn by an internal struggle between his faith and a desire to be honest with himself. Many others would follow him.

Mormonism, Roberts said, must "stand or fall" on the truth of Joseph Smith's account of the Book of Mormon and his claim that it was a history of an ancient people inscribed on a cache of gold plates.

Unless leaders of the church resolved the kinds of problems raised in the study, he predicted prophetically, the problems would remain to haunt the church and "now and also in the future" undermine "the faith of the Youth of the Church."

As controversy swirled around publication of Roberts's study, church leaders resumed their assault on contemporary historians. In a speech relayed by satellite to tens of thousands of teenage Mormons during the summer of 1985, President Gordon B. Hinckley attacked scholars who were "poking into all the crevices of our history, ferreting out little things of small import and magnifying them into great issues of public discussion, working the media in an effort to give credibility to their efforts."

He was followed by Apostle Russell M. Nelson, who argued: "In some instances, the merciful companion of truth is silence. Some truths are best left unsaid."

On August 16, Apostle Dallin H. Oaks told an assembly of religion instructors at Brigham Young University that young people should be instructed to be suspicious of articles and broadcasts regarding church history, because such reports, often prepared quickly and limited by time and space, were inadequate to report complex topics of history or reveal whether, for example, the recently discovered letters had been subjected to sufficient scientific testing to determine their authenticity. He also warned young Mormons to be cautious of bias and half-truths in news reports and the works of "partially committed Latter-day Saints." Oaks said:

"The fact that something is true is not always a justification for

communicating it. By the same token, some things that are true are not edifying or appropriate to communicate."

Criticizing *leaders* of the church was especially onerous. "Evil speaking of the Lord's anointed," Oaks said, "is in a class by itself. It is one thing to deprecate a person who exercises corporate power or even government power. It is quite another thing to criticize or deprecate a person for the performance of an office in which he or she has been called of God. *It does not matter that the criticism is true."*

31

In early September, Curt Bench asked Mark Hofmann if he was interested in buying a book recently unearthed from an old safe at Deseret Book. It had been in the safe since 1973 when the store had acquired it as an incidental part of another transaction, then had put it away and forgotten about it. It was an ordinary *Book of Common Prayer,* an Anglican missal similar to thousands that could be found in used bookstores, but Bench pointed out it had been signed by a Nathan Harris and suggested he might be Martin Harris's brother. Mark agreed and offered to buy it for $50.

A few days later Hofmann returned to the store. He said he had found a short poem in the rear flyleaf of the book written by Martin Harris himself, which raised its value considerably, and he had then sold it to the church for $2,000. Since neither of them had known about the poem when they agreed on the price of $50, Hofmann said he felt it was only fair that he split the profit and pay Deseret Book $1,000 for the book instead of $50. Vaguely remembering an inscription in the back of the book, Bench informed his superiors of the financial coup and Hofmann's generosity.

27 August 1985

Dear Raymond:

As you know, we have wrestled with the printed version of the "Oath of a Freeman" which you put into our hands some weeks ago. (It is here and safe, by the way.) We have pulled and tugged this way and that and are quite well satisfied that it is a mid-seventeenth-century, American printing of the "Oath." But, why it was printed, where, when and by whom we cannot say.

You will recall that in my letter of August 12, 1985, I suggested that before we could make a final decision we would require additional indications of its seventeenth-century American origin to be provided by the owner—all evidence available to us at this point has been developed by the Library of Congress for their own purposes, the results not being available to the public (nor can they legally be used by the owner without the permission of the Library of Congress), or by AAS for our purposes.

Properly, you inquired of me that if positive proofs were supplied at the expense of the owner (such as those suggested by us) would AAS buy the "Oath." The answer is a qualified "Yes," if:

1. The price is lowered drastically to a level that reflects its true importance, and

2. If the Council of the Society approves its purchase at their meeting on October 15, assuming that the proofs are in by that date.

The price of $1,500,000 is insupportable, in our view, by what can be actually determined about its printing. I do not believe that the owner will *ever* be able to categorically state that it was printed on the press in Cambridge, Massachusetts, in mid-March 1639 as the first piece struck off from the first press in what is now the United States. That being the case, we would be prepared to pay $250,000 for it, assuming further tests are not negative and upon full disclosure of a provenance that is adequate to establish its American origin and is verifiable by other documentation.

I look forward to your response to this statement of our intentions.

> Sincerely yours,
> Marcus A. McCorison
> Director and Librarian
> American Antiquarian Society

Hofmann told Ray Wapner that he didn't want to take less than $1 million for the Oath. Wapner and Justin Schiller said he probably wouldn't have to: The letter was only a bargaining ploy. But they said the letter meant the sale probably could not be consummated until the Society's governing board met on October 15.

Suddenly, Hofmann realized, his financial condition had deteriorated perilously.

He had spent money he didn't have. He owed a million dollars he didn't have.

Confident that the sale of the Oath would be completed by September 1, he had given Al Rust a check for $132,100 to settle their accounts. It would bounce. He had sent an $8,544 check to the Internal Revenue Service for back taxes that would bounce—and the IRS was demanding $28,413 in additional overdue taxes.

On September 1, he was obligated to pay Deseret Book $116,000 for the General Dunham letter. He had promised Dorie's cousin, Ken Woolley, $85,000 on September 3 as his long-delayed profit from a document transaction the previous spring. In the spring he had borrowed $90,000 from a Salt Lake City orthodontist to buy children's books; he was obligated to pay back most of the loan October 4. There were other debts totaling more than $100,000, and a travel agency was threatening to sue him because he had given it a bad check. On top of everything else, he owed $200,000 October 1 as the down payment on his new house—and he still owed First Interstate Bank $185,000.

He called Thomas Wilding, his college classmate whose investment group had doubled its money during two previous transactions and told him that the Morgan Stanley Library in New York City had agreed to buy Charles Dickens's manuscript for *The Haunted Man* for $500,000 on October 16. The deal would net them a sixty-percent profit in less than five months.

Now he said he had an opportunity that dwarfed any previous deals. If Wilding and his investors were interested, they could share in it:

After pledging Wilding to secrecy, Hofmann said that he had recently sold a copy of the first document printed in America—the most sought-after document in U.S. history, the Oath of a Freeman—to the Library of Congress for $1 million. He explained its discovery while he was browsing in a New York bookstore.

What he had not told anyone before, Hofmann continued, was that a *second* copy of the Oath of a Freeman had also been found. It had been discovered by a document dealer whom he knew in Boston, Lyn Jacobs, and he was willing to sell it for $500,000.

"If the first Oath was worth a million," Hofmann said, "the second ought to be worth a million and a half."

"If it's worth over a million dollars, why would Jacobs sell it for $500,000?" Wilding asked.

Hofmann said Jacobs already stood to make a fortune on his find and needed cash. Wilding invited Harold Vincent and Vincent's wife and parents to dinner to let Hofmann explain the proposition to them.

After Hofmann had repeated the details, they said they were interested but wanted a second opinion before committing such a large sum of money. Hofmann suggested a call to Justin Schiller in New York, whom they had consulted before investing in the Dickens manuscript.

As he dialed, Hofmann cautioned them not to say anything about a *second* Oath of a Freeman: It would drive down the value of both if Schiller knew two existed.

Schiller, regarding the callers as wealthy Utahans who were prospective investors in the *first* Oath of a Freeman, patiently answered their questions about its origins, historical significance and value.

The conversation suppressed whatever doubts Wilding and Vincent had had about making the investment, and they pledged to raise the money soon so that Hofmann could fly to New York and buy the document before anyone else did.

Three days later, Kenneth Rendell called Hofmann from Kansas where he was traveling on business and inquired if Hofmann was

certain he wanted *hieratic* hieroglyphics. Hofmann affirmed that
was what one of his clients wanted.

As the world's largest seller of papyrus, Rendell knew most collectors preferred the artful, finely drawn symbols of early hieroglyphics but a few liked large, showy pieces with less sophisticated
artwork that could be hung on a living room wall like a photograph. If that was what his buyer wanted, he told Hofmann, he
would send him two examples on approval priced at $5,000 and
$5,500. If Hofmann's customer wanted both, he could have them
for $10,000. Hofmann made an additional request: His client
wanted to keep the transaction totally confidential. Rendell agreed
not to mention it to anyone.

On September 12, Hofmann, Wilding and Vincent embarked on
a tour of Salt Lake Valley banks to collect cashier's checks totalling
$173,870 from members of the investment group who had agreed
to invest in the Oath of a Freeman. In addition, they decided to roll
over part of their profits from a previous investment, bringing their
total stake in the Oath to $206,000.

When they were at First Interstate Bank collecting one of the
checks, Wilding was puzzled when a bank executive, Harvey Tanner, walked over to Hofmann and asked to speak to him in private.
As Tanner led Hofmann to his desk he looked upset. Then Hofmann sat across from Tanner and had what appeared to be a tense
conversation that lasted several minutes.

On the sidewalk outside, Wilding asked:

"What was that about?"

Hofmann explained that he had cosigned a loan that was over-
due, but it was a minor problem that he had taken care of. Before
they went to a nearby branch of the Valley Bank to collect the final
cashier's check, Wilding said he had to return to his office for an
appointment, but Vincent accompanied Hofmann to the Rocky
Mountain State Bank so that Mark could exchange the checks for
a single cashier's check with which to buy the Oath of a Freeman.
Then Hofmann was to leave immediately for New York, meet with
Jacobs and pick up the Oath.

Wilding had been at his desk only a short time when he received
a telephone call from Hofmann. Hofmann said that after Wilding
had left them, Harold Vincent had become nervous about the in-

vestment; if he still had cold feet, Hofmann offered to take over his share of the investment.

A few minutes later, Wilding looked up from his desk and saw Vincent enter his office. There was an expression of confusion on his brother-in-law's face.

Vincent was a rugged-looking man with sandy hair, wide shoulders and a weathered complexion that suggested he had spent much of his lifetime outdoors. A hook was in place of the hand that had been lost in the sawmill accident.

Vincent said Gary Smith, Wilding's partner, had just told him Hofmann might have lied about the incident at First Interstate Bank. In a telephone call after Hofmann, Wilding and Vincent left the bank, bank executive Harvey Tanner told Smith to be wary about dealing with Hofmann; Elder Hugh Pinnock of the First Quorum of the Seventy, he said, had arranged a loan for $185,000 for Hofmann at First Interstate Bank that was almost a month overdue.

It was not the story Hofmann had told them.

"Something smells," one said, and then Wilding and Vincent decided to find Hofmann.

They drove to the Salt Lake City airport but discovered that, contrary to what Hofmann had told them, no more flights to New York were scheduled that day. They drove slowly through the airport parking lots but could not find his car. Then they drove to his home, but he wasn't there.

Tom Wilding lay awake that night unable to sleep, worried about losing the money invested by his friends and relatives.

At dawn the next morning, Friday, September 13, 1985, he got out of bed early, drove to Hofmann's home and parked at the curb. At 7:30, Gary Smith arrived and, together, they knocked on the door.

When Dorie Hofmann responded to their knock, they demanded to see Mark and a few moments later he appeared at the door in his bathrobe.

He was amazed, he said, by their visit.

There was *nothing* to worry about, he said. By the time he had finished his banking the previous day, he said it had been too late for him to catch a flight to New York. He said he and his oldest son were leaving for New York in a few hours. To reassure them their money was safe, he showed them a receipt for a $142,270 cashier's check made out to Lyn Jacobs as payment for the Oath.

"Where's the rest of the money?" they demanded.

It was safe in the bank, he said. The check was a down payment. When they asked him about the $185,000 loan at First Interstate Bank, he admitted it was overdue but said it was not a serious matter and blamed the problem on clients who were late in paying debts to him.

His guard up and his patience frayed, Wilding said he and the other investors had decided to back out of the investment in the Oath of a Freeman and wanted Hofmann to return the money they had given him the previous day. Hofmann seemed unperturbed by the news.

If they didn't want to invest in the Oath, he said, other investors would be glad to, and he promised to meet them at the Rocky Mountain State Bank when it opened at 10 and return the money.

Wilding felt uneasy.

"I'll wait here and go with you at 10," he said.

At 10 o'clock, a curious day-long odyssey began—a tour of banks, bookstores, office buildings and other places where Hofmann tried to raise money to pay back Wilding. At the first stop, the Rocky Mountain Bank, Hofmann asked a teller for everything in his account. She gave him a check for $18,000, which he gave to Wilding.

Hofmann had spent most of the money he had collected the previous day from Wilding and his associates to pay debts: He had purchased a $100,000 cashier's check and given it to Deseret Book for the General Dunham letter; he had drawn a $40,000 cashier's check for Dorie's cousin, Ken Woolley, to settle part of that debt. And most of the balance had gone into his own overdrawn checking account.

It was true Hofmann had also purchased a $142,270 cashier's check for Lyn Jacobs. But he had immediately returned it to the bank and kept the receipt, which he showed to Wilding.

Al Rust was sitting in a booth that he and his son had rented for a weekend coin show at the Salt Palace auditorium in Salt Lake City when he saw Mark approach him almost in a run.

"I've got to talk to you."

They walked to the auditorium lobby and sat down. In the five years Rust had known Hofmann this was the first time he had seen him not in command of himself.

Rust said:

"Calm down. What's the matter?"

As they spoke, Tom Wilding was sitting in a chair about 100 yards away, watching the conversation.

"I owe the bank $185,000 and they're going to foreclose on me —take our house, our cars . . . everything," Mark said.

"You owe a *bank* $185,000? Your check to me has bounced twice. You owe *me* $132,000."

"The Library of Congress still hasn't paid me for the Oath of a Freeman," Hofmann said. "They need more time to authenticate it. I told the bank I need more time, but when you sent through your check for collection, they decided to foreclose on me."

Rust was genuinely concerned for the welfare of his friend.

"Mark, I don't have any more money to give you. How much do you need to get off the hook?"

"A hundred thousand, today."

"Your book collection is worth more than that. Why don't you try to borrow on it?"

A few minutes later, Hofmann stood before Curt Bench at the Deseret Book Store.

Bench had never seen him so upset; he knew that Mark was heavily in debt but he hadn't realized how bad it was; Mark's lips were quivering.

"I have to raise $100,000 right away to save my house," he said. If Deseret Book would loan him $100,000 and take his books as collateral, he promised to repay the store $150,000 by January 1.

Bench, like Rust, felt compassion for his friend. He was familiar with Hofmann's book collection; he knew it was probably worth $375,000. Deciding that it would be a safe and profitable investment for his company, he told Hofmann he would raise the matter with his superiors and asked him to come back at 4 o'clock. He said he was optimistic a deal could be made.

But when Hofmann returned at four, Bench said his boss said he needed more time to consider the proposal and would not give him a decision until Monday. As he left, Wade Lillywhite, the store's rare book buyer, told Hofmann that if he couldn't raise the money, he knew a Salt Lake City businessman who might lend it to him against his book collection as collateral.

There were now two possibilities he could raise the money on Monday, Hofmann told Wilding, who had been watching the conversation from a few yards away. But Wilding said he was not satisfied with possibilities. He said he wanted the investors' money *now*.

After almost a full day with Hofmann, he had come up with only $18,000.

When they returned to his office at 6:30 P.M., Harold Vincent was waiting.

"Where's the money we gave you *yesterday?*" both demanded.

Hofmann responded with a blank expression, the blend of detachment and smug diffidence that other clients had come to know long ago.

"Where's the money?" Vincent demanded.

He had given Hofmann much of the insurance payment that he had received in exchange for his hand and part of an arm.

It was his retirement nest egg—and Hofmann was now just looking at him with a bored expression.

There was *nothing* to worry about, Hofmann said casually. A friend had flown the check to Jacobs that morning, and they already owned the Oath of a Freeman.

"You said *you* were going to take the money to New York," Wilding said. "You're lying again."

Hofmann told them to calm down.

"I just decided to have someone else take it back instead," he said. He hadn't told them before because he thought they might do something to spoil the negotiations.

"This is *serious,*" Vincent said. He was furious at Hofmann's chilly arrogance.

Hofmann gave his accusers another look of disinterest.

It was too much for Vincent.

The woodsman lunged at Hofmann, grabbed him by his shirt and threw him against a wall, and as he hurtled toward the wall, Hofmann felt the fist of Vincent's one good arm smash into his face.

Now this was a case in which you were given the result and had to find everything else for yourself.

Sherlock Holmes in *A Study in Scarlet*

32

On the afternoon of October 16, 1985, a senior executive of the First Interstate Bank in Salt Lake City received a telephone call from a General Authority of the Church of Jesus Christ of Latter-day Saints.

"Mark Hofmann just got blown up," the church leader said. "Don't say anything to anybody about the $185,000 loan to Hofmann."

Only moments before, a security man at the bank had hung up his telephone after speaking to the Salt Lake City police chief.

"It's too late," the bank executive said. "We just called Bud Willoughby and told him we had a $185,000 note outstanding with Hofmann for the McLellin Collection."

Several blocks away, policemen and federal agents searched the blackened wreckage of a Toyota that had been destroyed by the third bomb to rattle windows in Salt Lake City in two days.

Jerry Taylor, an agent of the U.S. Treasury Department's Bureau of Alcohol, Tobacco and Firearms, had flown to Salt Lake City the night before from his office in San Francisco and was examining charred pieces of pipe, wire, batteries and other debris from Tuesday's bombings when the third bomb exploded.

A bespectacled man in his mid-forties with a mustache and curly dark hair flecked with gray, Taylor had spent more than twenty years—first in the Navy, then in the Treasury Department—becoming an expert on the infernal devices that men and women make to kill and maim one another. He had already made some tentative conclusions about the bomb that had killed Steven F. Christensen, a thirty-one-year-old Salt Lake City businessman.

It had been a device of deadly simplicity: Several ounces of smokeless black powder had been confined in a short length of galvanized iron pipe that was capped at both ends; the powder had been detonated by an unsophisticated but effective electrical circuit employing flashlight batteries, an igniter like those used to start the engines of homemade model rockets and a mercury switch, a three-inch glass tube containing a drop of mercury and electrical contacts at each end.

The bomb was designed so that when it was tilted, the drop of mercury traveled from one end of the tube to the other and completed an electrical connection: Current flowed from the batteries through the mercury to the igniter, touching off the black powder.

Some bombs Taylor had investigated were meant to damage property—to blow up a car or destroy a building. This bomb had only one purpose, to kill a human being. Nails had been taped around the bomb to make it more lethal—not conventional carpenter's nails, but nails that had been forged at high temperatures to make them hard enough to be hammered into concrete.

When the bomb exploded, the nails and shards of shredded steel pipe became a burst of lethal shrapnel.

The bomb that killed Kathy Sheets almost two hours later did not have the lethal annex of concrete nails, but otherwise it appeared to be identical and, clutched tightly in her arms, just as deadly.

Within hours of the bombings, FBI agents and Salt Lake City investigators had made a list of dozens of prospective suspects. Most were investors in C.F.S., the company Steve Christensen had left two months before the bombings.

A few hours after his wife's death, Gary Sheets, who was placed

under police protection, told a newspaper reporter the killers had
no basis for accusing his company of fraud.

"We've had some troubles, a negative financial statement," he
said, "and we've lost some money in dumb investments; there's
been stupidity, bad judgment, too-fast growth and some poor management, but not fraud. Overall, we've been a good company. It's
sad to see this dream end."

Mark Hofmann was conscious but bleeding heavily when he was
wheeled by paramedics into the trauma room at LDS Hospital.

As he was undressed, a police officer, James Bryant, collected his
temple-garment underwear, trousers and a bloodied white shirt
embedded with tiny, dark particles that Bryant suspected were
scraps of upholstery from his car or parts of the bomb that almost
killed him. When Bill Hofmann arrived twenty minutes later, a
nurse told him that his son was in serious condition but would
probably survive.

For a man who had just had a bomb blow up in his face, she
said, his son was in remarkably good condition.

Mark shivered violently as he looked up at his father, who an-
nointed him with oil and gave him a blessing.

Bryant noticed that Mark's right hand was mangled, as if it had
been inserted into a butcher's chopping machine.

Mark told his father that he was unsure what had happened: He
could only remember returning to his car after a meeting in the
Church Office Building, opening the door and seeing something on
the seat start to fall. When he reached for it, it exploded.

Bill Hofmann looked over at the police officer and said:

"He and his family stayed overnight at our house last night
because they were concerned about the bombings."

He said his son had been scheduled to see a member of the First
Quorum of the Seventy in the Church Office Building at 10 o'clock
that morning, but the meeting had been postponed until 2.

Speaking slowly and stuttering at times, the younger Hofmann
said he had been followed before the bombing by a tan pickup
truck with a dented front fender whose license plate contained the
letters TW and at least one 3.

As a nurse pushed him toward the x-ray department, he urged
Bryant to contact two friends whose lives might also be in danger

—Brent Ashworth, a document collector who lived in Provo, and Lyn Jacobs, "the person who bought the salamander letter."

"Tell them to get out of town," Hofmann said.

Ashworth, in fact, was already preparing to flee the Valley of the Great Salt Lake.

For more than twenty-four hours, the Valley had talked of little except the bombings. The night before there had been an exodus of employees and former employees of Coordinated Financial Services fearful of Mafia assassins. Now, the news that Mark Hofmann, a dealer in controversial Mormon documents, had been injured and possibly killed by a third bomb spread over the Valley like a winter gale and put a new face on the earlier bombings.

Besides the Mafia, people were now worrying about the Danites.

The third bombing occurred on a Wednesday. Normally, Brent Ashworth would have met Hofmann at 2 P.M. at their meeting place outside a Walden bookstore at the Crossroads Mall. But Ashworth had had to attend a business meeting in Salt Lake City the day before, and as a result he had decided not to make a second trip from Provo that week.

Ashworth's friend at the Church Office Building who was an aide to a General Authority called him shortly after the third bombing and urged him to leave the Valley. He speculated—as Ashworth had already done—that all three bombings were connected and that the bombs had been left by religious fanatics who were outraged over the prying by historians into church history.

It had been a long time since there had been any evidence of the Danites, the band of ecclesiastical vigilantes who executed church dissidents and critics in the name of blood atonement during the nineteenth century, but rumors persisted that the secret society still existed.

"Some group has decided to take care of a few people," Ashworth told his wife. "Let's get the kids and get out of here."

They herded their seven children into a van and drove south as fast as they could from the Salt Lake Valley.

At the Church Administration Building, security measures, already tightened following Tuesday's bombings, were tightened again, and the gates of Temple Square were locked two hours ahead of schedule.

1.

Descendants of faith-driven pioneers who crossed the plains to Utah during the nineteenth century, Mark William Hofmann, *(above)* and Steven Fred Christensen were born in Salt Lake City in 1954. After serving a mission in Australia, Steve Christensen married his sweetheart, Terri Romney.

2.

The Church of Jesus Christ of Latter-day Saints was founded in 1830 by a farm boy in upstate New York, Joseph Smith, Jr. He said God appeared to him in a vision and an angel named Moroni led him to a cache of gold tablets that he translated into the Book of Mormon. He called it "the most correct of any book on earth and the keystone of our religion."

4.

3. Joseph Smith and his disciples found solitude in Nauvoo, Illinois. But in 1844 Smith was murdered at the jail in nearby Carthage.

5.

Martin Harris, Joseph Smith's first disciple, helped him translate the Book of Mormon but lost its first 116 pages.

6.

After Smith's death, Brigham Young led many of his
followers across the Rocky Mountains to a final gathering
place in the Salt Lake Valley. They prospered but their custom
of polygamy scandalized many people in the East. In 1896,
six years after the Mormons renounced the earthly practice of
polygamy, Congress granted statehood to Utah.

At nineteen, Mark
Hofmann left the Salt
Lake Valley to spend
almost two years as a
Mormon missionary in
England.

7.

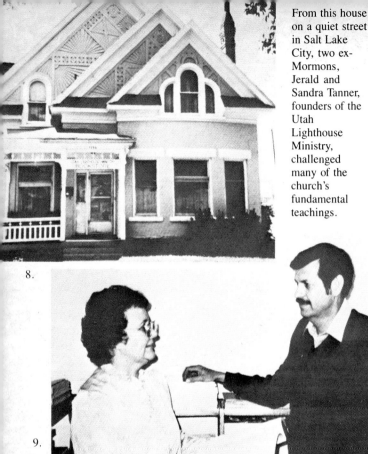

From this house on a quiet street in Salt Lake City, two ex-Mormons, Jerald and Sandra Tanner, founders of the Utah Lighthouse Ministry, challenged many of the church's fundamental teachings.

8.

9.

10.

Brent Ashworth, an attorney and collector of rare documents, regretted that the Vietnam War had prevented him from going on a mission for the church.

Beginning in 1980, the Mormon hierarchy was electrified by a series of discoveries of documents from the time of Joseph Smith. Among the church's top leaders were *(left to right)* Dallin H. Oaks, Gordon B. Hinckley and Hugh Pinnock.

On the morning of October 15, 1985, a booby-trapped package exploded on the sixth floor of the Judge Building in downtown Salt Lake City.

15.

Less than two hours later, a second bomb exploded in one of the city's most affluent suburbs, killing Kathleen Webb Sheets. Her husband, J. Gary Sheets *(right)*, was a legend in Salt Lake City's business community.

16.

17

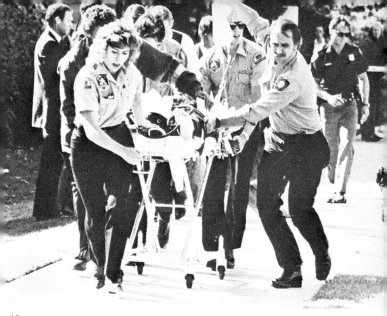

18.

The next day, a third bomb shook the Salt Lake Valley. This time the victim was Mark Hofmann, whose car was destroyed by the blast.

19.

20

Investigation of the bombings was directed by Theodore L. (Ted) Cannon, the Salt Lake County Attorney.

Defense attorneys Ronald Yengich *(left)* and Bradley Rich blamed the blasts on religious fanatics.

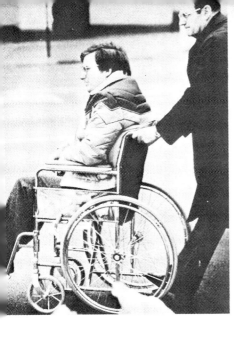

Although seriously injured, Mark Hofmann (photographed with his father) survived the explosion that destroyed his car.

Investigator Richard Forbes and prosecutors Robert Stott and David Biggs tried to unravel the mystery of the bombings. *(Left:* Forbes and Stott. *Right:* Biggs.)

The investigation
focused on Mark
Hofmann, shown
with his wife,
Doralee.

Hofmann was accused of the bombings, touching off court
proceedings that fascinated Utah, the Mormon community and the
larger world.

27.

Leonard Arrington headed the church Historical Department during a time historians called "Camelot."

28.

After the bombings, Lyn Jacobs *(above)* and Shannon Flynn were interviewed by the police about their knowledge of the "salamander letter."

29.

Investigator Michael George of the Salt Lake County Attorney's Office had a theory about the case.

30.

31.

Detective Kenneth Farnsworth headed the Salt Lake Police Department's investigation of the bombings.

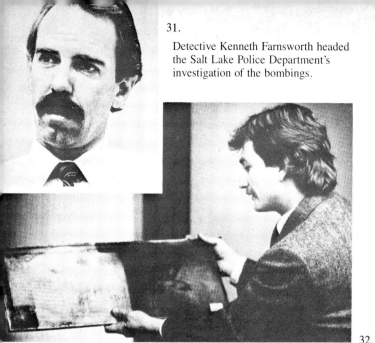

32.

Prosecutor Gerry D'Elia *(above)* was among those puzzled by the discovery of Egyptian papyrus in twentieth-century Utah. Kenneth Rendell *(below)* was the world's largest dealer in papyrus.

33.

Detective Jim Bell
helped make a mock-
up of the bombs, one
of which had a deadly
annex of hardened
concrete nails.

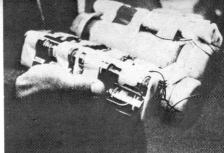

34.

36.

Aaron Teplick saw a
mysterious van near
the home of Kathleen
Sheets the night before
she died.

37.

Alvin Rust, *(right)*, and his son Gaylen enlisted in an effort to acquire a collection of long-lost documents from the early years of the church.

38.

The dean of American autograph dealers, Charles Hamilton, helped answer questions about the salamander letter.

W W Phelps Esq
Canandaigua

CANAN
25

39.

40.   41.   42.

George Throckmorton was mystified by the highly magnified images under his microscope.

Mark Hofmann was caught up in a whirlpool of accusation and intrigue that reached into the highest levels of the church. Members of his family, devout Mormons, rallied in support of him.

43.

44. Even after it seemed that all the questions
had been answered, Mark Hofmann
provided new mysteries.

45.

At the Metropolitan Hall of Justice, Bradley Christensen, the florist who had rushed to Hofmann's side and commanded him to live after noticing he was wearing temple garments beneath his shirt, told detectives that when he reached Hofmann he was virtually dead. He was certain, Christensen said, that the blessing and anointing had saved Hofmann's life.

Salt Lake City Police Department detective Jim Bell, after being awake most of the previous night collecting and cataloguing evidence and interviewing witnesses from Tuesday's bombings, arrived in the trauma room at LDS Hospital one hour after the third bombing. Physicians wearing surgical masks were examining x-rays against a glowing wall of lights. In one x-ray Bell saw a dark, round spot inside the skeletal outline of a bone.

"What's that?" he asked a physician after he introduced himself.

The doctor said it appeared to be a piece of shrapnel from the bomb that was embedded in Hofmann's right knee.

Looking through a glass partition, Bell could see Hofmann lying face up on a gurney, intravenous tubes extending from his body.

"Speak to him from his right side," a nurse said after a physician said Hofmann was well enough to be interviewed. Hofmann had lost hearing, at least temporarily, in his left ear, the nurse said.

Bell saw that Hofmann's face was freckled with blood, and more blood was oozing from a wound on his forehead. Near his right ear was a chip of blue paint.

He introduced himself and Hofmann asked him to speak louder.

"Where were you going when the bomb exploded?"

Hofmann said he had been on his way to see a lawyer to sell documents that were in his car when it exploded.

As he talked, two nurses pressed gauze on his forehead to restrict the bleeding.

"Where were you earlier in the day?"

Hofmann said he had eaten breakfast at a restaurant in town, "then I just drove around."

"Where?"

"Just around."

Bell asked for more details. Hofmann repeated: "Just around." Then, after a pause, he said he had spent part of the day in Emigration Canyon "thinking."

"Thinking about what?"

"Just thinking."

The nurses took Hofmann away for additional x-rays.

Bell was waiting in the trauma room when they returned and he asked Hofmann to describe what happened when the bomb exploded.

Hofmann said he had gone up to his car, opened the door and an object on the seat started to fall to the floor; then it exploded.

"Do you have any idea who might want to kill you?"

"No," Hofmann said.

Then he was wheeled away for a CAT scan to determine the extent of his head injury.

33

Zzzzzzzzzzzzzzzzzzzzzzz. . . . zzzzzzzzzzz.

Ken Farnsworth had heard the sound many times before, and he always hated it. It was the ugliest sound in the world, the buzz of a pathologist's saw cutting through the skull of a murder victim—not *cutting* it in the conventional sense of the word, with a sharp blade, but breaking it open with a vibrating bit whose trembling oscillations cracked the hard bone of the skull.

A few moments before, the pathologist had made a long incision in Steve Christensen's scalp and pulled back the skin of his face. He turned off the saw and, using a chisel, popped open the skull and removed his brain. He poked a pair of tweezers into the tissue and pulled out a blackened steel nail and held it up to Farnsworth. The nail had gone through Christensen's left eye, he said, and then lodged in his brain. The nail alone, the doctor said, would have been enough to kill him. Farnsworth had seen Christensen's brain. It didn't have to be explained to him.

He took a sip of coffee from the cup he had bought at a 7-Eleven store on his way to the medical examiner's office, then watched the autopsy proceed.

Normally, the pathologist said, he would have made three incisions across Christensen's torso, but only two were necessary. A long piece of shredded pipe had exploded into Christensen's chest and laid it open as neatly as a scalpel. Then it had penetrated his lungs and heart and came to rest under his left arm.

Ken Farnsworth was a gangly narrow-waisted man of forty with a deep cleft in his chin and a thin, handsome face. His forebears had come to Utah during the middle of the nineteenth century as part of the great Mormon migration from the British Isles, and they had begun enforcing the law in the Salt Lake Valley soon after they arrived. When he was a child, Farnsworth's parents drifted away from the church, but he had been raised a Mormon; indeed, he would remember, it was almost impossible *not* to be raised in the church when he was growing up in the Salt Lake Valley. When he wasn't attending religious instruction classes, the church and the social structure that was its appendage consumed most of the rest of his hours.

Farnsworth stood six feet three inches tall even as a high school student. He was athletically gifted and participated often in sports activities, most of which were run by the church. Along with most of the boys with whom he played as a child, he regularly offered his testimony in the Book of Mormon, was ordained into the priesthood when he was twelve and at nineteen went on a mission. After returning from his mission in France and Belgium, it seemed preordained that he would become a Salt Lake City policeman, as had his father and grandfather, two uncles and a cousin. For a while he resisted his father's solicitations to join the force, but after he spent three years at the University of Utah, his resistance faded and he joined the family business. Eventually Farnsworth, like his father, drifted away from the church, and he began to think of himself as an agnostic.

As he was leaving the medical examiner's office, the corpse of Kathy Sheets was wheeled into the examination room for her autopsy. Farnsworth checked her body quickly, finished his coffee and threw the cup in a trash can. He loved his job, but he never stopped being amazed by what human beings did to one another.

When Jim Bell returned from LDS Hospital to the scene of Hofmann's wrecked car, Jerry Taylor and other ATF agents said that the bomb that destroyed it appeared to be very similar to the two pipe bombs exploded the previous day. When Bell described Hofmann's story of grabbing for a package as it fell from the seat of his car, Taylor said the explanation troubled him. From what he could deduce from the wreckage, the bomb had been on the driver's seat or right beside it when it exploded.

"If he told you that," Taylor said, "he might be your man."

After KSL, a church-owned television station in Salt Lake City, broadcast a photograph of Mark Hofmann, a jeweler who worked in the Judge Building told a reporter that he resembled a man that he and his son had seen in the building's elevator with a package addressed to Steve Christensen on the morning of October 15. The jeweler, Bruce Passey, said the man was wearing a green jacket with leather sleeves like those worn by high school athletes in the Salt Lake Valley.

After obtaining a search warrant, detectives opened the trunk of Hofmann's Toyota MR-2 sports car. It was filled with stacks of charred paper and documents soggy from water hosed on the car by firemen; they found a felt-tipped pen, a piece of galvanized pipe, magazines and several ancient-looking books, including a first edition of *Uncle Remus* and two books by Jean-Jacques Rousseau. One policeman picked up a plastic envelope containing a thick, torn sheet of paper and showed it to another detective.

Neither knew how to list it on the inventory of evidence they were preparing. It was covered with bold drawings of costumed men, writings in an alphabet they had never seen before and dozens of unfamiliar symbols and characters.

Neither of them had ever seen Egyptian papyrus before.

Later that evening, a team of detectives entered Hofmann's home with another search warrant. In a hall closet they found a green high school letterman's jacket with gray leather sleeves. In the basement they found a locked room strewn with books, manuscripts, documents and, most curious of all, hundreds of small cards, each containing a single word from the Book of Mormon.

It was after three the next morning when Ken Farnsworth stopped at the LDS Hospital's intensive care unit to check on Hofmann's condition. He had slept less than three hours since the first two bombings and felt like it. The night-duty nurse said Hofmann's condition was improving and offered to rouse him if Farnsworth desired her to. But he said it was not necessary: "You patch him up, we'll execute him," he said.

The nurse gave Farnsworth a look of disgust as he left the room.

In the morning, detective Jim Bell confronted Hofmann in the LDS Hospital's intensive care unit and this time read from a small card marked "Miranda Warning" that was carried by Salt Lake City policemen. He said Hofmann could refuse to answer his questions and consult a lawyer before being interviewed.

Hofmann said he understood his rights and offered to answer questions.

Under Bell's probing, he repeated the account that he had given him the day before, about the bomb exploding as it fell to the floor of his car.

"Who do you think would want to kill you?"

"Nobody," he said.

"Did *you* bomb anybody?"

"No, I didn't do it."

Bell looked into Hofmann's eyes. He told him he knew *he* was the bomber. A witness had seen his green letterman's jacket at the Judge Building and a piece of pipe and rubber gloves had been found in his car.

"I just want to know *why* you killed these people," Bell said.

But Bell wasn't able to continue the interview. As soon as he asked the question, an alarm bell and buzzers erupted on the instruments that were monitoring Hofmann's vital signs and a nurse asked Bell to leave.

After serving a subpoena at First Interstate Bank, investigator Richard Forbes of the Salt Lake County Attorney's Office returned to his office carrying two steel safe-deposit boxes that had been rented in the name of Steve Christensen.

The first box was empty. Then Forbes opened the second box and looked inside. It contained one item, a sheet of Egyptian papyrus.

Three hours later, Shannon Flynn, one of Hofmann's document scouts, called the Church Administration Building and asked for an appointment with Gordon B. Hinckley.

Hinckley, he was told, was unavailable, but Apostle Dallin Oaks would see him.

When they met, Flynn asked Oaks what he should tell the police if they asked him about the McLellin Collection.

34

"How can we be of help to you?" Oaks, who had invited three church security agents and a stenographer to sit in on the meeting, asked. Flynn, a thick-waisted man with short hair, pudgy cheeks and a high-pitched voice that seemed out of place in a man who was fascinated with firearms and mercenaries, said: "I want to find what posture I need to take; the whole room is falling down."

He said Mark Hofmann had told him about the McLellin Collection and how the church had obtained a $185,000 unsecured bank loan for him to buy the documents. He needed advice from the church on what to say to the police about the loan and the documents.

Even now, the police were looking for him, wanting to ask questions about the bombings.

Oaks, a handsome, completely bald man of fifty-three who had once clerked for Supreme Court Chief Justice Earl Warren, began to question Flynn.

"Do you know anything about why he got that loan?" Oaks asked.

"I understand why he got it. I was involved with this. During the weeks before, he had purchased the McLellin Collection. He needed those funds to get that collection. . . ."

"Have you seen the McLellin Collection firsthand?" Oaks asked.

"No, only what he told me. I did see just a part, a papyrus. Mark said that several months ago when President Hinckley was in France he had spoken to him on the phone about the McLellin Collection and that he had also called Francis Gibbons [Hinckley's secretary] twice while President Hinckley was out of town. He told me President Hinckley had arranged the loan for him at the First Interstate Bank. . . ."

Flynn said he understood Hofmann had acquired the McLellin Collection to keep it away from the church's enemies and intended to donate it to the church before getting into financial straits when another transaction went sour.

"The Library of Congress deal?" Oaks asked.

"Yes. He was supposed to receive all the money up front. Instead he received a small portion of the total amount and he was to receive the rest over eighteen months. So he got some money but the rest wasn't coming. It just dragged on and on. . . ."

Oaks told Flynn he had already told FBI agents what he knew about the case and urged Flynn to do the same.

"Mark Hofmann has told you some things that are not true," Oaks said.

"You are a member of the church," he added. "The church has done nothing to hide in this transaction . . . you tell the police what you know."

From the Church Administration Building Flynn went to the Metropolitan Hall of Justice a few blocks away and told detective Jim Bell what Hofmann had told him about the loan and the McLellin Collection. The interview was summarized in an affidavit signed by Bell:

In September 1985, First Interstate Bank was requesting payment of the loan proceeds from Mark Hofmann and/or Hugh Pinnock. Shannon P. Flynn states that one evening a call came through the phone answering machine [of Mark Hofmann] from Gordon B. Hinckley, [First President] of the L.D.S. Church, asking about the loan and when it would be repaid by Mark Hofmann. Mark Hofmann finally told Steven Christensen and

Mr. Pinnock that he could not repay the loan. The authorities in the church, probably Gordon B. Hinckley, agreed to have the L.D.S. Church repay the loan if and when Mark Hofmann turned over the McLellin Collection. The transfer of funds and documents was supposed to take place at 2 P.M. Tuesday, October 15, 1985, at which time Mark Hofmann would repay the signature loan and the collection would be handed over to Steven Christensen, who in turn would place them in the hands of L.D.S. Church. . . .

Shannon Flynn was not the only person who sought the advice of Apostle Dallin Oaks following the murders of Steven Christensen and Kathy Sheets. Mark Hofmann had done exactly the same thing twenty-six hours before.

He arrived at Oaks's office at 2:45 P.M., less than seven hours after Christensen's death and, like Flynn, asked the church leader for guidance on what he should tell the police if he was questioned about the McLellin Collection.

In an interview with FBI agents David Barker and Rhead Richards, Jr., Oaks said he had informed Hofmann to do the same thing he had told Flynn: Tell the truth.

Oaks said he had told Hofmann the bombings appeared to be the work of "someone trying to enforce some business contracts" and, as far as he was able to see, the murders had nothing to do with the McLellin Collection or the church.

"Do you know anyone in your documents business who enforces contracts with bombs?"

"No," Hofmann said.

Oaks told the agents that the church wanted to acquire the McLellin Collection by donation and that Mark Hofmann had promised to donate it, but Hofmann encountered financial difficulties and Elder Hugh Pinnock had arranged for another church member to buy the collection from him and donate it to the church. The sale was to have been consummated the previous Monday, when Steven Christensen was to have examined the documents and ensure they were what they purported to be. But because Monday was a federal holiday, Oaks said, the transaction had been postponed until Tuesday.

When Hofmann visited the Church Administration Building a

few hours after the bombings, church leaders said they still wanted and expected the sale of the McLellin Collection to proceed the following day as scheduled. Oaks said he asked Hofmann if he could consummate the sale as planned. Hofmann said he was leaving for New York in two days, but that he was willing to remain in Salt Lake City long enough to close the deal. Oaks said he suggested to Hofmann that he contact the lawyer who represented the church member who was going to acquire the collection and assure him that the sale had not been postponed. And he said he told Hofmann that someone else would have to be found to check the documents now that Christensen was dead.

Oaks bid goodbye to Hofmann. As he did, according to a memorandum he made about the meeting, Oaks thanked him for his efforts "to sell the McLellin Collection to a buyer who was friendly to the church."

In an interview with FBI agents Barker and Richards, Hugh Pinnock gave the same story as Oaks and confirmed Shannon Flynn's assertion that he had arranged an unsecured $185,000 loan for Hofmann at First Interstate Bank, where he was a director, so that he could buy the McLellin Collection.

Pinnock said that when Hofmann subsequently failed to repay the loan, he had asked Steven Christensen to persuade Hofmann to do so. Hofmann, he said, admitted in early October that he was having serious financial troubles, and Pinnock said he told Hofmann that if *he* couldn't afford to donate the documents to the church, he should let someone else do it.

Pinnock said he then arranged for a friend, David Sorenson, a wealthy church member who was the president of the Nova Scotia mission, to buy the documents and donate them to the church.

He said Hofmann told him the documents were being held as security for a loan made by Al Rust, a local businessman, and when Sorenson provided the money Rust was owed, the documents would be released. The transaction was scheduled to be completed October 15, and Sorenson had retained a Salt Lake City lawyer to hand over the money to Hofmann after the documents were authenticated by Steve Christensen.

After Christensen was murdered, Pinnock said, there was no reason to suspect his death was connected to the McLellin Collection, therefore no reason to delay the transaction, and arrangements were made for Sorenson's lawyer to buy the documents from Hofmann the following morning at 10 A.M. Donald Schmidt, now retired as Church Archivist, agreed to substitute for Christensen and examine the collection before Sorenson's lawyer gave Hofmann a check for $185,000.

Pinnock said that when he arrived at his office on October 16, a telephone message was waiting for him from Dorie Hofmann, Mark's wife. The note said that the closing of the document purchase had been delayed until 2 P.M.

As he recounted his dealings involving the McLellin Collection, Pinnock said several times that he did not want to leave the impression that the church was trying to obtain the documents because they might embarrass the church, or that it had any real *interest* in the McLellin Collection. Pinnock, one FBI agent noted in his report, "stated that it was not really that significant of an item of interest for the church."

Sorting through the shards of shredded metal and other debris from the bomb that ended the life of Kathleen Sheets, Treasury agent Jerry Taylor found a cracked piece of black plastic and recognized it as part of a container used by model builders and others to hold flashlight batteries. On the back of it was a label, "Radio Shack."

Salt Lake City detectives visited a Radio Shack outlet and discovered that, unlike most retailers, clerks at the chain of electronics stores routinely asked customers their names and addresses when they made a purchase and listed them on the sales slip. The detectives decided to canvass all Radio Shack stores in the Salt Lake Valley and examine their receipts for the preceding week.

At 11:30 that evening, Scott Hallock, a policeman stationed as a guard at the LDS Hospital intensive care unit, heard Hofmann mumble something.

Hofmann said he wanted to make a statement and asked him for a tape recorder. Hallock telephoned the duty officer at the police station, who called detective Jim Bell at his home in the foothills overlooking the Great Salt Lake.

The same nurse who had been attending Hofmann almost twenty-four hours before, when Ken Farnsworth had promised to assure that he was executed, overheard the conversation and did not like what she heard. Convinced that the police wanted to railroad her patient in front of a firing squad, she called Hofmann's lawyer. And when she returned to Hofmann's bedside a few minutes later, she told Hallock he would be unable to talk to Hofmann for a while because she needed to attend to his medical needs.

"What are you trying to do?" the patrolman asked.

She said she was concerned about her patient's legal rights and proceeded to wash his face.

A few minutes later, Ronald Yengich, a Salt Lake City defense attorney who had been retained by Hofmann's father only a few hours earlier, arrived at the intensive care unit with an associate, Fred Metos. It was three minutes until midnight.

"I strongly advise you not to make any statement," Yengich told his new client, whom he had met only briefly.

Hofmann said he wanted his father to come to the hospital so that he could talk to him. While Metos left to telephone Bill Hofmann, Yengich sought to convince his new client that it was not in his best interest to make a statement, while the nurse adjusted his right arm, which was suspended in the air by a cable.

Hofmann said he wanted to think it over.

Metos, who had roused Bill Hofmann out of bed, returned and told Mark his father believed he should follow Yengich's advice. His parents were exhausted, he said, but they would come to the hospital in the morning to talk things over.

When Jim Bell arrived a few moments later with a tape recorder, Hofmann said he had decided not to make a statement. Bell and the patrolman left, leaving Hofmann alone with Yengich, Metos and his nurse.

The next morning, Bill Hofmann came to the hospital and told Mark that if he was a killer, he now had to die himself.

35

"If Satan got hold of you, son, and you've committed these acts, you should confess and ask for the firing squad so you can be with us in the next life."

The modern church disavowed blood atonement, the doctrine taught by Brigham Young and other nineteenth-century Mormon leaders that held that some sins—including murder—were so grievous that only the spilling of the sinner's own blood could atone for them and enable the sinner to enter the Celestial Kingdom.

Official pronouncements notwithstanding, however, many members of the church believed blood atonement was God's law, and Bill Hofmann was among them.

If Mark was guilty, his father said, he must admit his guilt and be executed so that the family could be reunited in the next world. In Utah, condemned criminals were given a choice of death by lethal injection or a firing squad. To atone, Mark would have to die before the firing squad.

"I didn't do it," Mark said. He said the only reason he had wanted a tape recorder was that the detectives were trying to frame him and he wanted to be sure there was a taped record of his account of what had happened before the bombing.

All of his problems, he told his father, would be solved if he could only raise $500,000 to pay off his debts. The Oath of a Freeman was certain to sell soon and then he would be in the clear. Dorie Hofmann asked what was going to happen about their new house: She had expected the $185,000 payment for the McLellin Collection for the house, and the payment was due to the seller in a few hours. Hofmann told her that he was sorry the house would have to wait.

As Hofmann was discussing blood atonement and the house Dorie had so dearly wanted at the LDS Hospital, almost two thousand people were gathered in the chapel of Steven Christensen's ward in Centerville and singing "The Poor Wayfaring Man of Grief," the hymn that had given Christensen, when he was a young missionary, a religious high he would never forget.

In a eulogy, a friend to whom Christensen had recently confided that he was desperately trying to help the General Authorities prevent embarrassing documents from falling into the hands of the church's enemies told those gathered at his funeral:

"I think that when all of the facts in this case are known, it will be shown that Steve died as a martyr for his church."

Before the funeral, police dogs had sniffed floral arrangements in the chapel while looking for another bomb; there would have been more flowers but Terri Christensen had requested that in lieu of flowers, Steve's friends make a contribution to his favorite charity, the Mormon History Association. Four hours later, the family of Kathleen Sheets and a huge throng of friends grieved over her passing at her ward in Holladay. Hugh Pinnock delivered one of the eulogies and Gary Sheets tearfully said goodbye to the woman who had been his wife for twenty-seven years.

Later that day, a General Authority of the church received a telephoned ultimatum from an executive of First Interstate Bank. "You created this mess," the bank executive said. "You come down here and pay off the loan."

While examining the records of a Radio Shack outlet at the Cottonwood Mall in a suburb south of Salt Lake City, detectives found a receipt for a battery holder and a mercury switch that had been sold October 6 to a customer who identified himself as "M. Hansen, 2056 East 3900 South, Salt Lake City." When they checked the address, they discovered it was a vacant lot.

At the Metropolitan Hall of Justice Brent Ashworth met that evening with Police Chief Bud Willoughby after he had checked his family into a hotel near the Salt Lake City airport under the name "Joe Smith."

Despite its special connotation in the gathering place of the Saints, it was a name that in Utah, as everywhere else in America, served as a nom de plume for hotel guests seeking anonymity.

Brent Ashworth's family had been on the run four days and they were exhausted. After Ashworth had called him from a small town in southern Utah, Willoughby said he thought it was safe to return to the Salt Lake Valley, and when they met he urged Ashworth to tell investigators everything he knew about Hofmann.

Ashworth said Hofmann had often lied to him about document transactions, but added, "Frankly, I think you guys have got the wrong guy."

At 1:15 A.M. the next morning, Shannon Flynn, Hofmann's twenty-seven-year-old friend and document scout, was arrested for illegal possession of a machine gun after federal agents and Salt Lake City detectives found an Uzi submachine gun in his home that appeared to have been modified to operate as an automatic weapon. Also seized at his home was a copy of *The Anarchist's Cookbook,* a book that included instructions on how to make a bomb. At a press conference the next day Willoughby promised more arrests soon. "We are not done by any means," he said.

In fact, the sense of euphoria that had followed discovery of Hofmann's letterman's jacket and produced off-the-record predictions to reporters that he would be arrested soon had receded even though there had been several encouraging developments: An eighth grader who lived near Kathy Sheets's home said that the night before she was killed he had gotten out of bed to get an aspirin and had seen a Toyota van outside similar to the one owned by Hofmann. Among thousands of items found in Hofmann's home was an envelope with the name "Mike Hansen" on it, providing a possible link to the receipt found at the Radio Shack store. And amid the debris at the first two bombings detectives found scraps of brown wrapping paper on which someone had addressed the bombs to Steven Christensen and Gary Sheets; ATF experts planned to compare the writing to Hofmann's handwriting.

Other developments, however, had been disappointing.

Janet McDermott-Reynolds said she did not recognize Hofmann as the man she saw on the sixth floor of the Judge Building before the bomb explosion. The identification of Hofmann by the jeweler at the Judge Building was of questionable courtroom value because he had seen a photo of Hofmann on television before making the identification. Dorie Hofmann said her husband had been at home with her the night before and on the morning of the first two bombings. Detectives discovered the piece of pipe found in Hofmann's car was not the same width as the pipe used to make the bombs. And hundreds of young men in the Salt Lake Valley, they learned, owned letterman's jackets almost identical to the one found in a closet at Hofmann's home; in fact, a few hours after the first two bombings one had been found abandoned in a dumpster in Salt Lake City. There was another setback: An attorney for the church, which owned LDS Hospital, had won a court order preventing investigators from compelling the nurse who had summoned Hofmann's lawyers to the hospital and was with them when they later spoke to him privately to repeat what Hofmann had said during this meeting. Above all, there was no apparent motive linking the two murders.

Willoughby said his investigators were examining every possible motive, including a possibility that the bombings might have been linked to forgery of the salamander letter.

After hearing news reports based on his comments that speculated that anyone who had come in contact with the salamander letter might be in jeopardy from religious hit squads, Elwyn Doubleday, the New Hampshire stampless dealer, called Willoughby and said he was worried. The salamander letter, he said, wasn't a forgery; he had sold it approximately two and a half years before for $25 or $30. And dealer Kenneth Rendell telephoned the Salt Lake County Attorney's Office and told David Biggs that the letter had been exhaustively tested and there was no indication it was forged. Rendell said it was ridiculous to link the killings to the salamander letter.

Despite the reassurances, the police investigators agreed that it was essential to be absolutely certain about the salamander letter, and on Monday, October 21, 1985, it was removed from the First Presidency's Vault and carried by two FBI agents to Washington for an examination at the FBI's National Crime Laboratory.

As he often was, Ron Yengich was mad.

At thirty-five, he was already Utah's best-known defense lawyer, a reputation won with acquittals in several prominent criminal trials. With long hair, a bushy mustache that swept from his lips to his jowls and penetrating eyes that could menace unfriendly witnesses like claws, Yengich's appearance and disposition suggested an irritable lion.

Belligerent, smart, impatient, determined to dominate those around him, he was the son of a Utah copper miner who had been raised a Catholic, had attended a Jesuit college in Kentucky, had been graduated in 1975 from the University of Utah College of Law and had marched in the antiwar and antiapartheid marches of the 1970s.

As a child he had learned what it was like to be an outsider. Many parents of Mormon children had refused to let their children play with Yengich because he was a Catholic; he despised it that school assemblies ended with a Mormon prayer; in high school, while Mormon boys were released from classes for religious instruction, he had to spend part of his Saturdays at catechism class. He was outraged by a system that he was convinced discriminated against non-Mormons, that gave the greatest opportunity and best jobs to those with old Mormon family names such as Snow, Kimball, Christensen, Anderson and Larson. The experience, he would say later, produced in him a deep anger against the church and Utah's power structure, which it dominated. The anger helped propel his work as a defense lawyer, where daily he did battle with the state establishment.

Yengich was furious.

He had read story after story in the newspapers, usually attributed to anonymous sources, claiming Mark Hofmann was a killer. But no charges were brought against him and as time passed and the speculative stories continued, Yengich said it was becoming impossible for Hofmann to get a fair trial in Utah.

"If they had a case, you can bet they would have filed it by now," he told reporters. "I've never experienced this type of wait in a high-profile case for criminal charges to be filed."

Yengich also knew how to use the press and he decided to plan a counterattack.

In New York City, Justin Schiller and Raymond Wapner welcomed three visitors from Salt Lake City—Thomas Wilding, Harold Vincent and a lawyer, John Ashton—to their gallery on East Sixty-first Street. After a few pleasantries, Wilding opened a briefcase and withdrew a piece of paper about the size of a postcard and showed it to the dealers.

Schiller and Wapner couldn't believe their eyes.

It was the Oath of a Freeman.

It couldn't be, they said.

The Oath of a Freeman was locked in their safe-deposit box.

36

When they returned to Provo after being on the run for almost a week, Brent and Charlene Ashworth were demoralized, tired and still worried that Brent's life was in peril. Relatives urged them to leave town again for a brief vacation without the children. After resisting several days, they surrendered to the family pressure and flew to San Diego for a rest at a relative's La Jolla condominium.

The Ashworth children were forbidden to ride their bicycles on the sabbath. But the relatives who were looking after them while their parents were gone did not know about this rule, and on the first Sunday after the Ashworths left for La Jolla, their four sons went for a bicycle ride near their home. Their son Sami, who was seven, was leading the family convoy of bikes when a teenage driver turned a corner and ran him down. A doctor said Sami Ashworth would probably not live through the night, but he survived the night and plunged into a deep coma.

Conducting their own investigations paralleling that of the police, news reporters began to show interest in the relationship between Hofmann and high-ranking leaders of the Church of Jesus Christ of Latter-day Saints.

Mike Carter of *The Salt Lake Tribune* was the first to disclose that Hugh Pinnock had arranged an unsecured $185,000 loan for Hofmann almost four months before the murders. When Carter asked Pinnock about the loan, the church official said it "was not out of the ordinary." When Carter asked an official of the bank his opinion of the propriety of the loan, the bank executive refused comment. Later, Carter disclosed that Mark Hofmann had met frequently and privately with President Gordon B. Hinckley and quoted Don Schmidt, the retired Church Archivist, as saying he had often been bypassed by the church's higher-ups in the acquisition of documents, some of which he had never seen. Then investigators leaked to reporters that Hofmann and Shannon Flynn had visited Dallin Oaks following the first two bombings. In a community where ordinary members of the church rarely met privately with a head of the church, these were stunning disclosures.

On October 23, 1985, the church called a press conference to respond, as President Gordon Hinckley said, to "questions, speculations and innuendos" regarding Mark Hofmann. No one could remember a precedent for such a press conference; indeed, no one could remember a member of the First Presidency ever opening himself to questions from the press under such circumstances.

Hinckley revealed that since 1980 the church had acquired "forty-some documents" from Mark Hofmann, including two he had purchased directly and one, "which the press has been wont to call 'the salamander letter,' " he had accepted as a gift from Steven Christensen.

Hinckley said he knew Christensen only vaguely while Hofmann had come to his office "occasionally, certainly not frequently." During one such visit the previous June, Hinckley said Hofmann had mentioned the McLellin Collection to him and more recently had tried to sell "the Kinderhook Plates."

The Kinderhook Plates were corroded copper tablets bearing unusual symbols unearthed from an Indian burial mound near Nauvoo that had been a source of embarrassment for the church in the nineteenth century.

After the discovery in 1843, Joseph Smith said he translated symbols on the plates and found them to be a kind of sequel to the

Book of Mormon. He said the symbols told the story of the Indian buried in the mound. His ancestors were among the lost tribes of Israel, and he was a "descendant of Ham through the loins of Pharaoh, king of Egypt," Smith said.

Later, a group of anti-Mormons revealed that they had manufactured the plates and buried them in the mound as a hoax.

"My recollection of this episode of history was dim," Hinckley told the reporters. "But I saw no reason why we should have them and so indicated to him."

Apostle Dallin Oaks was the next speaker. He told the reporters he had authorized Elder Hugh Pinnock to help arrange a loan for Hofmann at First Interstate Bank to buy the McLellin Collection and that after Hofmann was unable to buy the documents, he gave his permission to Pinnock to ask another member of the church to buy them.

The church member, he said later, called him and asked whether he should in fact buy the documents and donate them to the church and Oaks said that he had endorsed the idea.

But the church Apostle said these events should not lead to any inferences that the church wanted to suppress the McLellin Collection. It was not going to *buy* the documents, he said, only accept them as a *gift*.

"To have the church involved in the acquisition of a collection at this time would simply fuel the then-current speculation reported in the press that the church already had something called the McLellin Collection or was trying to acquire it in order to suppress it," he said.

"With the benefit of hindsight and in the feverish context of a murder investigation and in the glare and innuendo of publicity accompanying the recent investigation," Oaks said, "a normal, though confidential, proposed commercial transaction has been made to appear sinister and underhanded."

A reporter asked Pinnock:

"Do you feel it is proper for a high-ranking official of the LDS church to help secure a loan for any member of the church?"

"When they came to me that Friday afternoon, and when at that time I called two banks," Pinnock said, "I had not thought it improper. I was calling on what I thought was a legitimate transaction. I will say that there come into our offices many people asking questions but we would certainly not use our office for a favor for someone that was inappropriate."

"Would you do it again?"

"No," Pinnock said.

Another reporter asked: "Why is the church so intent on getting the papers? Is it to secure them in the right hands so that they are not taken advantage of and make the church look bad? And where does the money come from to purchase these letters?"

"Why, you say, is the church so intent on getting the papers?" Oaks answered. "I thought it was clear from my statement that the church was very intent on *not* getting the papers."

Several reporters looked at each other, confused by his answer.

Two days later, the church's Public Communications Department issued a press release. It stated that Hugh Pinnock had decided to repay Mark Hofmann's loan to First Interstate Bank, using his private assets, not church funds. "Although I am not legally obligated to the bank," Pinnock told the press, "I feel morally and ethically responsible to make certain the bank does not suffer any loss as a result of the loan to Mr. Hofmann."

As the murder investigation moved closer to the church hierarchy, Bud Willoughby, the Salt Lake City Police Chief, a non-Mormon, told detectives Ken Farnsworth and Jim Bell: "Work this case like any other. Let the chips fall where they fall."

On the same day that Hugh Pinnock said that he was going to repay Hofmann's loan at First Interstate Bank, Ted Cannon, the Salt Lake County Attorney, encountered a prominent leader of the Utah legislature who said, with a friendly smile, "Go easy on the Brethren."

"We'll take it where it goes," Cannon said. "I'm not afraid of Dallin Oaks."

Later, when Cannon reported the exchange in his journal, he wrote of himself: "Kind of a stupid riposte to a well-meant caution."

David Biggs, one of Cannon's deputies, made a notation in his journal on the same day: "Bombshell today (no pun intended) Writing on boxes is not Hofmann's. Hofmann has accomplice(s). Who *and* why?"

A few days later, Ken Woolley, Mark Hofmann's cousin by marriage, noted in his journal that the 1775 letter in which Daniel Boone described his expedition along the Wilderness Road had sold at auction at Sotheby's for $29,000. The winning bidder, he later learned, glued the letter to the pelt of a coyote.

On the same day Daniel Boone's letter was being auctioned in New York—October 31, 1985—Mark Hofmann was rolled out of the LDS Hospital in a wheelchair and driven home to recuperate from his injuries. A few hours later, federal authorities filed charges against him for illegal possession of a machine gun based on the discovery of components for Shannon Flynn's Uzi found in Hofmann's home. Hofmann pleaded innocent and after posting $50,000 bail was allowed to go home and continued his recuperation. His lawyer, Ronald Yengich, promised Hofmann would not leave the Salt Lake Valley.

37

By the first weeks of November an army of almost one hundred lawmen had enlisted in the murder investigation: detectives from the Salt Lake City Police Department and Salt Lake County Sheriff's Department, agents of the FBI and the Treasury Department's Bureau of Alcohol, Tobacco and Firearms, prosecutors and investigators from the County Attorney's Office.

It was not a compatible army. Indeed, it was evolving into a group of militias commanded by rival warlords.

Competing to solve the murders, investigators raced to be first to interview people who knew Hofmann, Christensen and Sheets, then concealed what they had gleaned during the interviews from other agencies investigating the murders. Some witnesses were asked to repeat what they knew about the principals in the case to four different teams of investigators. And when detectives talked to some potential witnesses they discovered security officers for the church had been there before them. Meanwhile, the Salt Lake City detectives could not fathom what the FBI agents, most of whom were Mormons, were doing on the case. The Bureau's jurisdiction was limited to possible links between the murders and organized crime. But the FBI agents assigned to the case exerted a proprietary right to investigate everything about the case, including the church's links to the bombings. City detectives caught them eavesdropping on their conversations and suspected they were spies who passed information to the church's director of security, a former FBI man.

The Salt Lake City Police Department investigators decided to collaborate with Treasury Department explosives experts but shunned detectives for the Sheriff's Department, who looked with suspicion on County Attorney Ted Cannon. Cannon, who had his own team of investigators reporting directly to him, had once called the Sheriff's investigators "run-of-the-mill detectives" and implied that those employed by the city weren't much better.

Cannon was a broad-shouldered, big-chested man of fifty-three whose hair had already turned white. Handsome and articulate, he had the kind of looks that might have cast him as a judge in a television series. In fact, he was casting himself for such a role.

Cannon was a descendant of George Q. Cannon, a legendary nineteenth-century Mormon Apostle who served time in prison for polygamy, and had reached his position of power in the Salt Lake Valley via an unusual route. The son of a prominent local newspaper editor, he had married at eighteen, gone to college, worked several years as a research micropaleontologist in the oil fields of Utah and at twenty-eight decided he wanted to be a lawyer. He took a job as a printer for a company that printed Salt Lake City's two newspapers, the *Tribune* and *Deseret News,* to support his family and after a thirteen-year battle to finish law school, earned his law degree in 1973. Then he began a political rise in the Salt Lake Valley that almost carried him into the governor's office.

Hired as a prosecutor for Salt Lake City, he declared war on X-rated movie houses and "adult bookstores." Other cities had had trouble closing such establishments because defense lawyers argued they were protected by the Constitution's guarantee of freedom of expression. But Cannon became extraordinarily successful in shutting down pornography outlets in Salt Lake City because of an unusual system he helped devise for selecting jurors. Under his system, which led to the highest rate of convictions in pornography cases in the country, associates surveyed local Mormon bishops to determine the moral outlook of potential jurors. He then used the information to select jurors who were likely to convict the pornography merchants that he brought to trial.

After a new state attorney general who was pledged to combating pornography was elected in 1976, he hired Cannon as his deputy and Cannon became even more prominent as a crusader against moral decay. The industriousness that had helped Cannon become a lawyer at forty-one—like his zeal in fighting sin—was a quality prized in the Salt Lake Valley. In 1978 he was elected County Attorney and soon he was being touted as a Republican candidate for governor.

By the fall of 1985, however, Cannon had acquired more than enough political enemies to end the Cannon-for-governor talk. Twice he had tried unsuccessfully to convict a local Democratic county official of misuse of public funds, but the defendant's lawyer, Ronald Yengich, not only prevailed in the courtroom but succeeded in portraying Cannon in the newspapers as a politically motivated prosecutor bent on a vendetta. Cannon then made more enemies by hinting to a reporter that several local lawyers—including Yengich—and a local television reporter trafficked in cocaine, an allegation that was later found to be groundless.

Despite his problems, Ted Cannon remained a powerful and prestigious figure in the Salt Lake Valley. After more than seven years as County Attorney, he was getting burned out from the job and faced the decision of whether to run for reelection when his second term expired late in 1986.

He expected several judgeships in the Valley to become vacant during the following year and decided that after the bombing case was settled it would be a good time to go on the bench.

To serve as a nerve center for the investigation, a windowless room was set aside in a building near the Salt Lake courthouse occupied by the County Attorney's Office, and each morning Cannon conducted a meeting there to review progress on the case.

Using a blue crayon, Cannon in early November printed on a sheet of clear plastic a list headed *"Theories of the Case,"* and projected it on a screen:

Revenge
Religion
Finances
Crimes of Passion (sex, jealousy)
Documents
Reputation [Hofmann] (doc.)   Sheets (CFS)
Power
Crazy

Cannon marked an *X* with a red crayon beside the first two words on the list as the most likely candidates for a motive. Members of his staff then reviewed what they knew about the murders. When they were through, he said:

"None of it hangs together."

The bombings had been ruthless and well planned. They had the look of killings motivated by revenge. But none of the possible scenarios fit all the facts in the case.

There were several reasons to suspect Gary Sheets: Several of Christensen's friends said Christensen told them shortly before his death that he expected to testify before a grand jury against C.F.S. and was complaining about what he considered questionable practices at the company. Christensen was clearly a threat to C.F.S.

Moreover, there were reports the company had $5 million worth of life insurance policies on Christensen, enough to settle a lot of its financial problems. Only a few hours after his wife was murdered, Sheets had appeared on television and, referring almost casually to "this thing that happened to Kathy," said C.F.S. investigators had nothing to worry about.

That evening, many people in the Salt Lake Valley turned off their TV sets expressing the same reaction: *He was so cold; his wife had just been murdered, and he's upholding the reputation of his business!*

Other evidence, however, led away from Sheets as the murderer. The scent of the Mafia could be detected all over the case: Several C.F.S. employees said Sheets had been threatened by investors in Las Vegas not long before the bombings and shortly after he sent a letter to the company's 1,400 investors informing them C.F.S. was all but bankrupt.

If someone had decided to kill Sheets for revenge, Christensen was a logical second target because he had been running the company until early August. In mid-November, Cannon wrote in his journal:

> AFT is now swinging toward Sheets as a victim and a Las Vegas vengeance motive for the bombings over losses to L.V. investors in C.F.S. FBI claims to be out of case—but nobody really believes it. By next week the pressure will build on us to file. Many players. It's as muddy as ever. . . .

But what was the connection between Sheets and Hofmann? Cannon asked.

According to Sheets, he had never met Hofmann. Hofmann's name was not on the list of C.F.S. investors. Nor did Hofmann, as far as they could find, have a connection to the Mafia or Las Vegas.

Cannon turned to the second item on his list:

The detectives had begun to establish a detailed chain of events showing that Hofmann and Christensen during the months prior to the bombings had been heavily engaged in the acquisition of secret documents for high officials of the church, one of whom had arranged an unsecured $185,000 bank loan to buy the documents. Regardless of what had been said at the church press conference, there was every indication it was trying to suppress the documents.

Even after the fatal bombings on October 15, church leaders had pressed Hofmann to acquire the McLellin Collection. The documents were reputed to contain information damaging to the church. But no one had ever seen them.

There were indications that Hofmann had been engaged in a clandestine commerce in documents with senior officials of the church for years. Yet, several days before he was murdered, Steven Christensen told friends that a General Authority had asked *him* to acquire documents for the church because Hofmann had become too greedy and the Brethren no longer trusted him. Christensen told the friends that he had been ordered not to keep a journal about this work in order to keep it secret and that the church would ensure that he had a $500,000 line of credit to acquire documents. He told one friend: "I feel like I'm in an episode of *Miami Vice*," and when he excused himself from a meeting shortly before resigning from C.F.S., he told another friend that he had to rush to a meeting with President Hinckley to discuss a group of documents "that makes the salamander letter look like a priesthood manual."

Shannon Flynn told detectives that a few days before the bombings Hofmann told him he was going to sell Gordon Hinckley the Kinderhook Plates. But how all of these elements created a motive for murder was a mystery.

Hofmann was heavily in debt. A lawyer for Thomas Wilding said Hofmann owed investors he represented over $400,000. Al Rust, the coin dealer, said he was owed $132,000. First Interstate Bank said Hofmann owed it $185,000. He owed other debts. But when Ken Farnsworth and Gerry D'Elia flew to New York City to interview Justin Schiller, they were told Hofmann was about to come into a great deal of money; Schiller and other document dealers in Manhattan said Hofmann's reputation in the trade was impeccable.

Officers of the American Antiquarian Society confirmed that they were negotiating to buy the Oath of a Freeman, and a spokesman for the Library of Congress said it was potentially "one of the most exciting finds of the century."

In Salt Lake City, historians, leaders of the church, college professors—almost everyone who knew Hofmann—said that while he was eccentric and unpredictable, he was not a killer.

There wasn't a coherent pattern linking the players in the drama, including the curious cast of characters orbiting around Hofmann: Lyn Jacobs, a Harvard Divinity School student who wore a ring in one ear; Brent Metcalfe, a self-taught historian who had been fired by the church's Security Department; Shannon Flynn, a gun buff who was obsessed with weapons and read *Soldier of Fortune* magazine; and Rick Grunder, a rare book dealer now living in Bloomington, Indiana.

Hofmann had his own theory about the case: When friends had visited him at the hospital, he attributed the bombings to religious fanatics who, he claimed, were dedicated to exterminating anyone connected to the salamander letter and anyone who threatened the church. Telephone tipsters blamed modern Danites.

At one of their morning meetings, investigator Richard Forbes told Ted Cannon that he was working on a new theory: that the murders were committed by a ring of homosexuals.

He said several of the men with whom Hofmann associated in

Utah and New York were homosexuals. "It looks like Hofmann
might be a switch-hitter," he said.

The implication was clear to others in the room. Homosexuals
were pariahs in the Mormon church, which regarded homosexuality as an aberration that could be corrected by marriage to an
attractive woman.

For homosexuals in the Mormon community, there was enormous pressure to live a double life. Men with homosexual desires
were pressed into marriage; if they persisted in having homosexual
relations and the church discovered it, they were excommunicated.
It was not implausible, the investigators said, that a group of gay
Mormons, perhaps motivated by revenge, had concocted a plot to
embarrass or blackmail the church and it had led to murder.

"Why don't you think of a way to work polygamy into the case
next?" Cannon joked.

Forbes, the department's specialist on polygamists and Mormon
fundamentalists, said he was already working on that angle.

38

Light snow and hail fell on Salt Lake City as more than six thousand mourners filed into the Tabernacle in Temple Square on a chilly Saturday morning in early November. Outside, thousands more stood in the cold, trying to share a moment of history with those inside.

As the 325 voices of the Mormon Tabernacle Choir filled the huge church, many thousands, possibly millions, of other Mormons participated vicariously through satellite-borne radio and television transmissions in the funeral services of Spencer Woolley Kimball, President, Prophet, Seer and Revelator of the Church of Jesus Christ of Latter-day Saints. The following day, according to tradition, Ezra Taft Benson, as the oldest member of the Council of Twelve Apostles, was elected his successor.

Benson took command of an institution with more than 5.8 million members in almost one hundred countries that was growing at a rate of nearly six percent a year, many of them recruited by a full-time corps of almost thirty thousand young missionaries. It was an institution that had come far from Palmyra, Nauvoo and the rugged canyons of the Wasatch Mountains that had led the pioneers into the Salt Lake Valley. In the White House, Mormons were among Ronald Reagan's closest advisers. Mormons held important positions of power in the Federal Bureau of Investigation and the Central Intelligence Agency. In business, sports, medicine, education, entertainment and other fields, Mormons were achieving success and prominence that was helping to move their faith further and further into the mainstream of American life. It was also an organization whose most conservative leaders were still passionately haunted by history. The church dismissed as unimportant the salamander letter and Joseph Smith's purported reference to a "clever spirit" in the 1825 letter to Josiah Stowell and a continuing tide of historical studies into its first prophet's claims of supernatural powers that enabled him to find gold and silver buried in the earth. But inescapably these images clashed with the glorious story repeated thousands of times daily by Mormon missionaries around the world about a divine Prophet visited by the Lord and His Son and by an angel who asked him to translate a cache of sacred gold plates into the Book of Mormon.

It is likely that in the fall of 1985, many in the church hierarchy hoped that the trying times they had been through were over and the job of enlisting the peoples of the world in the Lord's Elect could at last go on undistracted. But the murders of Steven Christensen and Kathleen Sheets generated a new wave of journalistic scrutiny of the church that Apostle Dallin Oaks would call a "feeding frenzy" and "some of the most sustained and intense LDS church-bashing since the turn of the century."

Shortly after the bombings, Dean Jessee, the church Historical Department's handwriting expert, called Elwyn Doubleday in Alton Bay, New Hampshire, and said he was updating an article about the salamander letter. He wanted to reassure himself that it was genuine. Doubleday gave him the reassurance he wanted: He explained that he had acquired the letter of 1982 after the death of Royden Lounsbery, an Ithaca, New York, florist and longtime collector of postal memorabilia; Lounsbery had originally obtained the letter as part of a collection of thousands of early-nineteenth-century stampless covers from upstate New York communities that had been saved by a family in Palmyra named Phelps, apparently relatives of W. W. Phelps, to whom the letter was addressed. Jessee was further reassured when he examined a *Book of Common*

Prayer containing a brief inscription by Martin Harris that the church owned; the inscription matched Harris's handwriting in the salamander letter. Still, Jessee wondered if there was anything more he should know about the letter before updating the article, and he decided to call George Throckmorton, a document examiner for the state Attorney General's office.

On the fifth floor of the Metropolitan Hall of Justice, a sand-colored high-rise separated from the county courts building by a large plaza, Salt Lake City detective Jim Bell spoke at a meeting that had been called to review what detectives knew—and did not know—about the bombings.

He said he suspected the church was concealing information about Hofmann and the murders.

"They're hiding something; the church is doing everything it can to make this as difficult as possible. I've never seen anything like this in a homicide investigation."

As he started to go on, a senior administrator of the Police Department lunged out of his chair and reached for Bell, his fist in the air, shouting, *"Don't keep saying 'they.'"*

Another policeman grabbed him and pulled him away from Bell.

The administrator, his face red with anger, slammed his fist on a desk and said:

"Who's 'they'? Don't keep saying 'the church' and 'they.' There are five millions of us!"

The church's resistance to letting detectives interview the LDS Hospital nurse who had overheard Hofmann's midnight conversation with his lawyers had been the first in a series of occurrences that convinced many of the investigators that they were being stonewalled by leaders of the church.

Detective Jim Bell was thirty-two years old and not a member of the church. His parents had brought him to Utah from Toronto as a child, and for as long as he could remember he had wanted to be a cop. After graduating from high school, he majored in police science at Weber State College, worked as a street patrolman, then was made a detective. Wiry and shorter than his partner, Ken Farnsworth, he had dark hair and rounded dark eyes and he often wore a dour expression that made him look sad.

Bell was too young to have burned out from the pressures of a job that often made detectives apply for a pension after twenty years. But he was a cynical man for someone so young. He expected almost anyone he interviewed, especially in a murder case, to lie, no matter what his religious convictions were.

Meanwhile, a team of lawyers was being assembled to oversee the investigation.

Ted Cannon assigned Robert Stott, his department's most experienced prosecutor of capital cases, to direct the bombing case and assigned two colleagues, David Biggs and Gerry D'Elia, to assist in the prosecution.

Stott was the forty-one-year-old son of a Utah steelworker who had chosen, like Jim Bell, what he wanted to do with his life when he was still a small boy.

As a child he had discovered it was easier to win arguments with his mouth than his fist and he decided to become a lawyer, a *criminal* lawyer. He went to Brigham Young University, then the University of Utah College of Law, interrupting his education only to become a Mormon missionary. It was one measure of Bob Stott's devotion to his church than when his mother died while he was serving his mission in Texas's Rio Grande Valley, he did not come home for her funeral.

When he graduated from law school, Stott was an idealist eager to defend the rights of the downtrodden. In the Salt Lake Temple he married a nurse who worked at the University of Utah hospital and they moved to Las Vegas, where he became a public defender for Clark County. After several years of representing indigent defendants who were unable to afford their own lawyers, Stott was disillusioned: He had learned that most clients who claimed their innocence really deserved to be convicted, some of them of dreadful crimes. His disillusionment, along with a dislike for raising a family in Las Vegas, brought Bob and Deanie Stott back to the Salt Lake Valley, where he took a job as a deputy county attorney.

During the next decade Stott convicted or helped convict a string of notorious defendants—serial murderer Ted Bundy; murderer Ervil LeBaron, the leader of a band of Mormon fundamentalists who believed in the doctrine of blood atonement; Joseph Paul Franklin, a sniper who killed two black joggers in an outburst of racial hatred; and Arthur Gary Bishop, who had coldbloodedly murdered five little boys.

Stott was a stocky man with a round face, sandy hair and a sense of self-confidence he did not attempt to hide; he was slow to make friends, methodical, cautious and, some observers said, colorless in the courtroom. But his track record in the courtroom was one of the best in Utah.

Stott attributed this largely to a lesson learned early in his career: Victories in difficult cases were never won at a trial but in the preparation for it. He was a stickler for pretrial preparation and skeptical of the evidence that policemen brought to him claiming to have proven a suspect's guilt. Stott had seen good defense lawyers destroy seemingly impeccable witnesses and irrefutable evidence and did not want to enter a courtroom until all his targets were lined in a row and he had the ammunition to knock them down.

He also believed that in complex criminal cases there came a time when prosecutors had to take charge of an investigation. It wasn't up to detectives to decide when the task of gathering evidence was complete; that was the prosecutor's job. And because police agencies were by nature competitive, he felt the investigation should be coordinated by a prosecutor, a philosophy that did not endear him to detectives.

Like Stott, David Biggs, the second prosecutor on the case, had been raised a Mormon. But as a college student he became perhaps the nearest thing his culture produced to a hippie. After entering the University of Utah in 1968, he grew a beard, let his hair grow nearly to his shoulders, joined peace marches, rode a motorcycle, wrote a thesis on Sartre and helped pay his college expenses by working as a potter. After deciding not to go on a mission he attended law school, then moved to California to work as a small-town prosecutor and later a public defender. He and his wife, Trish, his high school sweetheart, returned to Utah in 1981 and he took a job in Salt Lake City as a public defender. Four months before the bombings, he was hired as a prosecutor for Salt Lake County.

At thirty-five, the former Mormon hippie, a first cousin of Brent Ashworth's, was a sedate and conscientious lawyer who wore three-piece suits and blended into the gray landscape of Utah's legal profession. But there was something illusory about this visage: Along with his wife, he missed the more casual lifestyle of California, and he was not always comfortable with the church's authoritarian control over the lives of its members. His years as a rebel had left him skeptical of institutions and established authority, including the church.

Ted Cannon expected the investigation to lead, one way or another, into the highest echelons of the church, and he was troubled by what that meant. He did not expect the church to try to exert overt pressure on Stott and Biggs. But he knew it didn't have to. He had been raised in the church; he knew what that meant. He knew that with a glance or hint a church leader could evoke a sense of obligation that could cloud the mind of a man.

By every appearance Ted Cannon was a faithful Mormon. He attended sacrament and priesthood meetings, visited the temple and met his tithing obligation. But in many ways he had become what Utahans call a cultural Mormon: Strands of skepticism had appeared in the fabric of beliefs that had been woven into his mind since childhood, yet he remained in the church because it was a part of his culture. He was comfortable in its social milieu, he agreed with its moral values and he admired the climate of decency it sought to create. Besides, membership in the church was politically advantageous, and when he mad married a second time, it was to a woman who was deeply committed to the church.

He suppressed his intellectual doubts about the doctrinal claims of the church and explained this accommodation pragmatically. "A lot of Mormons," he said, "have to carry water on both their shoulders."

When Cannon placed Bob Stott in charge of the prosecution, he did not tell him that he expected Gerry D'Elia, the third prosecutor assigned to the case, to play an unusual role.

D'Elia lived with his girlfriend in Park City, a few minutes from the ski slopes that had first lured him to Utah from New York. He drove to work in a pickup truck with a camper shell in which his chocolate-brown Labrador often rode as a passenger. As he drove to work, D'Elia often wondered about the alien culture he had entered.

In the courtroom he was quick, brash and combative, every bit a
New Yorker, qualities that many of Utah's defense lawyers admired but often secretly reveled in because they knew his con-
frontational style annoyed many of the people who served on juries
in Utah.

As irreverent about God as Stott was devout, as unpredictable as
he was cautious, D'Elia resented Stott; he believed emphatically
that he should have been left in charge of the case because bombings were within his jurisdiction as the department's arson specialist. Like Bell, D'Elia was suspicious of the church and angry at its
power in Utah, and he rarely stopped complaining to his colleagues
about what he interpreted as efforts by the church to obstruct the
investigation and about excessive deference to church leaders. Like
Bell, he had been warned about a doctrine in Utah called *Lying for
the Lord*. It held that when a Mormon believed he was doing the
work of the Lord, it was not a sin to lie.

The role that Ted Cannon cast for D'Elia was devil's advocate.
He wanted someone to help insulate Stott and Biggs from the kinds
of pressures that he knew could be imposed on a faithful member
of the church.

In his journal, Cannon noted the assignments and wrote after
discussing the case with Don Harman, his chief investigator:

We are agreed that Hofmann is in it, that he's not alone . . .
beyond that we just need to be patient and put it together . . .
there's still too much too loose and unknown. My thought remains that we need to get a "feel" for all these players better
. . . that from one-dimensional to start they're becoming two
dimensional . . . especially the older players like Sheets. He is
emerging as somewhat chameleon-like . . . the younger ones
are probably what they seem . . . wheeler dealer, young guys
playing big time. The real problem is that every single person in
it has something to hide. . . . the church either misspending
church $$ on junk, or at the least embarrassed by the financial
part of the papers; Hofmann's friends their own shady stuff and
homosexuality; J. Gary Sheets his corporate piracies, and *some-*

one out there . . . Hofmann and more than one other: *murder*.
No motive scenario yet explains it all. . . .

  Enuf for tonite.

If nothing else, however, the murder investigation had begun to
open a door on Mark Hofmann's double life.

39

"Give me, if you can, your impression into Mark Hofmann's beliefs," David Biggs asked Shannon Flynn. "You said he was LDS, correct?"

"Yes."

"During the period of time you knew him, did you come to know whether or not his beliefs in that area were changing?"

"I wouldn't say changing, but I knew of their type."

"How would you describe it?" Biggs asked.

"To my understanding, he was completely atheistic."

"Tell me what prompted you to say that."

"That's what he told me," Flynn said.

"What was the content of the discussions? What was he talking about?"

"Well, it would usually be brought up in reference to me because it has become common among document dealers, at least in the Mormon community and people dealing with the history of the church, for them to lose faith and essentially turn away. I usually did not demonstrate that kind of sentiment and it has been a source of curiosity to most people to find out why. . . ."

Biggs asked him to go on.

"He told me some of the things that led him in that direction: A lot of it was the schooling at Utah State, taking psychiatry courses and chemistry and biology, those kinds of things. I don't know which ones in particular, but those kinds of things. The things that we normally ascribe to being religious are most often proved, scientifically, not to be, and I think it was with him a conclusion after a number of years, that it was impossible to know if there was a God and, philosophically speaking, that is correct: It isn't possible to know. It's also impossible not to know. But since he felt there was nothing to give him an indication that there was, he chose to believe that there was not a God. . . ."

His affection for guns and reports that he was knowledgeable about explosives had made Flynn a prime suspect as Hofmann's accomplice.

As Biggs and Ken Farnsworth questioned him, Flynn repeatedly denied involvement in the bombings and insisted Hofmann was innocent, too. But he offered a different view of his friend than the investigators had heard before.

Flynn said he had traveled often to New York City with Mark for auctions, to sell documents and to buy rare books. As soon as he got on an airliner in Salt Lake City, he said, Mark looked around to see if he recognized anyone, then ordered a Scotch.

In New York, he said Mark once got so drunk that he and Lyn Jacobs had to hold his head over a sink while he vomited.

Biggs and Farnsworth had heard of a "ten-mile Mormon"— someone who drives ten miles out of town and orders a drink. But Hofmann, more than most members of the church, had appeared devoted to the church and its way of life.

"Help me along in these areas," Biggs appealed. "Seems that his whole life is centered around the LDS faith; seemed that his wife is very active in the LDS church. . . . He went on a mission. As I understand it he wore temple garments. Attended the temple. Went to church regularly. Can you see my confusion?"

Flynn answered:

"I had the sad duty of telling his parents that he didn't believe in the church anymore, and they were shocked and amazed."

It had happened three days after the bombings. Flynn said he had been at LDS Hospital when Ronald Yengich asked him in the presence of Mark's parents to rate Mark's belief in the church on a scale of one to ten.

"I said: 'Well, I would probably put him at about two or one.' " Mark's parents, he said, refused to believe him.

"Did you ever hear Mark Hofmann tell you that it was to his financial benefit to be a Mormon in Salt Lake City as far as it regards his document dealings?"

"I never heard him tell me that, but I understood that," Flynn said. "I don't believe that it was a primary motivating factor.

"I believe his family and friends were the primary factor. I don't think he's the bomber, though."

Judy Smith, the college classmate whom Mark had come within eight days of marrying in 1977, said she believed he had lost his faith long before they ever met.

"Then why did he go on a mission?" she was asked.

"Social pressure . . . pressure to conform. He didn't want to disappoint his parents, especially his mother. He's devoted to her."

"We broke up," she told Treasury Agent Joyce Seymour, "because of differing views of the LDS religion. Mark professed to be atheist and wished me to share this belief. I could not—and would not—raise children to share his belief. He felt the LDS religion was a fairy tale and he wanted all Mormons to know that they had been misled, that they were involved in a false church and there was no God."

Although she loved Mark, she said she knew their marriage would not survive.

Mark married someone else a few weeks after they stopped dating. Then, she said, she lost contact with him until just a few weeks before he was injured in the bombing.

She said she spotted him in a crowd at a rock concert at Park City the last weekend in August. When their eyes met, they were about fifteen feet apart; they looked at each other and Judy said she turned and walked away.

The following morning, she said, Mark called her at an insurance agency where she worked and said it was important that he speak to her.

"Are you married?" he asked.

"No," she said in a voice that was as cold as she could make it.

Mark said he wanted to talk to her again about their relationship and breakup. She replied:

"Six years later, I'm not interested."

Mark said he was happy in his marriage, had three children and was buying a large home in Holladay.

"Is it okay if I call you again?" he asked.

"Well, okay."

The next morning, Mark called from his car telephone and asked her to meet him for lunch in an hour.

"Is there anything specific you want to talk about?"

"I just want to explain things."

When Judy Smith turned down his invitation, Mark exploded.

"Why can't you understand I just want to talk to you and explain things?"

"You're married and have kids," she said.

"Why don't you just listen to what I want to say?" he shouted. "Please."

The conversation ended as acrimoniously as some of their arguments over the church during the final months of their courtship.

As he continued to shout over his car phone, she hung up.

Mark still loves me, she thought—and in a way she knew she still loved him, too.

She hadn't told him that. Nor had she told Mark another secret. Judy Smith, like Mark Hofmann, no longer believed in the teachings of the church. She hadn't mentioned it to him because she knew it was too late.

40

The discovery of Hofmann's double life did not solve the murders. Indeed, much of the sand was washing away from beneath the fragile foundations of the case that investigators had already tried to build against him. Dorie Hofmann passed a lie-detector test during which she insisted Mark was at home with her on the morning of the bombings and the night before; one by one, his closest friends and suspected accomplices—Lyn Jacobs, Brent Metcalfe and Shannon Flynn—passed lie-detector tests in which they said they knew nothing about the bombings. Called before a federal grand jury, Hofmann's friends agreed he was innocent. Meanwhile, virtually everyone who knew Hofmann in the world of rare books and historical manuscripts—from Charles Hamilton and Kenneth Rendell to Leonard Arrington and Donald Schmidt —had come to his defense publicly and insisted that he was innocent.

Handwriting experts for the Bureau of Alcohol, Tobacco and Firearms studied the writing of Jacobs, Flynn, Metcalfe and Dorie and Mark Hofmann and found no evidence that any of them had addressed the packages to Christensen and Gary Sheets based on their examination of the scraps of brown paper found at the scene of the bombings.

The detectives had discovered that "M. Hansen"—the name on the Radio Shack receipt—was an extraordinarily common name in the Salt Lake Valley; the Salt Lake City telephone directory alone listed seventy-two subscribers with the initial and surname.

Then Hofmann passed a lie-detector test with flying colors, further jeopardizing their case against him. The polygraph examiner who tested Hofmann said he had cleared the test by such a wide margin there was no possibility he was guilty of murder. David Raskin, a University of Utah professor who had received national acclaim as a polygraph expert after testing a string of celebrity defendants such as auto magnate John DeLorean, agreed, saying that the test confirmed Hofmann's claim that he was a victim, not a bomber.

The test had been arranged by Ronald Yengich.

To counter the flood of anonymous news reports depicting his client as a killer, Yengich had launched a counteroffensive that demonstrated he could be an effective manipulator of the press. Saying he suspected "religious crackpots" were responsible for the bombings, he dribbled out tips to reporters to undermine the whispered leaks of police officials, and before long some of the reporters began to suggest in print that Hofmann was the innocent scapegoat for a divided team of incompetent detectives.

After Yengich released the findings of the polygraph examination, community opinion began to shift to Hofmann's corner, further disorienting an already troubled and fractious murder investigation.

The task force of detectives and prosecutors assigned to the case met at 10 each morning in a fourth-floor room at the County Attorney's Office they called the War Room. Lining its walls were photographs of the Judge Building and the home of Gary and Kathleen Sheets and computer printouts and flow charts on which the investigators had tried to trace the personal relationships of the growing cast of characters in the investigation along with the convoluted financial dealings of C.F.S. and Hofmann's dealings with the church. One of the participants in these meetings was a thirty-

three-year-old man with curly black hair, dark eyes and a boyish
face that he hid partly behind a dark beard.

As a college student, Michael George had helped pay his expenses by working as a janitor at Holy Cross Hospital in Salt Lake
City. One day while he was mopping a kitchen floor, Elaine Mep-
pen, a student from Idaho Falls who was studying to become a
hematologist, asked him:

"Are you a Mormon?"

"No, are you?" he answered.

After she said she was not a Mormon either, they began dating.
Two years later they were married.

Among prosecutors, Michael George was considered the best
investigator in Utah, one with a special knack for drawing confes-
sions out of people who had something to hide.

He was soft-spoken and self-effacing, qualities that concealed a
fast and inquisitive mind and a sense of empathy that helped him
relate to the problems tormenting people who were caught up in
the whirlpool of a murder investigation, and that often had a disarming effect on witnesses and suspects whose trust he sought.

Michael George's mother was Italian, his father French. "I
claim the Italian," he said. Like Yengich, he had known what it
was like to grow up as an outsider. His parents had brought him to
Utah in 1961 when he was nine years old after his father's employer, a manufacturer of explosives and rocket motors, transferred him from Michigan. Until then, George had never met a
Mormon. In his first weeks in Utah he came under pressure to join
the church and to attend recreation programs run by the Primary
Association and Boy Scout programs that also happened to include
religious instruction. When George demurred, playmates ostra-
cized him. Later, some of the girls he dated invited him to church
activities. When he turned down the invitations, the girls' parents
often forbade them from seeing him again. It was a systematized
process of discrimination, he would say later, that increased his
love for his own faith, Roman Catholicism.

After high school, George was eager to find an occupation that
promised excitement and variety. He found it in law enforcement.
He earned a sociology degree at the University of Utah in less than
three years, joined the Salt Lake County Sheriff's Department and
began a five-year assignment as an undercover narcotics agent. In

college, George wrote a paper advocating legalization of illicit drugs. But as a street narc, he saw lives destroyed, families ruined, children abandoned as a result of drug abuse. Arresting hundreds of drug dealers, he became the most productive narcotics agent in Utah history. After the first of their children was born, Elaine George began to urge him to get off the violent streets of the drug world, and in 1980, he became an investigator for the Salt Lake City County Attorney's Office.

Richard Forbes, Michael George's partner, was twelve years older than he was and a descendant of Mormon pioneers who crossed the plains to Utah in 1847. After being raised a Mormon, he drifted away from the church, then later reembraced it with a zeal that sanctified it as the most important element of his life outside his family. Indeed, he regarded the church and his family in many ways as one and the same. To Dick Forbes, being a Mormon meant not only being part of a close-knit community of people sharing similar moral values but being secure in the knowledge that if he and the other members of his family led worthy lives, they would be reunited in eternity.

Except on matters of the soul, Dick Forbes and Michael George were the best of friends.

41

As strange as it seemed, Ted Cannon said, the three bombings had the earmarks of the Danites, the nineteenth-century avenging angels who swore an oath of vengeance against the church's enemies and enforced it by slashing their throats.

After Hofmann passed the lie-detector test, Cannon suggested a new look at the possibility religious fanatics were responsible for the murders. On a yellow legal pad, as others in the War Room made notes, the County Attorney listed the pros and cons of possible motives:

"PRO-CHURCH GROUP: 'Protect Mormonism' from further negative publicity on salamander or other documents; punish finders; cut off the flow of further docs. such as salamander.

"However bizarre, this theory makes the most consistent motive across all three bombings . . ."

Sheets and Christensen had financed research on the salamander letter, he said; Hofmann had helped find it. An acquaintance of Kathy Sheets had informed a detective she had attended a meeting of members of her ward in which she expressed apprehension over a letter that showed early church leaders had preached the doc-

trine of blood atonement despite denials by the church's current
leaders.

The salamander letter, he said, had caused enormous embarrassment to the church. What stronger motive for murder, he asked,
could there be for a fanatical protector of the faith?

"If Christensen's interest and assignment was to obtain documents in order that they might never again 'see the light of day,' as
reported," Cannon wrote, "and Kathy Sheets' reaction to the
blood atonement letter was that it should be suppressed as reported
(and her views were taken to be shared by Gary, this is a possibility). The problem? No one apparently knew of their dealings or
attitudes outside their own circle. . . . Forbes will check with his
sources to see what, if any, the polygs knew of all this."

Cannon next wrote:

"*ANTI-CHURCH CRACKPOT GROUP:* ensure public exposure
of docs. supposed to be embarrassing to church, i.e., prevent what
was perceived as likely to be further 'suppression.' "

That was a possibility, too, he said.

They were going round and round and getting nowhere.

Cannon asked the investigators to compile a chronology of
Hofmann's activities during the month before the bombings to
learn if it illuminated a motive for murder.

In their home in suburban Salt Lake City, Mark and Dorie Hofmann tried as best they could to lead a normal life. Dorie's cousin
Ken Woolley volunteered to help pay Mark's legal expenses, and
Mark's parents pledged money for their living expenses. Members
of their ward offered money and food and clothing for the children.
As the weeks passed, Hofmann began to invite friends to his home,
to ride around the Salt Lake Valley in his van and to use his mobile
telephone again. He told his friends he was consulting with new
experts in an effort to authenticate the Oath of a Freeman and
predicted it would sell soon and enable him to solve his financial
problems. During a visit to Hofmann's house in mid-November,
Curt Bench noticed that, as usual, he was wearing his white temple
garments and afterward made a notation about the visit in his
journal:

Mark seemed to be in good spirits—"considering the circumstances" (as he said). His right knee was completely wrapped and bandaged and has a number of screws and pins in it as well as muscle transplants from his calf area. His right middle fingertip is missing down to first joint and fingers are still somewhat scarred. Shoulder is hurt fairly badly (in fact still has large piece of bomb shrapnel which they can't remove at all ever apparently). He constantly had to lift his right arm with his left and he held it up in a 90 degree angle. Hearing is not good in left ear but right almost normal.

During Bench's visit, Dorie Hofmann bitterly attacked Ken Farnsworth and other Salt Lake City detectives. She claimed they were "twisting facts and telling lies" and were determined to execute an innocent man. Mark listened to Dorie impassively, then urged her to calm down and told Bench the investigation would prove his innocence. He said he hoped to resume his document business full time soon and added that he might write a book about his experiences.

"I've already had offers for book and movie rights," he said.

As members of the task force reinterviewed witnesses and assembled their chronology, one point quickly stood out from the others: Mark Hofmann, Steven Christensen, Hugh Pinnock and Dallin Oaks during the final month before the bombings were obsessed with acquiring the McLellin Collection to keep it out of the hands of "the enemy."

Yet there was no sign of it.

No one they interviewed had ever seen the McLellin Collection.

Another point was equally clear: During the weeks immediately before the bombings, Hofmann was under enormous and increasing financial pressure. If the McLellin Collection had been sold as scheduled on October 15, he would have owed the proceeds from the transaction to four different parties: First Interstate Bank, Alvin Rust, Thomas Wilding and the family from whom he and Dorie Hofmann were buying the $550,000 home in Holladay.

Wilding told investigator Dick Forbes that after his brother-in-law, Harold Vincent, hit Hofmann and hurled him against a wall of his office September 13, Hofmann begged for time and promised to return the money he had taken from them by 3 P.M. the following Tuesday. "He said no one had ever hit him before," Wilding said.

When Hofmann confessed four days later that he was unable to settle the debt, Wilding demanded the deed to his home and the title papers for his cars and took some of the biggest prizes in his collection of rare books, including first editions of *Uncle Tom's Cabin, The Adventures of Sherlock Holmes, Dracula,* and *Pinocchio.*

A Salt Lake City lawyer hired by Wilding prepared two promissory notes that Hofmann signed: One, for $188,488, called for the return of the investors' payment for the Oath of a Freeman. The second, payable October 16, was for $226,677—their investment and profits on the sale of Charles Dickens's manuscript for *The Haunted Man.* In all, Hofmann owed Wilding and his investors more than $415,000 and the amount was to increase by $4,000 daily after October 16 if he failed to pay the debt.

Although the agreement relieved the pressure on Hofmann from Wilding and his investors, pressure increased on him from church officials to repay the loan they had helped arrange for him at First Interstate Bank. On September 24, Curt Bench told the detectives, Steve Christensen had called him and implored him to pass an urgent message to Hofmann: Dallin Oaks and Hugh Pinnock were furious that Hofmann had defaulted on the loan and were planning to inform President Hinckley about it the next day.

Mark could be *excommunicated* and possibly go to jail, Christensen said.

Bench found Mark at his home that evening. As they sat outside in Bench's car, he repeated what Christensen had told him. Hofmann listened quietly, thanked his friend and said he expected to straighten out the problems soon.

The intensity of Christensen's concerns, however, troubled Bench and he decided to break a pledge of secrecy he had made to Hofmann on another topic: He told Christensen that Mark had offered to sell him the Facsimile Number Two, the piece of papyrus containing Egyptian symbols that Joseph Smith had purportedly translated to produce the Book of Abraham, for $40,000.

Hofmann, Bench said, had confided to him that it was part of the McLellin Collection but he had to sell it because of financial pressures. Astonished by a revelation that Hofmann was trying to sell one of the documents he had promised to the church, Christensen went to Hofmann's home and ordered him to turn over the papyrus. After Hofmann surrendered it, Christensen showed it to Hugh Pinnock as a sample of the treasure contained in the lost McLellin Collection. The church leader advised him to put it in a safe-deposit box. He also urged Christensen to keep pressure on Hofmann to repay his loan at the bank and to produce the remaining documents from the McLellin Collection.

When Hugh Pinnock arrived home after a late meeting on the evening of October 3, Hofmann and Christensen were waiting for him in his living room.

Hofmann said he would not be able to donate the McLellin Collection to the church after all: The Library of Congress had been unable so far to conclusively authenticate the Oath of a Freeman. Although the American Antiquarian Society had offered $250,000 for the Oath, Hofmann said he was no longer able to afford to donate the McLellin Collection to the church. He said the documents were still sequestered from those who would do harm to the church in a safe-deposit box whose only key was in the possession of Alvin Rust. But he said the risk was growing daily that the documents could fall into the hands of the enemy.

Pinnock said he had a solution to the problem: He would find someone else who could afford to buy the documents and donate them to the church. The next day he called his friend, David Sorenson, who, after the proposal was endorsed by Dallin Oaks, agreed to provide the $185,000 needed to buy the McLellin Collection.

As the detectives pieced together their chronology of the final months before the bombings, they learned Wilding and investors applied more pressure on Hofmann as each day passed. Finally, in early October, Hofmann, in what appeared to be an attempt to buy time, told Wilding he was on the verge of selling an important collection of documents to the church for $185,000 and promised to give the proceeds to him when the deal was consummated October 11.

When Hofmann arrived at Wilding's office on the morning of October 11, a Friday, however, he admitted that he did not have

the money. Instead he placed a typewritten letter on Wilding's
desk that he said proved he would have it soon: The letter, signed
by Steven F. Christensen and David West, an attorney who had
been hired by Sorenson to handle the transaction, affirmed that
$185,000 was being held in a trust account for Hofmann for the
acquisition of a collection of documents and that the money would
be available to him the following Monday, October 14.

Wilding showed the letter to his lawyer, who said it appeared in
order but suggested that they call Christensen, whom he knew, to
secure additional reassurance the money would be paid. Hofmann
pleaded with them not to call Christensen, saying the pending
transaction with the church was extremely confidential: He had
promised not to reveal its intention to acquire the documents and if
anyone knew he had broken his word, the deal could be aborted.
Wilding agreed to wait for the money until Monday and not call
Christensen.

A few hours after this meeting ended, the detectives learned,
Hofmann called Wilding and said they would not be able to complete the deal as scheduled on Monday because it was a holiday
and the banks would be closed. He promised, however, to bring the
money to Ashton's office on Tuesday, October 15.

On Tuesday morning at 11 o'clock, as news of Steven Christensen's death was flashing across the Valley, Hofmann arrived at the
lawyer's office and said that because Christensen was not available
to authenticate the documents, the transaction would have to be
delayed again. Then he went to the Church Administration Building, where he told Dallin Oaks the same thing.

But the church Apostle said he saw no reason to put off the sale
and suggested it take place the following day. Oaks advised Hofmann to contact Sorenson's attorney and assure him that the sale
of the McLellin Collection was still on despite Christensen's murder. Oaks said someone else would have to be found to examine the
documents now that Christensen was dead and they agreed on
Donald Schmidt.

In all, the detectives estimated, Mark Hofmann owed almost $1
million on October 15. Somewhere among those zeroes, Ken
Farnsworth suggested, there was a motive for murder. But Ted
Cannon pointed out that according to Justin Schiller and Raymond Wapner, Hofmann was almost certain to receive at least $1

million for the Oath of a Freeman. If Hofmann's financial problems were soon to be solved, where was his motive for murder?

In his journal on the night of November 27 prosecutor David Biggs wrote:

It has now been over a month since the deaths and bombings and nothing seems as clear as it was on 10/16/85 after Hofmann was blown out of his MR2. I feel that all the pieces of the puzzle are at our fingertips but the placement is askew. If I could just rearrange them into a different permutation, *all* would be clear. . . . it's just like trying to fit a size 11 foot into a size five shoe. maybe it will always be a size 11!! Murder isn't logical or sensible. Stop trying to make it such!

The following morning, Thanksgiving Day, Biggs picked up a copy of *The Salt Lake Tribune,* and discovered that the McLellin Collection had been found.

It was in Texas, and its owner said he had never heard of Mark Hofmann.

42

The first search for the McLellin Collection had begun in the 1870s, when John Logan Traughber, Jr., a schoolteacher and farmer from Carroll County, Missouri, decided to write a book about Mormonism.

In addition to other early leaders of the church, he interviewed and corresponded with William McLellin, the onetime Apostle and confidant of Joseph Smith who left the church in 1838 in a dispute over Smith's assertion of absolute authority over the Saints. After McLellin died in 1883, Traughber traced his widow to a remote Texas frontier town and inquired whether she had saved any of her husband's writings. Yes, she replied to his letter, she still had many of his papers, although some had been burned and others had been given away. On November 5, 1884, Traughber, who was then thirty years old, went to the railway depot near his home in Norborne, Missouri, and after paying fifty cents in express charges, took home the McLellin Collection. The widow of the former church Apostle had sent him as a gift many of her husband's papers and loaned him others, including his daily journals covering six years in the 1830s.

John Traughber never completed his book about Mormonism.

But he spent more than twenty years studying McLellin's life and
papers and distilling his research into a handwritten manuscript
that filled more than three hundred pages of legal-sized paper.
Before his own death in 1908, Traughber wrote, perhaps prophetically:

> I hope the long and industrious life of Dr. McLellin has not been
> in vain, and that the record he has made concerning Mormon-
> ism will prove to be of as much worth to mankind as he had
> desired it should, but it may be in a different way than he had
> expected. . . .

When he died Traughber left his widow and six children virtually penniless except for an unusual legacy: the notebooks and
other writings of William E. McLellin along with his own lengthy
manuscripts, letters, pamphlets, newspaper clippings and other
material about McLellin and the early years of Mormonism.

Because she did not want the fruit of what had been her husband's life's work wasted, Traughber's widow sent his manuscript
to *The Salt Lake Tribune* in 1910 in the belief that the newspaper
might want to publish it. But it returned the material unpublished.

Even after twice remarrying, Traughber's widow tried to have
his work published, but she was unsuccessful. Following her death
in 1954 at the age of eighty-six, the documents fell into the possession of her youngest son, Otis, then a forty-nine-year-old salesman
of heavy equipment in Texas.

Stuffed into cardboard boxes, they were all but forgotten by the
family until the spring of 1977 when Otis Traughber received a
letter from a young graduate student in history at Yale University,
Dennis Michael Quinn.

Quinn had written similar letters to every person named
Traughber that he could locate in Texas after finding a letter in the
New York Public Library written August 21, 1901, by John Logan
Traughber, Jr., from Tyler County, Texas. Traughber's letter, sent
to another writer who was interested in Mormon history, related
that he owned a collection of materials once owned by William
McLellin. In his letter sent to Texans named Traughber, Quinn
inquired: "If you have the manuscript diaries, letters and other
materials once possessed by J. L. Traughber, or if you know of

someone who might know about these items, please provide me with this information."

After receiving the letter, Traughber placed a telephone call to New Haven in an effort to contact Quinn. But for unknown reasons the message was never passed on to him. Instead, it reached an archivist at the Yale library who replied with a letter to Traughber advising him of Quinn's mailing address in Salt Lake City.

This turn of events looked fishy to Traughber. He was willing to cooperate with a Yale scholar but he was suspicious of someone from Salt Lake City and suspected the Mormons were trying to obtain his father's work. Because of his suspicions he never replied to the letter and forgot about the old documents until he read reports about the Salt Lake City bombings. Then he collected his musty family legacy and placed it in a safe-deposit box.

Dawn Tracy, a reporter for *The Salt Lake Tribune,* tracked him down in Houston by following the lead Quinn had unearthed in the New York Public Library. She used the church's genealogical records to identify John Traughber's descendants, and they had led her to Otis Traughber in Houston. Impressed by her resourcefulness, Traughber agreed to show her the McLellin Collection.

As had been rumored, William E. McLellin's writings were not kind to Joseph Smith. Although he did not disavow the Book of Mormon, he wrote of the Prophet as a corrupt, even murderous dictator who seduced young girls under the guise of divine revelation and directed the Danites to kill dissidents who disagreed with him.

McLellin, who joined the church in 1831, asserted Smith had invented much of what he subsequently preached to his followers, including the claims that he had been personally ordained into the priesthood by John the Baptist, that he had translated papyrus "taken from the bosom of an Egyptian mummy" into the Book of Abraham and that an angel had given him special devices, Urim and Thummim, to translate the Book of Mormon.

In a kind of creed in reverse, McLellin listed fifty-five points about Mormonism that he did not believe: "I do not believe in disembodied spirits communing with man, as Angels do. . . . I don't believe in the doctrine of plurality of Gods and God-making,

as J. Smith taught in Nauvoo. . . . I don't believe that God himself was once a man as men are now. . . ."

"Mr. Traughber, are you familiar with papyrus?" asked John
Foster, a Salt Lake City detective. He had flown to Houston with
Treasury agent Michael Taylor after the *Tribune* reported its dis-
covery of the McLellin Collection.

A non-Mormon, Otis Traughber had a gleaming bald scalp
fringed by white hair. At eighty, he still visited his old office almost
every day even though he had been retired for several years.

"I'm fairly familiar with it," Traughber answered, puzzled by
the question about Egyptian papyrus.

"I'm not a—I don't know that I ever saw a papyrus—"

Foster showed Traughber a photocopy of one of the Egyptian
symbols that Joseph Smith said he had translated into the Book of
Abraham scripture and asked if there was anything resembling it
in the collection of documents his family owned.

Traughber shook his head, still puzzled by the line of inquiry.

"Any hieroglyphics . . . Egyptian handwriting?" Foster asked.

"Not that I know of."

Traughber said he might have seen pictures of papyrus in books,
but he didn't *own* any.

Foster inquired if he had ever discussed selling the McLellin
papers to a man named Mark Hofmann.

"No," Traughber said.

Traughber said he had never heard the name until he read news
reports of the Salt Lake City bombings. Nor, he said in response to
questions, had he ever heard the names Shannon Flynn, Lyn Jacobs, Brent Metcalfe, Gary Sheets, Kathleen Sheets, Dorie Hoff-
man or Steven Christensen.

After the *Tribune* published excerpts from the McLellin papers,
the church issued a statement declaring that McLellin's comments
were not surprising. From its beginning, it said, the church had
faced dissidents, critics and malcontents: "Still, the church moves
forward and continues to grow, primarily because it is the Lord's
Church and also because of the appeal of the gospel of Jesus Christ
and the way of life it offers."

* * *

George Throckmorton was a policeman who had drifted, by accident and ambition, into the specialized field of examining questionable documents. While working as a street cop in the Utah city of Ogden, he became interested in the scientific aspects of gathering evidence and enrolled in a program of study in forensic criminology at the Chicago Institute of Applied Science and proved adept enough to be asked to return as an instructor. After returning to Utah he became a criminologist at the state crime laboratory in Salt Lake City; then, in early 1985, he was appointed by the Utah Attorney General to a job investigating fraudulent checks, contracts and other paperwork generated by white-collar criminals.

A slender, forty-two-year-old man with fragile features, a gray beard and mustache, Throckmorton, like almost everyone else in Utah, had closely followed news reports of the October bombings, and some of the things he had heard troubled him.

In new articles, historians and Salt Lake City policemen frequently quoted Massachusetts document dealer Kenneth Rendell as saying the salamander letter's authenticity had been established without question. Experts had dated its paper and ink, he said.

Throckmorton knew of about two hundred specialists in the country who were expert examiners of questioned documents, but he had never heard of Rendell. Moreover, he believed it was all but impossible to accurately date ink or paper used in a document.

He expressed his skepticism to several reporters in Salt Lake City, but they paid little attention to him. Nor did police officials show any interest when he mentioned his reservations to them.

"I don't know if this letter is genuine or not," Throckmorton told Captain Bob Jack of the Salt Lake County Sheriff's Department, who was directing his department's portion of the murder investigation. "But I do know the reports that have been issued about it are not accurate: You can't date paper and ink and nobody qualified that I know of has ever examined it."

Jack told him not to worry about it. He said there was no reason to believe the salamander letter was a fake, and besides, it had been sent to the FBI laboratory for a thorough examination.

A few days later, Throckmorton received a telephone call from Dean Jessee of the church Historical Department. He said he was preparing a research paper on the salamander letter and wanted to meet with him and discuss how old documents were authenticated. This surprised Throckmorton. Jessee had often been cited in the newspapers as the church's leading expert on authenticating its historical documents. Throckmorton agreed to come to Jessee's home to look over a photo of the salamander letter along with Rendell's reports on the testing of the letter. After reading the reports, he called Albert Lyter and William Krueger, the experts Rendell had employed to examine the letter's paper and ink.

They reaffirmed what they had stated in their reports: There was nothing about the letter that was inconsistent with an 1830 date of origin. But both said their conclusions fell short of declaring the letter authentic. Krueger said that while it was difficult to do so, it was possible to age paper artificially; Lyter said the salamander letter had been written with iron gallotannic ink, which had been in use since the seventh century, and it was virtually impossible to determine exactly when it was actually inscribed on a sheet of paper.

On a Sunday evening several days after these conversations, Throckmorton returned to his home in a Salt Lake City suburb following a day at church.

After finishing dinner, he relaxed in a reclining chair in his living room, turned on a television set and, while giving the screen an occasional glance, looked over Xerox copies of the salamander letter and other documents pertaining to church history loaned to him by Jessee.

Throckmorton had never examined a document dating from before 1929 and had examined only a few that were more than a few years old. But as he leafed through the photocopies of nineteenth-century letters and manuscripts, he was puzzled. Brent Ashworth's letter written by Joseph Smith to General Dunham appeared, for example, to have been written on stationery that was slightly larger than letters Smith had written to his wife and lawyer shortly before his death in the Carthage Jail. A devout Mormon, Throckmorton tried to imagine himself inside the cell with Joseph and wondered where and how he could have obtained sheets of writing paper of two different sizes.

The next day, he called the County Attorney's Office and spoke to investigator Michael George.

"Mike, everybody's been saying the salamander letter has been authenticated. But it hasn't been authenticated by any reputable agency or examiner that's recognized by the professional associations I'm familiar with, and these reports we've been hearing that they've dated the paper and ink, well, you can't do it."

Something in Throckmorton's voice excited George, and he asked him to meet with Ted Cannon and the three prosecutors working on the case the following afternoon at 2 o'clock.

For the first time, George Throckmorton thought as he hung up, someone had grasped what he had been trying to convey.

43

"I can buy authentic paper—I could steal it out of a library book printed in 1830; I can make iron gallotannic ink," Throckmorton said, "and when I'm done I'll have paper of the proper time period and ink of the proper time period, but that doesn't mean I have an authentic document. These documents may be fine, but I wouldn't take it for granted that they're genuine."

Throckmorton was persuasive and hit a responsive chord.

For weeks, Ted Cannon had been puzzled by Mark Hofmann's miracle-like success at unearthing priceless documents. "How did one guy find so many old letters and manuscripts?" he asked repeatedly at the brainstorming sessions in the War Room that now often lasted several hours a day.

Forgery had been near the bottom of their list of possible motives for murder. Every expert they had consulted until Throckmorton said the salamander letter was genuine without question.

Perhaps, the prosecutors and investigators in the War Room speculated, there was a conspiracy no one had yet imagined in which Hofmann and other people had forged documents and they were linked somehow to the murders.

If he could arrange to borrow him from the Attorney General's staff, Cannon asked Throckmorton, would he be willing to join the task force?

Throckmorton accepted the offer under two conditions: He would have to have access to originals of the documents, and he would not take the job unless a document expert who was not a Mormon was retained to help him.

"I'm a Mormon," he said. "If I say the salamander letter is genuine, I'll have half the church saying I'm against them, and if I say it's forged, then I'll have half the church against me."

Cannon agreed to the terms and Throckmorton placed a call to William Flynn, a document analyst at the Arizona State Crime Laboratory in Phoenix.

Flynn was puzzled by Throckmorton's first question:

"What religion are you?"

"I'm not a practicing member of anything," Flynn answered.

"But what *are* you?"

"I was raised a Catholic."

Perfect, Throckmorton said.

At forty, Bill Flynn had spent almost half his life as a professional document sleuth, first in Philadelphia, then in Phoenix. With careful and thoughtful eyes, dark hair that was receding above his temples and a way of expressing himself that was slow and precise, Flynn could easily be taken for a college professor in midcareer. But like Throckmorton, his trade was examining bad checks, altered wills, forged records and other pieces of paper used as tools of fraud or deception.

When Throckmorton offered him an opportunity to enter a mystical world of angels, golden plates and white salamanders, Flynn jumped at the chance.

In a telephone call, Dean Jessee told Kenneth Rendell that criminologists were going to take another look at the salamander letter. Rendell laughed. Forensic document examiners, he said, were adequate for evaluating forged checks or another modern documents, but they were out of their depth when it came to examining nineteenth-century historical documents.

In early December the Utah State Supreme Court rejected an appeal by the county that would have forced the nurse who eavesdropped on the hospital conversation between Hofmann and his lawyers to talk to county prosecutors. The court said the conversation was as privileged as any between a lawyer and client.

Despite this setback, there was an uptick in morale in the War Room after Throckmorton's visit: Perhaps, at last, the prosecutors were circling around a motive for murder.

A few days later, they met with Justice Department lawyers, who were still conducting a federal grand jury investigation of the bombings.

The county prosecutors explained that while they were continuing to focus on C.F.S. investors and religious fanatics as suspects in the case, their investigation was narrowing again toward the likelihood that Mark Hofmann, probably with the help of others, killed Steve Christensen and Kathleen Sheets.

The senior federal prosecutor seemed unimpressed. All the evidence pointed to the murders as brutal acts of revenge by angry C.F.S. investors, he said. Hofmann may have been a wheeler-dealer in the document business. But he had an untarnished reputation in the community. His criminal record consisted of exactly one charge, a 1970 arrest for shoplifting that was never prosecuted.

In what sounded more like a reproach than a question, he inquired:

"What motive could Hofmann possibly have for doing it?"

Taking a deep breath, David Biggs answered:

"We believe there's a possibility of a massive fraud and cover-up involving the forgery of documents."

The federal prosecutor looked at Biggs as if he had stepped off another planet.

If forgery was involved, why would Hofmann kill Kathleen Sheets? he demanded.

If Hofmann was the killer, why did he blow himself up?

The federal prosecutor said he had just spoken to an FBI agent who told him the Bureau's document examiners in Washington had just completed their preliminary analysis of the salamander letter. It was genuine, he said, not a forgery. "Frankly," he said, "we don't think you've got the right man."

The skepticism in Salt Lake City's Federal Building was not the only evidence of disharmony in the fragile alliance of law enforcement agencies that had been hurriedly assembled on the afternoon of October 15.

For weeks, Police Chief Bud Willoughby and Sheriff Pete Hayward had accused Hofmann publicly of murder, but no charges had been filed against him. Ronald Yengich's counterattack had turned public support in favor of Hofmann, a cause enhanced by his passing of a lie-detector test and by several leaked tips by Willoughby and Hayward that turned out to be wrong after they were reported in the newspapers.

Arguing that the continuing avalanche of publicity could jeopardize the prosecution and Hofmann's right to a fair trail, Ted Cannon appealed to Yengich, Willoughby and Hayward to call a truce in the battle being waged in newspaper columns and on the airwaves. But he only intensified the battle. Willoughby and Hayward not only were Cannon's longtime political foes but faced growing pressure from the public and press to solve the murders, and they fired back: They said they had a *responsibility* to inform the community about the progress of important investigations and claimed their detectives had already given Cannon enough evidence to bring charges against Hofmann and other people.

At the street level, the lead investigators—Ken Farnsworth, Jim Bell, Michael George and Dick Forbes—maintained cordial relationships. But the rising level of enmity between their bosses produced mounting pressure to keep secrets from each other.

Meanwhile, Salt Lake Police Department officials, like the federal prosecutors, rejected the county prosecutor's theory that the murders might be linked to forgery.

If they were going to prove forgery was at the root of the case, Bob Stott said, the County Attorney's Office would have to do it alone, and they would have to keep their work secret until they had enough evidence to prove it.

The situation was not helped by a widening division among the members of the prosecution team.

Gerry D'Elia began to side with Farnsworth and Bell, who argued that there was sufficient evidence to charge Hofmann with murder. But Stott insisted that only when they knew his motive for murder would they file charges against Hofmann; Ted Cannon said he would support Stott in the conflict.

Cannon, meanwhile, had other problems to deal with.

The owners of a suburban office building damaged by a fire had
filed a $2.5 million negligence suit against the county claiming
lawyers on Cannon's staff had suppressed evidence showing the fire
originated in space leased by Salt Lake County. Because it was
impossible for Cannon to investigate his own office objectively,
plaintiffs in the lawsuit asked for the appointment of a special
prosecutor and grand jury to investigate the prosecutor's office.

Cannon ridiculed the proposal, but the matter was not to end
there.

As the final weeks of 1985 approached and members of the
bombing task force labored to build a case against him, Mark Hofmann entertained friends at home, attended church in his wheelchair or on crutches, pressed Justin Schiller and Raymond Wapner
to sell the Oath of a Freeman and conceived his fourth child. During one visit with Curt Bench, Hofmann predicted the American
Antiquarian Society would buy the Oath soon and help solve his
financial problems. Later, Bench wrote in his journal:

> Mark thinks someone tried to kill him but doesn't know who or
> why. Says he goes from theory to theory, says whole thing is so
> bizarre and incredible as to be hard to believe—like "Twilight
> Zone."

44

David Biggs looked across the large desk of Gordon B. Hinckley and said he thought there was a possibility some of the documents the church had acquired from Mark Hofmann were forged.

The president of his church smiled paternally at Biggs and said he believed that Hofmann, as slightly as he knew him, was not a murderer or a forger. Then, in what appeared to be an afterthought, he said: "We relied on the integrity of Mr. Hofmann, and if we relied on his integrity wrongly, it's to his eternal detriment."

Biggs felt a chill shoot down his spine and thought: If there *is* an afterlife I wouldn't want to be Mark Hofmann.

In early December, the focus of the investigation shifted decisively toward Hofmann and the documents he had sold and traded to the church. Although the church informed the press it was cooperating with the investigation, many of the investigators and prosecutors working on the case told a different story when they returned to their offices each night.

When detectives arrived for an interview, church leaders often opened the meeting by inquiring if they were members of the church or, as they were leaving, handed them a hymnal or other publication. Senior church officials refused to meet with the homicide investigators several times unless an FBI agent who was a returned Mormon missionary was present, even though the Bureau's only apparent jurisdiction in the case was the possible role of organized crime in the murders or possible fraud involving the operations of Gary Sheets's company, C.F.S. Saying it was inappropriate for leaders of a religion to disclose such information to civil authorities, several General Authorities declined to provide their diaries to the detectives who wanted to establish when and how frequently Hofmann visited the Church Administration Building.

Early in the investigation, friends of Mark Hofmann and Steven Christensen repeatedly told the detectives that they had been present when Hofmann and Christensen received telephone calls from Gordon Hinckley. Toll records showed Hofmann placed several calls to Hinckley's office from his car telephone during the week before the bombings, including two calls on the Monday immediately before the explosions. But Hinckley spoke of Hofmann as if he barely recognized his name. Repeatedly when he was asked about the document dealer, Hinckley answered: *"I can't remember."* He said he couldn't remember what Hofmann had told him about the McLellin Collection, but said he was certain Hofmann had never mentioned that it contained any material that would be embarrassing to the church. And while it was true that he had purchased documents from Hofmann over the years, Hofmann could not have construed from anything he ever said that he was acting as an agent—formally or informally—to acquire anything for the church.

Hinckley and Hugh Pinnock denied Steve Christensen's claim made to several of his friends shortly before his death that *he* had been asked to acquire documents for the church. Hinckley said he had met Christensen only once and had only the vaguest recollection of him.

Hugh Pinnock sobbed as he related his dealings with Christensen regarding the McLellin Collection, and Ken Farnsworth, one of the detectives who was interviewing him, wondered if he felt a sense of responsibility, however unintended, for Christensen's death. He also wondered if the church was using Pinnock, expecting him to suffer the embarrassment surrounding the bank loan so others could escape it.

Farnsworth felt a different kind of compassion for Gordon Hinckley. He was visibly uncomfortable with the process he was being forced to undergo. He was not accustomed to having to answer questions, nor was he accustomed to being involved in a murder investigation. Clearly, he did not like the prospect of a subpoena to testify in court. It seemed to Farnsworth that Gordon Hinckley was caught in a dilemma of damned-if-you-do, damned-if-you-don't: If he didn't acquire the documents offered by Hofmann, there was a risk of embarrassment for the church; if he did accept them, there was the risk of a different kind of embarrassment for the church. And as he sat looking across his desk at a team of murder investigators, Farnsworth thought, Hinckley must have feared the possibility of even more embarrassment for the church he loved.

The salamander letter and several other documents Hofmann had sold to the church were still in Washington at the FBI laboratory. When Ted Cannon pressed the church to let his investigators look at the originals of those that were still in Salt Lake City, a lawyer for the church said that would be impossible, because some of the documents were extremely confidential and the church did not want to risk having them made public.

Cannon said that if the church declined to provide the documents voluntarily, he would subpoena them—and indeed, he subsequently did so. But, to head off a court fight over the subpoena, Cannon surrendered to a demand by the church's lawyers to keep the substance of the documents a secret.

"The content and meaning and interpretations to be placed upon what is iterated within the documents," Cannon wrote to Wilford Kirton, the church's lawyer, "is either immaterial or of secondary concern as far as this investigation is concerned. Nevertheless, aware of the possible antiquity of the documents and the import of what they contain, every reasonable measure will be employed to secure not only the documents themselves, but the contents thereof, from scrutiny or discussion by anyone outside the authorized investigative team. In no case will any member of the investigative team be permitted to discuss, describe or characterize the

contents of the said documents, or any of them, to media or indeed
any interested party whatsoever, since it is no proper part of the
investigation to make such interpretations and will neither add to
nor detract from the state's forensic case. . . ."

Cannon agreed to let church officials maintain a sign-in/sign-out
log identifying everyone who examined the documents and agreed
with the church's demands that members of his staff would have to
turn over to the church all notes, photocopies, photographs and
negatives made during examination of the documents. Cannon
ended his letter with an expression of thanks for the church's coop-
eration, a clause that brought snickers from many of those in the
War Room.

On December 11, Jerry Taylor, the Treasury Department bomb
expert, flew to Salt Lake City from his office in San Francisco to
review for the prosecution team why he believed Hofmann was the
bomber.

He said tests at the Bureau of Alcohol, Tobacco and Firearms
laboratory on Treasure Island in San Francisco Bay had left little
doubt that the three pipe bombs were made by the same hand and
that Hofmann's account of the bomb's detonating as it fell to the
floorboards of his car was inconsistent with the evidence. "He had
to have physically gotten into the car," Taylor said. "His right
hand was touching the bomb when it exploded."

Taylor said additional analysis of the handwriting on the bombs
still indicated that someone other than Hofmann had addressed
them, pointing strongly to the likelihood of a co-conspirator.

After he finished his presentation, Gerry D'Elia put him through
a mock cross-examination, a dress rehearsal for the time in a trial
when a defense lawyer would try to impeach his testimony.

When it was over, Farnsworth, pleased by Taylor's performance,
turned to Stott and asked: "Now, what do you think about filing?"

Stott was silent. It meant he wasn't convinced yet.

When the silence continued, Farnsworth shouted: "You got to be
shittin' me."

Stott had not been satisfied with several of Taylor's answers. He
was afraid a skilled defense attorney might be able to discredit him.
Weeks earlier, Taylor had said the door to Hofmann's car was
closed when the bomb went off, then changed his mind after Brad-

ley Christensen, the pedestrian who had blessed Hofmann as Hofmann lay bleeding on the ground, said he thought the door was open when the bomb exploded.

Farnsworth stood up, towering over Stott, and looked down on him, anger in his eyes. But Stott didn't retreat.

Policemen, he thought, were accustomed to intimidating people with their physical presence and getting their own way. He ignored Farnsworth.

It was one thing, he told the others in the War Room, to have circumstantial evidence that persuaded investigators and prosecutors of a defendant's guilt, another to convince a jury of that.

To bring charges against a defendant in Utah, he said the law required evidence of "a reasonable likelihood of conviction," and they didn't have it yet. There were a million ways a defense attorney could obscure their case and plant doubt in the minds of a jury. To acquit Hofmann, all Yengich needed was to persuade *one* of twelve jurors to have a reasonable doubt of his guilt. Besides, they still needed a motive.

Stott then excused himself to play racquetball, leaving Farnsworth and Bell in the War Room, seething.

When George Throckmorton and William Flynn arrived at the Church Office Building on the morning of December 17, two months after the bombings, church lawyers said a security guard was to be with them during the test, but they vetoed the demand and, behind locked doors and two security checkpoints, they set up a makeshift laboratory and began their examination of the documents. Their goal: to find a common denominator in Hofmann's documents that made them distinctive from other nineteenth-century documents owned by the church.

Three days later, they suspected something *was* different about some of Hofmann's documents. But they weren't sure what it was. Several took on a blue cast when they were exposed to an ultraviolet lamp. Although employees of the church Historical Department attributed the condition to the probable effects of a process used to de-acidify antique documents and prolong their life, not all the documents fluoresced with the same shade of blue.

Then, while looking through a microscope at the handwriting on one of Hofmann's documents, Throckmorton saw something he had never seen before.

He asked Flynn to take a look.

"What do you think this is?" he said, looking up from the microscope at his associate.

Flynn peered into the instrument and saw tiny fractures in the ink. Highly magnified, the surface of the ink looked like the mottled, cracked skin of an alligator.

"I've never seen it before," Flynn said.

When they examined the ink on other documents in the church's archives, they found several with similar microscopic cracking. But on others of approximately the same age the ink was as smooth as a sheet of ice.

All of the documents with cracked ink, Throckmorton said, appeared to have come from Hofmann.

He proposed a game:

"Hand me a document and don't tell me where it came from," he said. He leaned over the microscope, accepted a yellowed sheet of paper from Flynn and examined it.

The ink had cracks in it.

"This came from Hofmann," he said.

"Right," Flynn said.

"This didn't come from Hofmann," Throckmorton said a few moments later as he peered at another document whose ink was not cracked.

"You're right," Flynn said.

"This came from Hofmann," Throckmorton said as he examined another document whose ink was cracked.

"Wrong," Flynn said.

"There goes that theory," Throckmorton said.

Then he saw that the ink was cracked on another document not on the church's list of acquisitions from Hofmann.

"Well, it was a good theory while it lasted," Throckmorton said.

Flynn asked a church archivist to double-check the source of the documents they were examining. The next morning, the archivist sheepishly acknowledged that the list was wrong: Mark Hofmann had been the source of several additional documents, including the two on which Throckmorton had identified cracked ink.

Throckmorton and Flynn were now confident that some of

Hofmann's documents had unusual qualities, but didn't know why or how important they were. They agreed to take a recess and think about it over the Christmas holidays. In Phoenix, Flynn checked all the textbooks on handwriting and forgery that he could find. None said anything about cracked ink.

In Utah, county judges are required to hold a hearing every two years at which any citizen can request the appointment of a grand jury to investigate allegations of malfeasance by government officials.

On December 31, 1985, more than twenty people with a variety of grievances appeared before the twelve judges of the Third District Court and asked them to convene Salt Lake County's first grand jury in eleven years.

One of those who appeared before the judges was the County Sheriff, Pete Hayward, who requested an investigation of his old political enemy, County Attorney Ted Cannon. Hayward complained that weeks before, detectives from his department and the Salt Lake City Police Department had presented Cannon with more than sufficient evidence to file murder charges against Mark Hofmann. But for reasons known only to Cannon, he was refusing to do so.

The judges said they would consider the requests for an investigation and announce their decision early in the new year.

Ted Cannon and Bob Stott agreed that *if* the bombing murders were connected to fraud or forgery they would have to find out *why* and *how*. The testimony of forensic experts like Throckmorton and Flynn would not be enough to convince a jury that the documents were forgeries; Hofmann would probably find other expert witnesses to testify the handwriting was genuine.

Investigator Dick Forbes was assigned to direct the search for evidence of fraud against Hofmann. Michael George was assigned to investigate the origins of the nineteenth-century letters, manuscripts and other documents that Hofmann had sold.

For both, it was the beginning of a journey backward in time.

45

At a public library in Palmyra, the town where Mormonism was born, Michael George located a journal of court proceedings covering the years 1827 through 1830 that contained the signature of Martin Harris, the wealthy disciple of Joseph Smith who mortgaged his farm to finance publication of the Book of Mormon. George Throckmorton wanted a sample of Harris's writing that had never been handled by Hofmann to determine if its ink was cracked like that on the other documents he had examined. The FBI still had the salamander letter and several other documents signed by Harris but was refusing to release them for examination in Salt Lake City.

When he telephoned the library, an administrator agreed to surrender the journal only if he was presented a subpoena. George knew a subpoena issued in Utah had no legal effect in New York, but decided not to explain this fine point of law to the administrator and promised to bring one with him.

As angry snowstorms pummeled the Wasatch Front during the first week of 1986, George called his wife, Elaine, and asked her to meet him at the Salt Lake City International Airport with a change of clothes because he had to leave on a midnight flight to Denver.

In Denver, he caught another plane to Chicago, then another to Rochester and landed there late the following morning. An hour later he was in Palmyra, chilled by the hard, subfreezing weather that he had left behind in Utah.

When he walked up the steps of the library, George was met by two state policemen who had been called by the library administrator. They were not pleased that he had entered their jurisdiction without first informing them. George apologized, and as he explained why a 150-year-old signature was needed for a murder investigation in Utah, he felt their resistance melt.

Then he noticed a young man taking notes.

"Who's that?"

Someone had invited a reporter.

"He leaves." George's anger flared. "Get him out of here."

The trip was intended to be so secret that even the Salt Lake City detectives who were investigating the bombings would not know about it. But when George arrived back in Salt Lake City, barely twenty-four hours after he had left, the news of his secret mission was in the newspapers along with the suggestion that his trip was a waste of time and money because the church already had samples of Martin Harris's handwriting.

The following morning, Throckmorton looked into his microscope at the ink on the document from Palmyra.

"It's not cracked," he said.

After being issued a subpoena, the church had released to Throckmorton and Flynn what it said were all of the documents it had acquired from Hofmann since 1980, including some that it had previously kept secret.

When the First Presidency's Vault yielded the letter presented to Gordon Hinckley by Hofmann in which Thomas Bullock accused Brigham Young of having tried to destroy the Blessing of Joseph Smith III, it caught those in the War Room by surprise.

"What else are they hiding?" Michael George demanded. "None of the church historians I've talked to—Don Schmidt, Leonard Arrington, Dean Jessee—even knew this existed. *They've never heard of it.* What else do they have? Who knows what's in the First Presidency's Vault?"

Throckmorton and Flynn moved their test instruments to the Utah State Crime Laboratory in a Salt Lake City suburb and, after more tests, reviewed for the prosecution team what they knew so far:

The paper used in all of the documents Hofmann sold to the church was manufactured during or before the nineteenth century. All were written with iron gallotannic ink, a compound of iron salts, tannic acid and other ingredients that was the Western world's basic writing solution for centuries until it was made obsolete by synthetic materials and the ballpoint pen during the twentieth century.

The majority of the church's documents from Hofmann appeared to be normal. But on several there were microscopic cracks in the ink. When these documents were illuminated by ultraviolet light, the ink appeared in many instances to have bled through the paper, and some revealed an otherwise invisible running of the ink, suggesting that they might have been washed in a solution and hung to dry. None of these qualities, Throckmorton and Flynn said, showed up on documents Hofmann had not sold, such as the letters Joseph Smith wrote in the Carthage Jail shortly before his death to his wife and lawyer, which had been loaned to the investigators by the Reorganized Church of Jesus Christ of Latter-day Saints.

Throckmorton and Flynn said there was reason to suspect the authenticity of as many as twenty-one of the seventy-nine documents sold by Hofmann that they had examined, including Joseph Smith's 1825 letter to Josiah Stowell, the Blessing of Joseph Smith III and Joseph Smith's last letter from the Carthage Jail that Brent Ashworth had begged Hofmann to sell to him.

Then Throckmorton and Flynn broke the bad news: Despite their suspicions, they could not prove the documents were forged; all they knew was that Hofmann's documents were *different.* But there was such a distinctive family resemblance to Hofmann's documents that *something* had to be wrong.

Flynn returned again to his home in Arizona, saying that he planned some experiments to learn if he could discover why they were different.

* * *

In mid-January, the Federal Bureau of Investigation sent a torpedo from Washington that threatened to sink the fragile case being assembled against Hofmann in Salt Lake City. The salamander letter, it said, was not a forgery.

46

The FBI laboratory's examination of the salamander letter had been long and exhaustive and its report left little doubt about the letter's authenticity. The Bureau's document analysts noted that they had encountered the same problem Kenneth Rendell had faced when he had set out to examine the letter more than a year before: a scarcity of writing samples in the hand of Martin Harris. But they said they had uncovered three signatures of Joseph Smith's early disciple in the National Archives and the church had loaned them two other documents he had signed and a copy of *The Book of Common Prayer* containing an unsigned poem attributed to Harris. The report concluded:

Although lack of sufficient known signatures and writing prevented a definite conclusion, similarities were observed which indicate these writings were probably written by the same person. . . . These writings appear to have been normally written and no evidence was observed which would indicate forgery or an attempt to copy or simulate the writing of another . . . there is no evidence to suggest that these documents were prepared at a time other than their reported dates.

The FBI said it had also examined an 1829 contract for the printing of the Book of Mormon signed by Martin Harris, Joseph Smith and printer E. B. Grandin that Hofmann had sold to Gordon B. Hinckley for $25,000 and had found no evidence of forgery.

In Salt Lake City, Bob Stott received the report with a groan.

Now, along with Charles Hamilton and Kenneth Rendell, the country's foremost experts on forgery, and all of the senior Mormon historians, the prosecutors had to prove that the FBI was wrong, too.

At the Salt Lake City Police Department and in the United States Attorney's Office in Salt Lake City, the report was viewed as further evidence that if Mark Hofmann was a murderer, the murders had nothing to do with forgery.

"It's up to us," Ted Cannon told the members of the prosecution team, which assembled in the War Room after copies of the FBI report arrived in Salt Lake City.

"If we're ever going to convince a jury that Hofmann's a murderer, the first thing we have to do is *prove* that his documents were forgeries."

With its examination completed, the FBI returned the salamander letter and other documents it had borrowed from the church, allowing them to be studied by Flynn and Throckmorton.

Now much experienced at looking for minuscule fractures on the surface of highly magnified ink, they took only a few minutes to conclude that the ink on the salamander letter was cracked, as was the ink used in the printing contract and the poem in *The Book of Common Prayer* that was found in a safe at Deseret Book. The poem read:

*If this book should wander, and if you this book should find
Then please to kindly remember that what you hold is mine.*

They said the handwriting of Martin Harris in the salamander letter was virtually identical to the handwritten script of the poem inscribed on the rear flyleaf of the prayer book.

"Whoever wrote the poem wrote the salamander letter," Flynn said.

The corollary to Flynn's remark was clear to other members of the bombing task force: If they could prove the poem was a forgery, it would be easier to prove that the salamander letter was forged; but if they found it *was* written by Martin Harris, they would be proving it was genuine.

The Book of Common Prayer had a strong pedigree supporting its authenticity. Before selling it to the church for a few hundred dollars, Hofmann acquired it from Deseret Book, which said it had bought the missal in 1973 from a Mormon book dealer named Rounds who lived in California; then it had been kept in a safe at the store for twelve years. Curt Bench of Deseret Book said he remembered seeing a brief passage written in the rear flyleaf of the book before selling it to Hofmann.

During interviews with Dean Jessee, Brent Ashworth and Donald Schmidt, Michael George and Dick Forbes had assembled a list of the facts that were known—and unknown—about the origins and histories of the best-known documents Hofmann had sold. Besides *The Book of Common Prayer,* several others had strong pedigrees, or, in the lingo of document collectors that they were beginning to use, they had a strong "provenance":

• The Anthon Transcript, whose discovery made Hofmann a celebrity, had been removed from a 1668 Cambridge Bible that had apparently been owned by an ancestor of Joseph Smith; Hofmann purchased the Bible from a man named White who had purchased it from an antique shop in Carthage, Illinois, that was owned by a relative of Joseph Smith. Dorothy Dean, a granddaughter of Smith's sister, had given Hofmann an affidavit certifying that after he said he had bought the Bible from a man named White she had checked the store's records and found an entry in a 1954 ledger: "Sold on August 13 to a relative of Ansel White in California— $6."

• The salamander letter had come from William Thoman, a document dealer in Cortland, New York, who had gotten it from Elwyn Doubleday, an equally reputable dealer in New Hampshire who specialized in postal memorabilia.

• According to Brent Ashworth, Joseph Smith's letter ordering the chief of his militia to rescue him from the Carthage Jail had been acquired from descendants of an early Mormon family named

Huntington. Nineteenth-century history books confirmed that such a letter may have been found and retained by a Mormon whose last name was Huntington.

• Hofmann gave Schmidt a notarized affidavit signed by a descendant of Joseph Smith's scribe Thomas Bullock—Alan Lee Bullock, who was born September 22, 1918, and resided in Coalville, Utah—attesting that the Blessing of Joseph Smith III had come from a collection of early Mormon material owned by Bullock's descendants.

• The 1825 letter in which Joseph Smith described his money-digging techniques to his former employer, Josiah Stowell, had come from Charles Hamilton, a respected New York document dealer, according to Hofmann.

Dick Forbes had a skill other detectives might have envied. Like many Mormons, he had learned to peel back the leaves of history to trace his origins in the church's genealogy library, a repository of records listing births, deaths, marriages, property transfers and other milestones of human life covering many nations and many centuries. The library enabled Mormons to identify ancestors for whom they became proxies at baptisms, marriages and other temple rituals conducted to ensure that they someday joined their progeny in the Celestial Kingdom.

A soft-spoken and amiable man with short hair that was a seamless blend of silver and black, Dick Forbes had become expert at using the information in the library to research his own ancestry. But the experience had also taught him how to identify and locate people whose names arose during criminal investigations. It had paid off many times, no more so than in cases involving Utah's fundamentalist groups, some of whom still murdered under cover of the doctrine of blood atonement.

After Forbes gave Michael George a crash course in how to use the huge storehouse of information, they set out to find leads in the mountain of data that might help them solve the murders. They located several Alan Bullocks and several people named White who might have purchased the 1668 Cambridge Bible and identified relatives of a Californian named Rounds who had once owned a bookstore in Glendale, California.

* * *

While they worked to assemble the pieces of a genealogical puzzle, the pressure on Ted Cannon to file charges against Hofmann or to arrest someone else for the murders of Steven Christensen and Kathleen Sheets was unrelenting. News reporters began to speculate that Hofmann was a scapegoat for prosecutors who had embraced a faulty theory and had become too stubborn to admit they were wrong.

Gerry D'Elia suspected Stott was refusing to move faster because he was intimidated by leaders of the church and looking for ways to avoid calling Gordon Hinckley, Dallin Oaks and Hugh Pinnock as witnesses in a trial. "He's scared—all he cares about is looking good in the eyes of the leaders of the church," he told Ken Farnsworth, with whom he sided in what had become increasingly contentious and bitter battles each day in the War Room.

D'Elia savored needling Stott about the church.

After their investigators learned that the papyrus Hofmann had shown Curt Bench and Steve Christensen as a sample of the McLellin Collection was an ordinary Egyptian funereal document that had been sent to Hofmann on approval by Kenneth Rendell, D'Elia ridiculed Joseph Smith's claim of translating a similar example of the Book of the Dead into the church scripture called the Book of Abraham and called the papyrus "the curse of the mummy."

When one of her friends quoted Dorie Hofmann as saying "Mark is as honest as Joseph Smith," D'Elia said he agreed with the sentiment completely and hung up a sign with the quotation on a wall in the War Room near a note predicting Hofmann would soon find a document proving that Jesus, before his crucifixion, had summoned the "Hebrew Legion" to rescue him from the cross.

At a meeting in the War Room in mid-January, Ken Farnsworth demanded that the prosecutors take a vote on whether they believed Hofmann was a murderer or not.

"I don't think you guys believe he's guilty," he said angrily.

The outburst caused everyone in the room to start shouting, reminding Stott of a revival meeting. But he refused to vote.

"The key is not whether I believe he's guilty: It's do we have enough evidence to convict?"

"Everybody tells us Mark Hofmann is the most respected document dealer in America, that's he's a wimp, that he wouldn't hurt a flea," Stott said. "We've got to prove that he had a motive for two of the most brutal murders in America.

"Jerry Taylor says, 'That man's our bomber.' But you can't stand up in front of a jury and say, 'That man's our bomber.' We have to prove it."

The suspicions of Throckmorton and Flynn about cracked, runny ink did not prove Hofmann headed a conspiracy of forgers: They had to prove the stories he told about the salamander letter and other documents were lies.

Why did Hofmann and his accomplices want Steve Christensen dead? Worse, no one had a plausible explanation why he would have wanted to kill Kathleen Sheets.

Cannon began to join D'Elia and Farnsworth in pressing for a vote on whether to file charges against Hofmann. Stott took Biggs aside and lobbied for more time. He said Michael George and Dick Forbes were about to make a trip to the East Coast and California to see if they could find any new evidence against Hofmann and, equally important, undermine Hofmann's support among Eastern document dealers. Afterward, Biggs wrote in his journal:

I sided with B.S. and against T.C. & G.C. We decided to wait and get the results of our investigators' interviews back east—this will enable us to firm up the motive (why?) as a cover-up and delaying tactic by the defendant so no one would learn of his forgeries. Massive forgeries it seems now!!!

47

For the second time in less than a month, Michael George arrived in Palmyra, the birthplace of Mormonism, in arctic weather. This time he was accompanied by Dick Forbes, for whom the trip was a pilgrimage.

Religion was a source of tension between the two friends. George, a devout Catholic, resented the power of the church that ruled the community in which he was raising his family. He didn't think much of many of its doctrines. One thing he feared about the future was the possibility that his two daughters, Maria and Theresa, might fall in love with a Mormon; that meant he and Elaine George would be barred from her wedding in the temple as nonmenbers of the church. He knew that if this happened he might lose his daughters in other ways, too.

Forbes's love of his church was deep and unadulterated by doubt. Early in his life, he had drifted away from the church; he drank and smoked. But after his son returned from his mission, Dick Forbes became the final conversion of that mission, and he and Sally Forbes remarried—sealed for time and all eternity—in the Salt Lake City Temple.

Nothing Forbes had heard during the investigation of the bombings had shaken his testimony in the church. His faith was rooted in his own witness and acceptance of Christ, not in documents or histories. He believed that if Gordon Hinckley or other General Authorities had suppressed documents that were critical of or potentially embarrassing to the church, they had done so to serve its best interests. He had tried to imagine himself in Hinckley's place and concluded: "If I were in that position and I saw something that would damage people's beliefs in the church, I would have to weigh in my mind what was the best thing to do."

Dick Forbes had been offended by what he considered cruel and insensitive remarks about the church and its leaders by Gerry D'Elia and other non-Mormons who were investigating the bombings. At first during the meetings in the War Room, he tried to defend the church. Then he decided it was best to remain silent, and when he went home at night and talked it over with his wife she agreed. No one had written it down, but Forbes and Michael George had long had a religious truce: Each respected the other's right to his own faith and both avoided religious discussions. Forbes thought of George as a man of decency whom he would have loved to recruit into the church. But because of their unspoken truce, he hadn't tried. Since the beginning of the bombing investigation, however, he had heard his friend join others in the demeaning of his church and its leaders, and it had hurt him. He felt that Mike George had broken the truce. Still, on a level that transcended theology, they remained the best of friends and, if need be, each would have trusted the other with his life.

Forbes suggested a visit to the Hill Cumorah after they returned the journal containing Martin Harris's signature that George had borrowed from the library in Palmyra on his previous trip. His partner quickly agreed. If George had been in Rome on a homicide investigation, he would have wanted to see Saint Peter's Square.

They watched a promotional film on Mormonism at a visitors' center operated by the church, then drove to the top of the hill and looked out at a snow-blanketed valley that stretched far into the horizon. It was a beautiful spot, George thought, even in a snowstorm. He looked over at Forbes. There was a glow on his face.

At that moment, Forbes was imagining what Joseph Smith had been thinking when he looked out from the hill after the angel Moroni had given him the gold plates.

It was here where the last battle of the Nephites had ended. It was here where it all began. He had never been happier.

Forbes was silent as they drove down the hill. But when they reached the bottom he said he wanted to take a picture looking up at the crest of the Hill Cumorah.

George watched him get out of the car, take a few steps, and vanish.

Outside, Dick Forbes was airborne.

He had slipped on a sheet of ice, and as he did, he heard the bones in his right leg crack three times.

George lifted him into the car and, after discovering the nearest hospital was more than fifty miles away, he headed for it through the blizzard. But Forbes protested, not because of the pain he was suffering: He had come two thousand miles and didn't want to leave before driving past the home of Joseph Smith, which they did before continuing to the hospital.

An hour later, George wheeled his partner into an emergency room in the town of Newark, New York, and saw a television set encircled by hospital employees. They watched as the space shuttle *Challenger* rose into space and exploded in disaster.

Doctors said Forbes needed orthopedic surgery and would have to remain at the hospital several days. But Forbes said he had too much work to do and asked them to put his leg in a cast; while the doctors went to work on Forbes, George reentered the blizzard and drove to the Rochester airport to pick up Gerry D'Elia, who was joining them for an interview that evening with document dealer William Thoman.

With Forbes in the rear of their rented car, his leg propped on the seat, they headed for Thoman's home near Syracuse. As the car started to move, George turned to D'Elia and said:

"He got tripped by a white salamander on the Hill Cumorah. You notice the salamander didn't bother us Catholics."

Thoman, a dentist who operated his dealership in stampless covers as an avocation, was friendly and said he was anxious to help the investigators. He leafed through his files and confirmed that, beginning in March 1982, Mark Hofmann had purchased scores of stampless covers from him by mail, including many dated around 1830 from Palmyra and other communities in western New York.

The investigators had brought a briefcase containing the originals of many of the documents sold by Hofmann, including the salamander letter.

Like card players playing a hand, they began laying them down in front of Thoman, one at a time.

The dealer studied the salamander letter, the 1825 letter about money digging purportedly written by Joseph Smith to Josiah Stowell and Lucy Mack Smith's letter to her sister-in-law, all of them stampless covers with postmarks from the Palmyra area.

Thoman said he couldn't remember selling any of them. He said he usually read the covers he sold, but didn't remember these or any mentioning the name of Joseph Smith. Nor could he remember handling any covers containing a reference to a white salamander.

The interview with Thoman was not enough to blow Hofmann's story out of the water. But for the first time they had something besides cracked ink to cast a shadow over it.

At dawn the next morning, George, D'Elia and Forbes arrived in New York City for a confrontation with Charles Hamilton that had two objectives: to find evidence that Hofmann was a forger and to recruit Hamilton to their side before charges were filed against Hofmann. Kenneth Rendell was to be next. If Hofmann was charged with murder, reporters would immediately call Hamilton and Rendell; if charges were filed against Hofmann and these dealers again declared publicly that his documents were genuine, Bob Stott said, their egotism would make it all but impossible for them to later retreat from that position, and that would make them hostile witnesses.

Forbes, in pain and barely able to navigate the icy sidewalks of New York City on borrowed crutches, remained at their hotel while George and D'Elia went to the East Sixty-third Street apartment of Charles Hamilton.

Like the interview with Thoman, the visit to Hamilton was being kept a secret from the homicide detectives investigating the bombings in Salt Lake City because Stott feared that if their bosses knew about the trip, they would leak information about it to the newspapers.

On their way to the meeting with Hamilton, George and D'Elia agreed on a strategy for the interview: act like country bumpkins, let Hamilton establish himself as an expert, show him enough respect to lower his defenses, then undermine his confidence in Hofmann by proving that Hofmann was a liar.

Speaking slowly with a hint of deference and seemingly unsure of himself, George had little trouble establishing himself as a bumpkin; D'Elia, on the other hand, underwent a different sort of metamorphosis. He and Hamilton hit it off immediately and George knew why: Both were New Yorkers. Hamilton reminded him of D'Elia. Both were opinionated, sure of themselves, assertive, loud. New Yorkers, he thought, spoke their own language, and it made him miss Utah.

Hamilton acknowledged that he knew Hofmann well and said that he had the highest regard for him. He was shy and socially backward but Hofmann knew the document business and he wasn't a murderer. Hamilton said he and his wife, Diane, had dined with Mark and Dorie Hofmann and liked them both very much.

"We wanted to talk to you about this Josiah Stowell letter that you sold to Hofmann," George said.

"I didn't sell it to him," Hamilton said.

Hofmann, he said, had brought it to him; he had looked at it briefly and had charged him $200 for a statement certifying that it was an authentic letter signed by Joseph Smith.

"Well, Mark says you sold it to him," George said. "That's what he told President Hinckley in Salt Lake City."

"Well then he's a goddamned liar," Hamilton said.

"Are you certain it was written by Joseph Smith?"

"Yes," Hamilton said.

The letter, he said, had all the characteristics of Joseph Smith's writing, albeit in a more immature script than his writing as an older man.

D'Elia handed the letter to him and asked him to fold it.

A few seconds later, Hamilton said:

"You dumb son of a bitch."

"Who?" George asked.

"Me," Hamilton said.

48

"This letter doesn't fold right," Hamilton snapped. He walked silently to a file cabinet and pulled out a stampless cover and showed Gerry D'Elia and Michael George how it was folded differently from the letter to Josiah Stowell.

"The *seal's* in the wrong place," he said. "God damn it, this thing is a forgery and I didn't see it."

His guests had previously reached a similar conclusion after comparing the letter to other stampless covers. Then they pulled more examples of Hofmann's documents from their briefcase, beginning with the salamander letter.

During their visit in upstate New York the night before, William Thoman had said he was puzzled by one characteristic of the salamander letter: the way *it* was folded. The sheets of stationery used as stampless covers during the early nineteenth century, he said, were folded and sealed so that all four sides were closed, like an envelope. The salamander letter was folded so that it was open on the right, making it possible to look inside.

Except for a few legal documents, Thoman said he had never seen a stampless cover folded that way.

When Hamilton looked at the salamander letter, he said the

same thing. "This is all screwed up," he said. "That's not the way it's supposed to be."

Hamilton glanced at Lucy Mack Smith's letter to her sister-in-law, Joseph Smith's letter from the Carthage Jail to General Dunham and almost a dozen other letters Hofmann had sold. He pointed out examples of similar handwriting supposedly written by different people and other discrepancies.

"They're all forgeries," he said.

George showed him the Anthon Transcript.

George Throckmorton and William Flynn had seen no evidence through their microscope of cracked ink on the document that had made Hofmann famous and were uncertain whether it was genuine or not.

"That's a forgery too," Hamilton said.

"It's got the same fingerprints as all the rest. God, I was a fool."

When George and D'Elia returned to their hotel, Dick Forbes said his broken leg was getting so painful that it was best he return to Salt Lake City. But during a telephone call, Bob Stott asked him to go with D'Elia to Boston to interview Kenneth Rendell. Mike George, he said, had to leave in the morning for California, and at least two people had to be with the church's documents at all times.

Over dinner that evening at a Manhattan rib house, Forbes, despite his pain, refused his friends' entreaties to break the Word of Wisdom and have a drink to deaden the pain. Midway through the meal, they saw smoke rising from the floor of the restaurant and discovered that their briefcase containing the church's priceless documents had been set afire by a heater. Although the plastic skin of the briefcase was melted and scarred, the documents survived the fire unscathed.

The following morning, Michael George flew to Los Angeles while Forbes and D'Elia drove to Boston to see Kenneth Rendell, the dealer Steve Christensen and Mark Hofmann had retained to examine the salamander letter. They expected a tough sell.

Since the bombings, Rendell, who had a reputation as a proud man, had repeatedly vouched for Hofmann and ridiculed speculation that the salamander letter was a forgery. He had publicly criticized the investigators and made it clear he thought some of them were yokels.

He was handed the same documents Hamilton had seen two days earlier and agreed to examine them under an ultraviolet lamp for indications of erasures, overwriting or other clues of forgery. On several, Forbes and D'Elia noticed a bright blue glow emerge from the paper when the light was shone on it.

Rendell, D'Elia thought, seemed upset, even depressed by what he saw.

He couldn't be sure, Rendell said, but it appeared that some of the documents were forgeries.

The last document D'Elia and Forbes gave him was the salamander letter. Rendell slipped it beneath the ultraviolet light but the three men were unable to see the same tint of cobalt blue emerge from the paper that they had seen on the other documents. Rendell said it didn't look like a forgery.

They asked if he thought the letter was folded in an unusual fashion. Rendell said the way the letter was folded wasn't especially important. There could be any number of explanations for that. It meant nothing.

Still, Rendell said, the strong possibility that several other documents sold by Hofmann were forgeries suggested that the salamander letter could be a forgery too—a case of guilt by association. Still, he emphasized as the Utahans left his office, there were also substantial reasons to believe the salamander letter was not a forgery.

When Michael George knocked at the front door of an apartment in a middle-class neighborhood of Glendale, California, on January 30, 1986, he knew that much of the case rested on how he posed his questions to the elderly couple that he was about to meet.

Working in the church's genealogical library, Dick Forbes had located Verna Rounds, proprietor of the bookshop that in 1974 sold Nathan Harris's copy of *The Book of Common Prayer* to Deseret Book. She was living in Fresno, an agricultural city in central California. In a telephone interview, Mrs. Rounds told George she had acquired the prayer book in 1973, along with Martin Harris's first edition of the Book of Mormon—the second copy of the book to come off Egbert B. Grandin's press in 1830—from a descendant of Martin Harris's named Magee who lived in Glendale, a city near Los Angeles.

It was this prayer book that contained the poem purportedly written by Martin Harris that Flynn and Throckmorton said perfectly matched the handwriting in the salamander letter. If they could prove the poem was forged, Flynn said he was willing to testify that the salamander letter was also very likely a forgery and that the same person had forged the letter and the poem.

The prayer book had been in Deseret Book's safe from 1974 until Hofmann bought it in September 1985, a few weeks before the bombings. Although Curt Bench said he remembered seeing a poem in the book, Michael George suspected Hofmann or an accomplice had added the poem after buying it, because he had caught Hofmann in a lie about the prayer book: Shortly after he had purchased it for $50, Hofmann returned to Deseret Book and told Bench that he had discovered the poem and was able to sell it for $2,000 because the poem was in the handwriting of Martin Harris. Generously, he said it was only fair that he give Deseret Book $1,000 as its share of the windfall. Officials at the church archives, however, said they acquired the prayer book from Hofmann in early October, almost three weeks later than he claimed, in exchange for minor Mormon currency worth about $500.

Hofmann had not only lied about the transaction but, for reasons George was unable to discern, had taken $1,000 out of his own pocket and given it to Deseret Book.

When he arrived in California, George's task was to prove that the poem attributed to Martin Harris was *not* in the prayer book when Deseret Book locked it away in a safe.

As he shook hands with Reginald and Frances Magee, a thought passed through the mind of Michael George: He was looking into the very roots of Mormonism.

Magee was the great-grandson of Martin Harris, the man who had taken Joseph Smith's drawing of "reformed Egyptian" characters to Professor Charles Anthon at Columbia College, who had transcribed the first portions of the Book of Mormon and had mortgaged his farm to finance its publication.

Both Magees were in their seventies. Reginald Magee was ill and not very friendly. Mrs. Magee, George decided, spoke for the couple, and he directed his questions to her.

Martin Harris, she said, had been the last member of their family who was a Mormon.

She said that she was a Jehovah's Witness and that they had been forced to sell her husband's ancestor's copy of the Book of Mormon for $600 because they needed money for medical expenses. The bookstore had also obtained the family's copy of *The Book of Common Prayer* that had been owned by Martin Harris's father, Nathan.

It was important for George to frame his questions about *The Book of Common Prayer* carefully: If he simply pulled it out and showed the poem to the couple, there was a risk that they might reply instinctively that the poem *could* have been in the book when they sold it, weakening the testimony they might give at a trial.

Advancing cautiously to the purpose of his visit, George began, as he often did in an interview, by going over some of the details of his investigation and explaining why his interview with them was important to it. Then he started to talk casually about the book without showing it to them, hoping to plant a picture of it in their minds as it was when they sold it.

From her reaction, George realized Frances Magee had a vivid recollection of the prayer book, which she said had been handed down through her husband's family for more than a century.

Finally, he extended the prayer book to the couple and asked her to leaf through it.

When she turned to the last page of the old book and saw the poem, she said:

"This wasn't there when we sold it."

"Are you sure?"

"I'm positive," she said.

"How can you be sure?" George asked.

"Number one, I read this book a lot—I prayed out of it—and I never saw this in it. Number two, I love poetry; I collect poems, and if it had been there before, I'd have copied it down and saved it."

"Would you testify to that?"

"Certainly," she said.

As he prepared to leave the Magees' apartment, George said that he had become fascinated by stories regarding the life of Martin Harris and that many of the people he had interviewed during the investigation believed that someday the first 116 pages of the Book of Mormon he transcribed would be found.

"They were destroyed," she said.

"How do you know?"

Frances Magee said her mother-in-law, a granddaughter of Martin Harris, had lived in her home for many years before she died and had often discussed their family's history.

According to her mother-in-law, Martin Harris's first wife, Lucy, was so angry with her husband for investing money in Joseph Smith that when he brought home the 116 pages of the Book of Mormon to show her what he had transcribed, she read them and said, "This is the work of the devil," and threw them in a fireplace.

George left for Fresno, confident that he had solved the 155-year-old mystery of the fate of the Book of Lehi. Her account of the disappearance of the 116 pages was similar to that offered by the church, but one that had been disputed for more than a century. Here was supporting evidence from the family of Martin Harris himself long after it had become estranged from the church.

After leaving the Magees, George called Bob Stott in Salt Lake City and told him he thought they now had the evidence needed to prove the salamander letter was a forgery, regardless of what the FBI said.

"If the poem wasn't in *The Book of Common Prayer* when Frances Magee sold it in 1973," George said, "it wasn't there in 1830 either."

En route to Fresno, Michael George stopped at a nursery to buy several bonsai trees. The Japanese art of shaping plants into tiny trees and miniature forests was the passion of George's life when he was not investigating murders and other crimes.

He found Verna Rounds late at night in a driving rainstorm living at the home of a daughter near Fresno. She was in her eighties, a lifelong Mormon, and it had been many years since the bookstore she had operated with her late husband in Glendale had closed, but she still remembered the transaction: She said she and her husband had purchased Martin Harris's Book of Mormon and

The Book of Common Prayer once owned by Nathan Harris from the Magees and had sold them to Deseret Book for about $5,000.

Like Frances Magee, she said she loved poetry and was sure she would have remembered a poem if one had been in the old prayer book.

"My daughter," she said, "says my memory isn't as good as it used to be—but if you ask me, I'm sure that poem wasn't there when we sold it."

49

The interviews in California, New York and Boston by Michael George, Dick Forbes and Gerry D'Elia had gone well. In Phoenix, Bill Flynn said he was unraveling the enigma of the cracked ink. The developments convinced Bob Stott that it was time to move:

On February 4, 1986, Mark Hofmann was arrested and charged with the first-degree murders of Steven Christensen and Kathleen Sheets and twenty-three counts of theft by deception and fraud against a list of victims that included Gordon B. Hinckley, Brent Ashworth, Thomas Wilding, Alvin Rust and the Church of Jesus Christ of Latter-day Saints. Dick Forbes, recovering at home with his leg in a cast after orthopedic surgery, was called to the office to join other investigators and prosecutors in signing the criminal complaints that they had all been seeking since October 15.

Standing on crutches, Hofmann was arraigned before Fifth Circuit Judge Paul G. Grant and then locked in a jail cell.

Outside the courtroom, Ronald Yengich told reporters:

"Now we finally have something to fight and a place to fight it in —a court of law; we will show that he was not guilty, and you'd better believe it."

Three days later, Judge Grant ordered Ted Cannon to release a previously sealed court statement that outlined the prosecutors' basis for their charges. It alleged that virtually all of the Mormon documents that had made Hofmann a celebrity—including the Anthon Transcript and the salamander letter—were forgeries. It quoted Curt Bench and other friends of Hofmann's as saying that in the weeks before the bombings Hofmann had admitted he was in desperate financial straits and quoted a business acquaintance of Christensen's as saying that shortly before the bombings he had overheard Christensen tell Hofmann behind closed doors: "You can't hide that!"

Missing from the prosecutors' probable-cause statement was an explicit explanation of why they thought Hofmann had murdered Steve Christensen and Kathleen Sheets. That was because they were still not sure what it was.

The prosecution team was confident Hofmann was involved in a scheme to forge documents; it was likely he was not a forger himself but the front man for a ring of forgers. There was substantial evidence of fraud: He had sold documents—including the McLellin Collection, which he apparently never had at all—to several buyers at once.

But proving that documents already authenticated by experts were in fact not genuine would be difficult in court; moreover, even if they satisfied a jury that Hofmann was involved in a conspiracy to forge documents, they lacked a bridge to connect forgery with murder. And they were still unable to pin a case on his co-conspirators, whoever they were.

They theorized that Christensen may have been killed because he stumbled across a forgery conspiracy and was silenced to keep him from informing others. Possibly a second bomb was delivered to the home of Gary Sheets because Hofmann wanted to mislead investigators and divert attention to the problems at C.F.S.

But there were many other scenarios that had to be explored, including the possibility that Christensen, Hofmann and some of the young males they knew were homosexuals involved in a scheme to defraud, embarrass or blackmail the church.

The question of whom the third bomb was intended for—if it was not intended for Hofmann—was the biggest mystery of all.

Gerry D'Elia predicted that at the root of the case they would find a con game—another example of the get-rich-quick schemes that made Utah the fraud capital of the country.

"You guys think Mormons have a divine right to get rich," he argued. "You trust anybody; you've got no street sense; you can't get used to the idea that some people *lie*. I could sell gold bricks out of the back seat of my car for a quarter and half the state would have stars in their eyes."

Never avoiding an opportunity to needle the faith of his Mormon colleagues, D'Elia said: "I thought your Prophet had a God-given ability to see the truth. How come God didn't *reveal* to him that the shit they were buying from Hofmann were fakes?"

As Stott predicted, news reporters turned to Charles Hamilton and Kenneth Rendell after the public disclosure of forgery allegations against Hofmann.

Hamilton declined to be interviewed, saying that he expected to be a witness at Hofmann's trial. Rendell told reporters he had been shown a dozen documents attributed to Hofmann and several appeared clearly to be forgeries. But he said he was still unconvinced the salamander letter was a forgery. "There's nothing to show it was forged," he told one reporter, "but that is not to say it is real." Experts who had authenticated the Joseph Smith III Blessing for the Reorganized Church of Jesus Christ of Latter-day Saints were interviewed and told reporters they remained convinced it was genuine.

The allegations that Hofmann's best-known documents were forgeries produced a wave of disbelief among Mormon historians, several of whom had insisted to reporters they thought the police had the wrong man.

Five days after Hofmann's arrest, he was released on $250,000 bond at a hearing in which Stott tried unsuccessfully to keep him in jail without bail. Mark's parents and an aunt posted their homes as security for the bond. "He's told me that he's not guilty and that he would like to have his name cleared and the Hofmann name cleared," Bill Hofmann testified at the hearing.

"If a bond needs to be given," he said, "his word's as good as any bond you're going to get; he's an honest businessman."

The defendant's father did not tell the judge what he had told members of his family, that he had had a revelation from God, who told him Mark was innocent.

When Mark arrived home from jail there was a large sign, made by his family, neighbors and friends from the ward, draped across the front of his house: *Welcome Home Mark.*

The next step in the legal process that would determine the guilt or innocence of Mark William Hofmann was a preliminary hearing. Under Utah law, prosecutors are required to convince a judge that there is reasonable cause to suspect a defendant is guilty of charges brought against him before he is held to answer for the crimes at a trial. Hofmann's preliminary hearing was scheduled for mid-April.

As the legal machinery was being oiled for the first round of court proceedings in the case of *The State of Utah* v. *Mark W. Hofmann,* two other legal proceedings were getting under way in Salt Lake City.

J. Gary Sheets, the chairman of Coordinated Financial Services, filed a notice with the United States Bankruptcy Court that he was insolvent. Then C.F.S. followed him to bankruptcy court: The company founded by Gary Sheets said it had debts of $174 million and assets of only $9.4 million.

In another part of Salt Lake City the first grand jury investigation in Salt Lake County in eleven years was getting started. Its targets were the Utah Power and Light Company, which was accused of abusing its status as the state's largest utility, and the Salt Lake County Attorney's Office, which was accused of abusing its powers as the state's largest prosecutorial agency.

"It's a political hatchet job," Ted Cannon said when he was informed of the decision to investigate him. It was a partisan attack, he said, engineered by Democrats. Neither the decision to conduct the investigation nor Cannon's response to it was received warmly by local Republican leaders, who feared it would produce a difficult and embarrassing reelection campaign for Cannon and the party in the fall.

Cannon, however, told his closest friends that he was unconcerned about the investigation because he had decided not to seek a third term and would seek a seat on the bench instead. He was to learn painfully that it was a dream he would not realize.

50

With a pair of needle-nosed pliers, Michael George bent a coil of copper wire around the limb of a tiny evergreen bush to shape it. He rose up to admire what he hoped in a year or two would look like a solitary pine tree growing on the crest of an earthen hill. As he left home and drove to the County Attorney's Office, he saw one of the wives of a neighbor who lived in his Salt Lake City suburb. George's neighbor had four or five wives. No one in the neighborhood could keep count of how many children lived in the house. As a cop in Salt Lake County for more than ten years, George had learned long ago that polygamy had not ended when the Mormon church renounced its earthly practice in 1890. Periodically, articles appeared in the Eastern press about colonies of polygamous Mormon fundamentalists living in isolated rural colonies in the West, but during his investigations George had interviewed enough businessmen, mechanics, lawyers and other men engaged in "plural marriage" to know polygamy was very much alive in the modern Salt Lake Valley.

As he drove to work, he thought about Mark Hofmann. D'Elia was right; the case had the earmarks of another Utah con game. But it was something more than that. If their theory about the case was right, Hofmann and his accomplices—if there were any—had not been content with selling forgeries and making a financial killing. They were trying to change the history of Mormonism according to their own vision. From the perspective of the church's hierarchy, it was a dark and ominous vision.

The church—or at least some of its leaders—was paranoid in its determination to restrict the flow of information about its past to members and potential converts, and Hofmann had exploited the paranoia. The church had made him a celebrity by focusing on his faith-promoting documents, starting with the Anthon Transcript in 1980. But a year earlier, he seemed to have secretly embarked on a different kind of mission. In 1979, Jeff Simmonds, the Utah state archivist, said he had purchased a document for $60 from Hofmann that was surely not intended to uplift the faith of ordinary Mormons.

When Simmonds first mentioned the "Second Anointing" to him, George had never heard of it, nor had several Mormons whom he consulted about it. Then he spoke to Jennie Glover, who was the department's computer analyst assigned to the case and a devout Mormon.

Almost in whispers, she said rank-and-file Mormons were not supposed to know about the Second Anointing. It was a temple ritual administered only by the Prophet and limited to senior church leaders—Apostles and members of the First Presidency, apparently—that guaranteed them exaltation in the Celestial Kingdom. Other Mormons had to wait until Judgment Day before learning if their earthly works made them worthy of becoming a god. Those given the Second Anointing were assured of becoming gods while they were still mortal. It was a secret ticket to heaven, a case of rank having its privileges.

Hofmann, Mike George thought, was a blackmailer who had lived a double life. After ingratiating himself with President Hinckley and other General Authorities by producing faith-promoting documents he turned against the church with a vengeance. During the race in 1981 by Utah and Missouri churches to get the Blessing of Joseph Smith III, he must have realized he had discovered a lever to exercise enormous power over his church and that he could menace and manipulate its leaders with nothing more sinister than a sheet of paper.

From then on, Hofmann rarely sold faith-promoting documents that spoke of angels and gold plates but instead produced documents that assaulted the faith of Mormons with visions of salamanders and black magic.

Hofmann was the antithesis of the pious scholar-dealer he presented himself as. According to Mark's former fiancée, Judy Smith, he had turned against the church in his early teens but kept it a secret because he did not want to disappoint his parents, whom he loved and feared at the same time. Bill Hofmann was devoted to the church, and George wondered if his son had set out to hurt it, because disillusionment and fear of his father had somehow been transformed into hate.

As he drove to work, George wondered what it was like for a young man to be raised in the church: to be drilled in its doctrines from infancy, to be told constantly he must lead a life of *perfection* in order to be worthy of becoming a god, to suffer the guilt it imposed for masturbation, petting or other transgressions that made him feel imperfect and then to decide as a teenager that he had been the victim of a scam, to decide, as he told Judy Smith, that Mormonism was a *fairy tale* like the story of Alice in Wonderland.

There was a deep hostility—maybe even rage—within Hofmann, and perhaps that explained it. But it still didn't explain everything about Hofmann.

George thought about the thousands of coded file cards, each with a word from the Book of Mormon that detectives found in his basement office; he had paid a former college classmate thousands of dollars to catalogue every word of the Mormon scripture. Why?

The only motive George could think of was to analyze—and copy—the syntax, grammar and word usage of the Book of Mormon.

He thought of Frances Magee's *Book of Common Prayer* containing a poem supposedly written by Martin Harris and of other documents with Harris's handwriting that Throckmorton and Flynn said were probably forgeries: the salamander letter, the purported 1865 letter to Walter Conrad, the printing contract for the Book of Mormon.

* * *

If Hofmann was a forger, George suggested to Jennie Glover as they shared theories on his motives, he had made *himself* Martin Harris.

If Throckmorton and Flynn were right, most of the extant samples of Harris's writing were in fact Hofmann's handwriting. If he had chosen to, he could have written virtually anything he wanted and it would have been accepted as written by Harris, who died in 1875.

Until the bombings, the provenance of these samples of Harris's writing stood on solid ground: Dean Jessee had authenticated one Martin Harris letter, Kenneth Rendell another. Until the bombings, historians regarded the documents as coming from different, independent sources, a factor that strengthened their pedigree: Lyn Jacobs, not Hofmann, was said to be the source of the salamander letter; the safe at Deseret Book had yielded *The Book of Common Prayer,* where it was supposed to have been stored for almost a dozen years.

It was then that George decided that he knew Hofmann's ultimate goal: He was going to forge the lost 116 pages of the Book of Mormon, the pages Martin Harris transcribed as Joseph Smith's scribe and then lost.

The church had based the full weight of its claim to legitimacy as God's only true church on the literal truth of the Book of Mormon and Joseph Smith's account of its discovery and translation.

Hofmann, writing as Martin Harris, could have shaped the lost Book of Lehi any way he wanted it to be.

He could have made it faith promoting and sold it to the church, perhaps for the $10 million he once told Brent Ashworth he would ask for if he ever found it.

Or he could have filled the lost Book of Lehi with inconsistencies and errors or a prologue in which Joseph Smith acknowledged what anti-Mormon critics had long claimed, that he had written it as a novel, causing the church's fundamental piece of scripture to forever lose its credibility. He could have sold it to the church to be hidden away and then—as he had done often with embarrassing documents—made sure its contents were made public.

It was possible, George thought, that Hofmann could have destroyed Mormonism.

Perhaps that is what he wanted to do—and to get rich at the same time.

51

County Attorney Ted Cannon had spent seventeen years as a printer before he became a lawyer. He had handled thousands of galleys of type, blackened his face and hands with ink, pied enough type to print a Gutenberg Bible. He sensed there was something wrong with the Oath of a Freeman. But he couldn't decide what it was.

It didn't look as if it was printed with hand-set type. Something was wrong with the alignment of the type. In the white space between two lines of the Oath, the spine of a *d* on the bottom line was taller than the tail of a *j* that dropped down from the upper line.

That was impossible, or it should be, he thought.

He said he didn't care what the Library of Congress said about the Oath of a Freeman.

"You know what?" he told others in the War Room. "I think this is a piss-poor pasteup job."

While Ted Cannon was trying to decipher what he thought might be typographical anomalies in the Oath of a Freeman, Salt Lake Police Department detectives Ken Farnsworth and Jim Bell continued their search for a man named Mike Hansen. For months they had been frustrated by an inability to establish a connection between the receipt for a mercury switch and battery holder bought a few days before the bombings at a suburban Radio Shack store by "M. Hansen" and the envelope marked "Mike Hansen" found in Hofmann's home. No fingerprints had been found on the shredded bomb components that survived the explosions, and they had nothing else to link Hofmann or his associates to the bombs. ATF agent Jerry Taylor said it was a good bet the bomber had purchased other parts for the three bombs at Radio Shack outlets. Their only option, Bell and Farnsworth decided, was more leg-work: They assigned a new group of police recruits to check by hand all sales receipts for the six months preceding the bombings. It was a difficult task made even more difficult by a clerk at one Radio Shack outlet who, bored with asking customers to identify themselves, invented several names that he wrote on the store's receipts to satisfy his boss. One of the names he chose to invent was "Mike Hansen."

The detectives checked out every purchase by his fictional Mike Hansen and interviewed dozens of men in the Salt Lake Valley who were *really* named Mike Hansen. But as spring arrived in the Valley, they had still not made a connection between M. Hansen and Mark Hofmann.

In late February, members of the bombing task force decided to take another look at the material, stored in dozens of cardboard boxes they had carted away during the searches of Mark Hofmann's home and other evidence they had accumulated since October 15. They laid it out in the Police Department's gymnasium and, when they were through, it covered most of the basketball court.

Their goal was to find anything important they had overlooked before.

There were thousands of items: huge amounts of printed material, yellowed documents in plastic envelopes, tattered books, receipts, letters, doodle-filled notes Hofmann had written to himself. One item found in the mountain of paper was a note in Hofmann's handwriting with the name "Mike Hansen," an address on Twenty-fifth Street and a telephone number. But there was no ref-

erence to what city the address was in. Nor was an area code listed
for the telephone number.

"We've got to figure out what this means," Farnsworth said.

They dialed the telephone number using the 801 area code for
Utah, as well as area codes in California and several other states.
The people who answered the telephone calls said they had never
heard of Mike Hansen.

Jim Bell said he had been in Denver and remembered that it had
a Twenty-fifth Street. He dialed the telephone number listed on the
note preceded by the area code for Colorado: 303.

A woman answered:

"Cocks-Clark Engraving."

Farnsworth identified himself as Mike Hansen and said the IRS
was auditing his income tax returns.

He said he had some business with Cocks-Clark Engraving and
needed a receipt for the transaction to show the IRS auditor. The
clerk promised to check the store's records. When Farnsworth
called back several hours later, she said she had found his receipt.
It was dated May 18, 1984, and cited an order for an engraving
plate entitled "Deseret Currency." Cordially, the clerk promised to
mail a copy of the receipt to a post office box whose address Farnsworth gave her, a box used for undercover operations by the Salt
Lake City Police Department.

Until the telephone call, the investigators had focused on handwritten—not printed—documents. The next day, Farnsworth suggested to David Biggs that they make a tour of Salt Lake City's
photoengraving shops to learn if Hofmann might have done any
business in their hometown.

Their first stop was an aged brick building in an industrial neighborhood several blocks west of Temple Square whose ground floor
was occupied by the Salt Lake Stamp Company. After several
hours of rummaging through its records, they discovered a receipt
for $9.83 dated December 12, 1984, issued to a customer named
Mike Hansen for the purchase of a rubber stamp. A clerk produced
a copy of the stamp, which read:

Austin Lewis
3108 Harper
Berkeley, Calif.

Neither had ever heard of anyone named Austin Lewis. Uncertain of the discovery's significance, they took the receipt with them in an envelope used to preserve evidence.

The next day, Biggs and Farnsworth introduced themselves to Jack Smith, a small, taciturn man who had spent forty years making photoengravings in the same premises for the DeBouzek Engraving & Colorplate Company several blocks east of Temple Square.

"We've got several suspected forgeries that we're investigating," Farnsworth said, "and I wonder if you might help us."

Smith said he would gladly do what he could to help.

Farnsworth removed a copy of the Oath of a Freeman from an envelope and showed it to him.

Smith looked at it a moment, then studied it again.

"I made that," he said.

52

Farnsworth felt himself levitate.

"What?"

"Sure."

Smith went to a back office and brought out a receipt. It showed that a customer named Mike Hansen had bought a four-by-seven-inch engraving on March 25, 1985, for $34.13. Attached to it was a negative of a photoengraving entitled "The Oath of a Freeman" that matched exactly the document in Farnsworth's hands, a photocopy of the Oath that Justin Schiller had offered to sell the Library of Congress.

"Wait a minute," Smith said. "I got something else."

He returned to the back office and came out with a receipt for $47.59 dated March 8, 1985. It had been issued to a customer named Mike Harris and also referred to the production of an engraving entitled "The Oath of a Freeman."

But Farnsworth and Biggs did not recognize the text that was printed beneath the title on the second engraving. It was a long patriotic hymn to America that began: *"Give thanks, all ye people, give thanks to the Lord. . . ."*

They looked at each other in mutual confusion. Then one of them pointed to the dates on the two orders:

From records provided by Hofmann's travel agent, they knew he had flown to New York City on March 11, 1985, shortly before showing the Oath of a Freeman to Justin Schiller and Raymond Wapner.

He could have taken a print of the engraving that he ordered March 8—the one with the patriotic hymn—and salted it with other merchandise at the Argosy Book Store; then he could have purchased it for $25 and obtained a receipt for purchasing "The Oath of a Freeman."

Next, he could have returned to Salt Lake City, ordered the second engraving, had a copy printed from it and flown back to New York and shown it to Schiller, Wapner and Zinman.

Or perhaps, they conceded, Hofmann—or "Mike Harris"—had decided to have an engraving made of the genuine Oath of a Freeman. It was a new mystery to add to the others.

Although the discovery was a triumph for Farnsworth and Biggs, it was not a total victory: When they showed Jack Smith a group of mug shots, he said he didn't recognize Mark Hofmann or any of his friends.

Declaring he had accomplished "most of the things I set out to do," Ted Cannon announced on March 6, five weeks before the preliminary hearing was scheduled to begin, that he would not seek another term as County Attorney at the upcoming November election. His announcement immediately set off a race to succeed him, along with other events that soon would affect the prosecution of Mark Hofmann.

Homicide detective Jim Bell was not aware of the cloud that was forming over the County Attorney's Office when he sat at his desk in early March and wondered about Mike Hansen. During a search by hand of more than 400,000 receipts, police recruits had found sales slips for thirty-seven mercury switches sold by Radio Shack stores in Utah and Nevada during the six months preceding the bombings. They had tracked down and interviewed the purchases of thirty-two of the thirty-seven switches, most of which had been incorporated as motion-sensing devices in homemade auto burglar alarms. The detectives had been unable to find or identify the buyers of five other switches. Radio Shack's security department had scanned computerized logs of transactions at hundreds of stores around the country but had been unable to identify any of the principals in the investigation as buyers of mercury switches.

Perhaps, Bell thought, Hofmann or a friend had shoplifted them. If that was the case they might never be able to tie him directly to the hardware used in the manufacture of the three bombs.

With nothing else to lose, Bell decided to canvass some of the stores where sales receipts had already been examined, in case any had been overlooked the first time, and dispatched a police rookie to the Radio Shack outlet in the Cottonwood Mall where detectives a few days after the bombings had found the receipt for a mercury switch and battery pack issued to "M. Hansen" on October 6. Bell instructed him to go over the store's receipts for October 7.

Within an hour, the rookie returned to the police station and he presented Bell with a receipt dated October 7, 1985, for the sale of a $1.19 mercury switch and a battery holder to a customer named "Mike Hansen" who gave the clerk an address for a vacant lot. Later, Farnsworth and detective John Foster found at a Radio Shack store in Logan, the city where Hofmann attended college, a receipt for a battery holder and a roll of electrical wire sold to a man named "Bill Edwards" on the morning of October 16, the day of the third bombing. Edwards, as far as they could determine, did not exist.

Meanwhile, the search for evidence at engraving companies continued.

In the records of the Utah Engraving Company in Salt Lake City, Farnsworth found receipts for the production of engraving plates for promissory notes dated in 1852 identical to several Hofmann had sold for $5,000 apiece to collectors of early Mormon money. The only difference was that the documents he had sold contained a signature and an X, the mark of a legendary—and illiterate—frontier mountain man, Jim Bridger. The order for the promissory notes was placed by "Lowell Petersen" of Ogden, Utah, a man who, as far as Farnsworth could determine, did not exist.

The records kept by Jack Smith at DeBouzek Engraving also produced more surprises, including a receipt for the sale of an engraving containing a handwritten inscription:

To Buck and his human friend Austin Lewis who once said his dog is the best man he knows of. With affection,

Jack London

The Bungalow, July 22, 1903

Farnsworth examined a first edition of Jack London's *The Call of the Wild* that Hofmann had given to Ralph Bailey, a Salt Lake City dentist, as collateral for a $40,000 loan. The book contained an autographed inscription that was identical to the engraving, along with a rubber-stamped claim that the book was owned by a turn-of-the-century San Francisco lawyer and socialist:

Austin Lewis
3108 Harper
Berkeley, Calif.

The stamp was identical to the one a customer named Mike Hansen had ordered at the Salt Lake Stamp Company.

In Denver the detectives discovered that the address on Twenty-fifth Street "Mike Hansen" had given to Cocks-Clark Engraving when he ordered engraving plates for frontier Mormon currency was virtually identical to that of Dorie Hofmann's brother.

Because Hofmann's travel records showed he had traveled to Kansas City, the detectives went there and interviewed employees at each of its engraving companies. A clerk at Heisler Engraving said that in June 1984 it had made twelve zinc etchings that reproduced the *Latter Day Saints' Emigrants' Guide,* a rare, 1848 frontier Baedeker written by Mormon scribe William Clayton that was used by Mormon pioneers to guide themselves to the Salt Lake Valley.

According to the store's records, the buyer, "Mike Hansen," paid for part of the $389.69 order with a check for $169.69 that was signed by Mark W. Hofmann.

None of the clerks whom the detectives interviewed at engraving shops in Utah, Colorado or Missouri could recognize photographs of Hofmann. But at last they had a link between M. Hansen and Mark Hofmann. After the investigators discovered "Mike Hansen" had paid for part of an order at DeBouzek Engraving with a $2 check signed by Mark Hofmann, investigator Michael George quipped:

"You know, I think this guy was playing a game of catch-me-if-you-can."

53

Gum arabic, that's what it was.

When Bill Flynn had returned to Phoenix from Salt Lake City, he had faced two problems: to learn if it was possible to alter the physical appearance of handwriting enough to convince experts that it was written more than a century ago, and to discover why the ink on most of Mark Hofmann's documents was cracked. He decided the only way to answer the question was to pretend to be a forger himself.

Flynn began by mixing batches of ink in his kitchen sink and applying it to paper. Since iron gallotannic ink had been used for centuries, it was easy to find a recipe. But when he applied it to paper and looked at it under his microscope, it was sleek, smooth and black, not the reddish-brown color of ink on nineteenth-century manuscripts—and it wasn't cracked.

He questioned every expert on forged documents that he could reach; none had ever seen microscopic cracks on the surface of ink. He read dozens of books on ink, paper and forgers, but found nothing about cracked ink. In one old textbook, however, he discovered that nineteenth-century forgers had sometimes chemically accelerated the oxidization of iron gallotannic ink in order to make it look older, and he decided to learn whether he could duplicate the process.

He placed a drop of an oxidizing agent—first household ammonia, then sodium hydroxide—on samples of the ink he had manufactured.

Both induced a reaction that turned black ink into a beautiful shade of rust, the same color he had seen on Hofmann's documents as well as on manuscripts he knew were *really* centuries old.

The same transformations occurred when he placed a document in a jar and exposed it to vapors from one of the two oxidizing agents.

The ink now looked *old,* but it still wasn't cracked.

Flynn decided to vary the formula for his ink; several recipes for iron gallotannic ink he had found called for the addition of sugars and other thickening agents to increase the ink's viscosity and give it more body, making it easier to use. In Charles Hamilton's book, *Great Forgers and Famous Fakes,* he found a 1770 recipe for iron gallotannic ink that included as thickening agents nutgalls, natural growths on oak trees, and gum arabic, a thick, gummy substance secreted by acacia trees.

There were no oak trees on the Arizona desert where he lived, so Flynn was unable to include the former, but he managed to secure the latter, and he brewed a new batch of iron gallotannic ink containing a small amount of gum arabic. He wrote a few words on a sheet of paper with the new ink, exposed it to sodium hydroxide, then looked through the microscope at what he had written.

As he expected, the ink had lightened in color and was the dark brown, antique rust that he had seen before. Then he saw something that made him squint into the microscope a second time.

He repeated the experiment, then did it again. Each time when Flynn looked into the microscope he saw the same thing: *The ink was cracked.*

He marked another piece of paper with the stroke of a pen and, while looking at it through his microscope, placed a drop of sodium hydroxide on the ink. For a moment the ink remained as smooth as a lake covered by ice. Then, as he watched, wrinkles appeared in the ink; the wrinkles spread rapidly into an intricate and sinuous spiderweb of strands and swollen rivulets, then collided and intertwined and hardened into something that looked very much like the mottled and crusty skin of an alligator.

The sodium hydroxide, Flynn thought, must have stimulated a chemical reaction that caused the gum arabic to rapidly harden, become brittle and crack as it dried.

In early November, when he had first assigned him to the case, Ted Cannon had worried that Bob Stott might be intimidated by leaders of the church, an organization in whose doctrine he believed without reservation. But as the investigation proceeded, it became apparent Cannon's concerns were unnecessary.

When church officials refused to allow George Throckmorton and Bill Flynn to examine some of the documents the church kept in the First Presidency's Vault, Stott joined Ted Cannon in ordering them to be subpoenaed. And as preparations for the preliminary hearing gained momentum in early April, he let it be known that he would not permit his faith to obstruct the prosecution of Mark Hofmann in other ways.

To most members of the prosecution team, it was plain that Mark Hofmann had blackmailed the church. It was equally clear that leaders of the church were terrified that Gordon B. Hinckley would be required to testify against him and would be forced to testify, under oath, about his dealings with Hofmann.

From the first weeks of the investigation, lawyers for the church sought to head off this possibility. After charges were filed against Hofmann, they sought to have those listing Hinckley as one of his victims dismissed. Hinckley, they argued, hardly knew Hofmann. He had acquired documents from him only as a representative of the church and therefore could not be considered a *personal* victim of the alleged frauds.

Shortly before the preliminary hearing was scheduled to begin, David Biggs and Bob Stott met with Hinckley and one of the church lawyers at the Church Administration Building and, as Biggs later reported to Michael George, the church President "sat Stott down and talked to him like a father to a son."

Hinckley said it was not in the best interests of the church that he be subpoenaed to testify at the preliminary hearing; he said he was sure they could understand this. He had far more *important* things to do as a member of the First Presidency's Office than to appear in court; Hofmann's hearing was insignificant compared with the important challenges that he faced in his job; they had no idea how many problems were posed by the church's responsibility to carry the restored gospel to the peoples of the world.

The meeting lasted almost an hour, and again and again he urged Stott to withdraw the charges against Hofmann naming him as a victim of fraud.

But Stott was as adamant at the end of the meeting as he had been at the beginning.

"We're not dropping the charges," he said.

As preparations continued for the preliminary hearing, the prosecutors and investigators reinterviewed people whom they expected to call as witnesses at the hearing. During one of these interviews, David Biggs realized that businessman Thomas Wilding was not being candid with him. Wilding hinted that he knew something about the case he could not discuss. Biggs tried persuasion, but it failed to dislodge the secret. Then he called Michael George and asked him to join the interview. George suggested that until he got there Biggs should apply pressure on Wilding's lawyer to persuade Wilding to talk.

The strategy worked. After a brief meeting with his lawyer, Wilding admitted that he had the Oath of a Freeman.

It was the first time the prosecutors had heard about a *second* Oath.

He said Hofmann had given it to him in mid-September at a time when he and Harold Vincent were pressing him to return their money. He hadn't mentioned it before, he said, because the Oath, plus a few of Hofmann's books, was the only thing of value they had to show for more than $400,000 given to Hofmann.

"We want it," Biggs said.

Schiller and Wapner were refusing to loan prosecutors *their* Oath of a Freeman for an examination by Throckmorton. Now the investigators had a second opportunity to determine if it was a forgery and compare it to the negative found at DeBouzek Engraving.

"I can't give it to you," Wilding said.

"We're not leaving this room until we get it," George said.

"It's not here."

"Well, wherever it is, we're going to get it and we're going to do it now," George said.

Wilding said Schiller and Wapner had promised to market it after they sold the first Oath. If news leaked out now about a second copy, the value of both would plunge. George said the prosecutors understood his concerns and would say nothing publicly about it until after it was examined.

"It's in Idaho Falls," Wilding said. Harold Vincent, his brother-in-law, had it.

Four hours later, Mike George and Tom Wilding were disembarking from a small commuter plane at the airport in Idaho Falls.

George promised the pilot they would not be long: "Don't leave without us," he said.

In the terminal, waiting for them, he could see the stocky figure of Harold Vincent, a disconsolate expression on his face.

Silently averting his eyes from George and frowning at his brother-in-law, the woodsman handed an envelope containing the Oath of a Freeman to the investigator.

During the flight back to Salt Lake City, Wilding asked: "What do you think are the chances it's genuine?"

"Close to none," George said.

It was after 10 o'clock when Wilding and George arrived at the home of George Throckmorton in a suburban housing subdivision south of Salt Lake City. Ken Farnsworth and Dick Forbes were waiting with Throckmorton. They ordered a pizza delivered to the house while Throckmorton took the document into another room where he had a microscope and other tools set up for examining documents.

An hour later, he returned. As they looked up from their cardboard tray of pizza, Throckmorton was holding the negative of the first Oath of a Freeman that Farnsworth and Biggs had found at DeBouzek Engraving.

Wilding's Oath of a Freeman, he said, had been printed from this negative made in Salt Lake City—not on a printing press in the Massachusetts Bay Colony in 1638.

Mike George looked over at Tom Wilding and felt sorry for him.

Three days later, the preliminary hearing for Mark Hofmann began.

54

At first only a few people in the courtroom heard the sobs.

Matter-of-factly, Janet McDermott-Reynolds described her arrival at the Judge Building on the morning of October 15, 1985, her elevator trip to the sixth floor, the unfamiliar man in the hallway. She testified about seeing a package propped against the doorway across from her office, her indecision whether to pick it up, then her rejection of the idea.

Under questioning by Gerry D'Elia, she described the terror she felt when the bomb exploded, shattering the wall of her office and hurling her to the floor, and of cowering behind her desk in fear for her life.

"Did you hear anything at that time while you were over at the desk?" D'Elia asked.

"Yes, I did."

"What did you hear?"

"A very high-pitched crying."

"What did it sound like?"

"A little child dying. . . ."

As the sobs grew louder, heads in the courtroom began to turn sympathetically toward Terri Christensen.

Indeed, almost all the heads in the crowded courtroom turned toward her except that of Mark Hofmann, whose face remained fixed straight ahead, a blank, vacant expression in his eyes.

For six months Terri Christensen's stoicism had amazed her friends. She had tried to accept the fate God had chosen for her. She was certain she would see Steve again in the Celestial Kingdom; their marriage had been sealed in the temple not just for time, but for time and eternity. She and Steve and their children were an eternal family. Someday they would be together again, and knowing that had eased her pain.

She had been pregnant when Steve was murdered and had decided to deliver his fourth child—Steven Fred Christensen, Jr.—by cesarean section on January 9, 1986, the day that would have been Steve's thirty-second birthday.

"Did Mr. Christensen move at all at that time when you were standing there staring at him?" D'Elia asked.

"I don't believe he moved."

"How about the noises that you heard from inside your office? Did you ever hear them again once you got to your door and looked at Mr. Christensen?"

"They were coming from Mr. Christensen and they were much deeper by now."

Until that morning, Terri Christensen had been brave and stoic. But as the preliminary hearing in the case of *The State of Utah* v. *Mark W. Hofmann* got under way on the morning of April 14, 1986, she was overcome by grief as Janet McDermott described the last moments of her husband's life.

She sobbed louder and louder, and when she was no longer able to control herself, Jennie Glover of the County Attorney's Office led her out of the courtroom.

Spectators and reporters had filled the courtroom in Utah's Circuit Court Building for the start of the preliminary hearing. Seated in the front row were Bill Hofmann and the defendant's wife, Dorie, who insisted to everyone they knew that Mark was innocent.

Taking turns examining witnesses, Bob Stott, David Biggs and Gerry D'Elia presented a case that they hoped would persuade

Judge Paul Grant to order Hofmann to stand trial for murder and fraud.

At a preliminary hearing, it was not necessary for prosecutors to present their entire case against a defendant or prove a motive; the prosecutors were required only to show that a crime had been committed and that there was reasonable cause to suspect a defendant was guilty.

For Ronald Yengich and his partner, Bradley Rich, the hearing provided an opportunity to learn as much as they could about the prosecution's evidence and to pinpoint possible vulnerabilities in it before trial.

Bruce Passey, the jeweler who worked in the Judge Building, testified that he saw a man resembling Hofmann in the building's elevator shortly before the first bombing. Aaron Teplick, a thirteen-year-old neighbor of Kathleen Sheets, testified that he saw a gold Toyota van—similar to one owned by Hofmann—near the Sheets home a few hours before the second bombing. Gary Sheets testified that his wife was "one of the most loved individuals I have ever seen . . . a great wife, a great companion, a super mother, a great grandmother; I used to tell people the best job of selling I ever did was to convince Kathy to marry me."

Detective Jim Bell and Treasury agent Jerry Taylor testified why they thought Hofmann's remarks about the location of the third bomb in his sports car implicated him as a bomber. Taylor displayed models of the pipe bombs; to demonstrate how they were detonated, he moved one slightly and it electrified a mercury switch that caused a buzzer to sound with a sudden, strident signal that sent a cold chill through the courtroom. Curt Bench, Alvin Rust, Thomas Wilding, Wilford Cardon, Richard Marks and other customers of Hofmann described their dealings with him.

Brent Ashworth testified about his transactions with Hofmann only two days after his son Sami had died in his sleep after spending most of the preceding six months in a coma.

Contradicting comments he made after the bombings, Lyn Jacobs testified that it was Hofmann, not he, who had purchased the salamander letter from dealer William Thoman. Frances Magee testified that the poem by Martin Harris was not in *The Book of Common Prayer* when she sold it to Deseret Book. Jack Smith of DeBouzek Engraving described selling engraving plates to a man named Mike Hansen, and a state fingerprint analyst testified that Hofmann's fingerprints had been found on one of the orders placed by Mike Hansen at the Salt Lake Stamp Company.

When a clerk from Cocks-Clark Engraving described selling an engraving plate to a Mike Hansen who offered an address in Denver on Twenty-fifth Street, Dorie Hofmann sucked in her breath so loudly that others in the courtroom looked at her.

The address was different by only one digit from the address of her brother, who lived in Denver. The next day she did not return to the preliminary hearing.

At the end of a week of testimony, David Biggs wrote in his journal:

> I really feel as if we've missed the "glue" that connects the pieces of this puzzle together. The pieces don't seem to want to stay together. We have evidence, motive, murder, but it is all just a degree off. I'm still trying to find out what the problem is.

His journal the next day recorded:

> Hugh Pinnock testified today and he seemed to me to be like a fish out of water—completely out of his element and gasping for air. I guess, like I would be if I were suddenly made a G.A.!! I felt for him and thought how Hinckley must feel anticipating the possibility of testifying. . . .

Although Charles Hamilton was not called as a witness because he was being saved for Hofmann's trial, Kenneth Rendell, the bearded Massachusetts document dealer who had examined the salamander letter, testified that he was the source of the papyrus found in Mark Hofmann's car and Steve Christensen's safe-deposit box after the bombings. He said the papyrus was not part of a group of documents known as the McLellin Collection but an ordinary Egyptian funeral document that most collectors of papyrus would consider second-rate.

Under questioning by D'Elia, Rendell recounted his tests to authenticate the salamander letter.

"What is your opinion today of the Martin Harris 1830 letter, as you have termed the salamander letter?"

"There is no black-and-white answer on the salamander letter," Rendell said.

He said that after repeatedly reexamining its handwriting, he had discovered nothing wrong with it.

"To my understanding, everyone who has examined that letter can find nothing wrong. No indication of forgery in the handwriting and there is nothing with the paper either. It's a question of the ink and if a chemical link can be made between the salamander letter and other letters or if there is something wrong that can be found in the ink, but from my standpoint, I can find no evidence of it being a forgery. . . ."

Rendell said that because he regarded some of the documents sold by Hofmann as forgeries, he would not currently offer the salamander letter to a client. But he said its authenticity was an open question. "I don't think there is sufficient evidence to prove it is genuine; there is also no hard evidence that it is not genuine."

The following day, the preliminary hearing was recessed for ten days because Hofmann broke his kneecap. While trying to walk without crutches, he fell and fractured the wounded joint that had been mended by doctors at LDS Hospital after the third bombing.

Among the first witnesses Hofmann heard when he returned to the courtroom in a wheelchair were William Flynn and George Throckmorton, who outlined their theories about cracked ink.

They did not testify that Hofmann's documents were forgeries, but when Bob Stott and Gerry D'Elia showed them, one by one, the documents they had studied, they repeated, in words so similar that they became a litany: "I do not believe that the writing on the document is authentic writing for that time period."

Out of hundreds of documents they had inspected, Flynn said, only the ink on those sold by Mark Hofmann was cracked.

Gordon Hinckley was not summoned as a witness after all.

Judge Grant, a devout Mormon, later attributed his absence to the trial attorneys' concern for Hinckley's health. But church spokesmen said Hinckley was not ill, and in fact the reasons were more complex than that. Ron Yengich, Hofmann's lawyer, was no more eager to have the leader of the church that dominated the community raise the specter of his having been blackmailed by his

client than the church wanted a man close to its Prophet to appear
to have been blackmailed.

Yengich agreed to accept a statement—a stipulation—in which
both sides in the case acknowledged that Hinckley, acting for the
church, had purchased the letter about money digging supposedly
written by Joseph Smith in 1825 to Josiah Stowell from Hofmann
for $15,000, and the original contract for the printing of the Book
of Mormon for $25,000.

There was no reference in the stipulation to Hinckley's other
dealings with Mark Hofmann.

The final witness was detective Jim Bell.

"Have you investigated the motive for the death of Kathleen
Sheets and Steve Christensen as part of your investigation?"
Yengich asked.

"Yes."

"And do you have any evidence . . . evidence indicating motive on Mr. Hofmann's part for the death of Mr. Christensen, and
if so, what is the evidence?"

D'Elia jumped to his feet with an objection.

The prosecution team did not want Bell to answer the question
for two reasons: They did not want Yengich to know their theory
for Hofmann's motive—and they were not sure yet what it was.

After a fifteen-minute argument over legal issues, the judge told
Bell to answer the question, and he did:

"It's my understanding that Mr. Christensen had gotten the information from additional people to Mr. Hofmann, that if he
couldn't produce the McLellin Collection . . . he would make
sure that he would be charged criminally, that he would be
charged civilly, that he would be excommunicated from the
church, and that he would no longer be dealing in Mormon documents, which is basically his livelihood, and if he removes Mr.
Christensen, that's one thing he removes, is that threat."

"Okay," Yengich said.

Continuing, Bell said it appeared that Hofmann was afraid
Christensen would learn that the papyrus he had given him as part
of the McLellin Collection had come from Kenneth Rendell.

"Any facts which show any motive for Mark Hofmann to kill
Kathy Sheets?" Yengich asked.

After another objection by D'Elia, the judge said he could answer.

"The only one would be a diversion."

"Are there any facts to indicate a diversion?"

"The fact that Mr. Hofmann contacted Mr. Brent Metcalfe over the phone and indicated that, 'hey, everybody can rest easy now because the bombings aren't related to the Mormon document end of it, they're related to the C.F.S. end of the deal.' "

"And that's the only fact?"

The only other possible link, Bell added, was Gary Sheets's collaboration with Steve Christensen in financing research on the salamander letter.

After eleven days of testimony by thirty-nine witnesses delivered over five weeks, the judge on May 22, 1986, ordered Mark W. Hofmann to stand trial in Utah's Third District Court for murder and fraud. "There is probable cause," he said, "to believe that all of the crimes have been committed and there is probable cause to believe that the defendant committed each of the crimes as alleged."

Outside the courtroom, Ronald Yengich predicted to reporters that when the case came to trial, Hofmann would be acquitted. "A preliminary hearing," he said, "is just the first reading of the script play."

55

In the spring of 1986, much attention in the world of historical scholarship was focused on a small, fortresslike building eighty miles northeast of San Francisco. The building contained a cyclotron. Inside, physicists at the Davis campus of the University of California had developed a procedure for chemically analyzing ancient documents without damaging them: A beam of protons was accelerated at high speed into a document; when the protons collided with atoms in its paper and ink, x-rays were emitted that the physicists analyzed to determine the chemical composition of the paper and ink in microscopic detail. The academic world was abuzz with the atom smasher's success at solving a string of historical mysteries.

Scholars had long debated the identity of the first European printer who used movable type. Most believed he was a German, Johannes Gutenberg, whose printing of the Bible during the mid-fifteenth century was thought to mark the birth of modern printing. But others argued that more crudely printed items of scripture found in Germany indicated others had used movable type before he did.

The physicists at Davis helped resolve the dispute: They focused their beam of protons at pages from a Gutenberg Bible and then at samples of some of the documents whose origins were unknown. Their chemical analysis showed that a secret formula for ink devised by Gutenberg had been used to produce both the Bible and the other printed items.

Later, the Davis scientists examined a map owned by Yale University, *Vinlandia Insula,* that was the subject of another scholarly debate. The map had supposedly been prepared about 1440 and contained a crude outline of part of North America, suggesting that other Europeans had discovered the New World before Columbus. In 1974, particles of ink taken from the map were found to contain titanium and as a result it was branded a fraud, because titanium was a modern element. But when the University of California researchers examined the map with the cyclotron, they found only minuscule traces of titanium in its ink and the earlier cloud over the authenticity of *Vinlandia Insula* was removed.

In the spring of 1986, the scientists at Davis revealed another triumph: They said they had examined what was purported to be the first printed document in America, the Oath of a Freeman. After side-by-side tests with a copy of *The Bay Psalm Book* printed by Stephen Daye in 1640, they said the ink in both documents appeared similar, and they said they had uncovered no indications of forgery in the Oath of a Freeman. Speaking to a reporter, one of the scientists said of Hofmann's document: "Nothing about it appears to be fishy; he may have stumbled onto the real thing."

On the Upper East Side of New York City, the news was greeted enthusiastically by Justin Schiller and Raymond Wapner. A few weeks after the bombing, Hofmann had sent them $10,000 to finance tests requested by the American Antiquarian Society before it would purchase the document; antiquities experts at the Library of Congress said the cyclotron test should resolve the remaining doubts about the Oath's authenticity.

Schiller and Wapner said the examination in California simply confirmed what they had always known: Hofmann's Oath of a Freeman was truly the first document printed in America. When investigators from Salt Lake City asked to borrow it for their own examination, their lawyer replied that it would be sacrilegious to risk damaging such a priceless remnant of American history.

In the War Room, the test in California was viewed as a devastating setback. If Hofmann's original Oath of a Freeman was genuine, it meant he was not in serious financial difficulty at the time of the bombings after all—and it would be more difficult than ever to prove at his trial that he had a motive for murder.

George Throckmorton said neither the cyclotron test nor the previous tests conducted by the Library of Congress had solved the fundamental riddle of the Oath of a Freeman: Exactly when was it printed?

He said he had heard reports of a new process whose inventor claimed an ability to date documents to within a few years of their origin, but he had been unable to track down the inventor of the process, whose name was Roderick McNeil.

As the Salt Lake Valley began to swelter under the heat that each spring reminded its inhabitants that Brigham Young had led the Lord's Elect to a desert, prosecutors were more certain than ever that Hofmann was the bomber, but far from certain they could convince a jury of that.

In law school, David Biggs, Gerry D'Elia and Bob Stott had learned the same axiom that Ron Yengich had learned: If you don't have the facts, argue the law; if you don't have the law, argue the facts.

Almost certainly, Yengich during pretrial hearings would challenge the legality of some of their most important evidence. After prosecutors had obtained warrants to search Hofmann's home, the detectives working on the murder investigation had seized dozens of boxes of evidence. A judge could rule they seized too much material based on the narrow scope of the warrants, making some of the material—including the envelope marked "Mike Hansen"— inadmissible as evidence.

Jim Bell's decision not to advise Hofmann of his right to have an attorney present during his first interview at LDS Hospital—when Bell thought Hofmann was the victim of a crime, not a perpetrator of one—was a potential problem: A judge could rule that the content of the interview was inadmissible; it was at this meeting that Hofmann gave his account of the bombings that Treasury agent Jerry Taylor later claimed showed he was the bomber.

There were other problems: Neither Throckmorton nor Flynn could testify with certainty that the handwritten documents were forgeries. Although persuasive evidence linked Hofmann—as Mike Hansen—to the forgery of some of the printed documents he sold, the issue of whether the handwritten documents were forged came down to a battle of experts: Flynn and Throckmorton versus many of the Mormon world's most prominent historians, who still insisted they were genuine; and Hofmann also still had the backing of Kenneth Rendell, not to mention the FBI National Crime Laboratory; both had said the salamander letter did not appear to be forged.

Moreover, the prosecutors were still unable to undermine Hofmann's stories regarding the provenance of three of his best-known documents; the Anthon Transcript, which he said he found in a Bible purchased in Carthage, Illinois, from a descendant of Joseph Smith's sister; the salamander letter, which stampless cover dealers Elwyn Doubleday and William Thoman said they had sold to Hofmann; and the Blessing of Joseph Smith III, which Hofmann said he had acquired from descendants of Joseph Smith's secretary, Thomas Bullock.

The scope of the suspected forgeries, involving dozens, perhaps even hundreds, of documents, was too large for one person and there was an unevenness in quality that suggested a second hand was at work. Yet they still had no idea who his co-conspirator was, nor had they resolved the mystery of whether a ring of homosexuals was involved in the murders.

And even if they could convict Hofmann of forgery, the evidence of murder was thin and fragile, especially the murder of Kathy Sheets. The whole case was circumstantial. Dorie Hofmann would testify he was home with her when the murders occurred. Their only eyewitness was the jeweler at the Judge Building, and Yengich's cross-examination at the preliminary hearing had demonstrated he might be able to raise doubts in the minds of jurors about the reliability of his testimony.

The only link between Hofmann and the three bombs was his alias as "Mike Hansen" when he bought engravings and the Radio Shack receipts with Hansen's name, but no eyewitness could identify Mark Hofmann and Mike Hansen as the same person. Finally, they knew that Ronald Yengich could point to any number of investors in Coordinated Financial Services who had motive enough to be considered potential assassins of Steve Christensen and Gary Sheets.

When the prosecutors, under intense pressure, filed charges against Hofmann in February, they did not link forgery, fraud and murder as elements of a single criminal conspiracy but treated them as unrelated crimes. It had been a mistake. It meant Yengich might be able to persuade a judge to schedule multiple trials, one for murder, others for various aspects of the purported fraud, which would drastically limit their ability to argue that the crimes were connected. Since they had difficulty trying to explain this connection to each other, the prospect of having to do so at several trials was daunting.

Several weeks after the preliminary hearing ended, their fears were realized: Judges of the Third District Court ruled that Hofmann would face five separate trials, with the first—for murder—scheduled March 2, 1987.

As the summer of 1986 passed, the trial preparations became progressively less important to many members of the Salt Lake County Attorney's staff than a state of chaos that began to grip the office, rooted in uncertainties about the future of Ted Cannon.

Morale in the office had plummeted after judges had decided to impanel a grand jury to investigate Cannon and the 120 people who worked under him. Then came his decision not to seek reelection, which touched off a campaign to succeed him between his deputy, Roger Livingston, and Michael Christensen, another prosecutor in the department. Both wanted the Republican nomination for County Attorney, which was usually tantamount to election. After Cannon sided with Livingston, the prosecutor's office split into rival camps, and the split produced an enmity that far exceeded ordinary intraoffice bickering and backstabbing. As it continued, rumors circulated that some of Christensen's supporters were meeting privately with the grand jury and informing on Ted Cannon. Meanwhile, some members of his staff began to complain that Ted Cannon was undergoing a personality change. A secretary in the department's investigative unit whispered that he had flirted with her and had suggested carrying their relationship beyond flirtation. Another woman saw Cannon in his office wearing a wicker basket as a hat. On July 6 Bob Stott noted in his journal:

Ever since he decided he wasn't going to run for office Ted has
been a changed man. It's almost like he has lost his inhibitions.
He is constantly telling jokes about other people and seems to
have lost his respect and demeanor. He swears an awful lot and
is constantly making jokes about other people and constantly
talking about his past performance and keeps reminding us that
he would have won the election if he had decided to run but
decided not to because he was tired of it. . . .

Stott soon learned that the problems in his office had only begun.

56

When Michael George and Dick Forbes boarded an airliner at the Salt Lake City International Airport on July 9, 1986, there were so many unanswered questions in their notebooks that they did not know which ones to attack first. They decided to start with David Smith.

Since the beginning of the investigation there had been an undercurrent in their interviews of people who knew Hofmann: Many suggested that he and some of his friends may have wanted to embarrass the church because of an outrage they felt over its treatment of gay Mormons. Smith was a printer and occasional dealer in Mormon material who had traded documents with Hofmann and several of his friends. But during the hectic race to prepare for the preliminary hearing, no one had had time to question him. In the minds of George and Forbes, he had become something of a mystery man. As a printer, he ranked high among their candidates as the second member of the conspiracy. The fact that he was a homosexual added to their interest in him.

They found David Smith living in a Houston neighborhood that during the preceding five years had been colonized by gay men. When they met him, they were disappointed: His candor and openness quickly persuaded them that he was not involved in forgery or murder.

Smith said he had once traded a document to Hofmann and had spoken to him several times on the telephone. Although he had often heard through the collectors' grapevine that Hofmann was searching for the lost 116 pages of the Book of Mormon and had said he would ask $5 million to $10 million for the missing pages if he ever found them, the printer said he had never met the legendary finder of lost documents.

Smith was in his forties. As often happened to homosexual men in the Mormon church, he had been forced into an early marriage after returning from his mission. His family and bishop had hoped the sexual appeal of a woman would smother his homosexual desires.

But after fathering six children, Smith told the investigators, he had left his wife to live openly as a homosexual. Once he had left his family, he had never seen his children again.

"How do you feel now about the church?" George asked.

"I have a deep love for it. I hope some day it'll change and we'll be accepted," Smith said. "I was raised as a Mormon and it gets ingrained in you. It's hard to leave even if you want to. . . ."

Smith said it wouldn't surprise him that some gay Mormons plotted to embarrass the church, but he said the ambition of most was acceptance by the culture in which they had been molded—and that they had been dependent upon—since childhood. It was difficult, he tried to explain, to escape the tug of a culture that had been so pervasive a force in one's life for so long. He said he was trying through an organization of gay Mormons called Affirmation to persuade it to accept homosexuals as they were—a likelihood, he admitted, that was probably remote.

As Forbes and George left Houston, they felt certain that Smith was not one of Hofmann's confederates. In the jet airliner that carried them to their next stop, George looked out at the arid Texas landscape and found it hard to forget David Smith.

In many ways, he thought, Smith was in exile. He was an outcast from a world to which he still desperately wanted to belong.

When Michael George and Dick Forbes arrived in Carthage, Illinois, the site of Joseph Smith's murder, their mission was to destroy the provenance Mark Hofmann had offered for the Anthon Transcript.

In 1980, Dorothy Dean, a granddaughter of Smith's sister Catherine, gave Hofmann an affidavit declaring that after he had mentioned the name "White" to her, she had looked at the sales records of her mother's antique store and found a reference to the sale in 1954 of an unidentified item for $6 to a "relative of Ansel White in California" and concluded that that was the transaction that led to the uncovering of the Anthon Transcript.

Ansel White, the detectives had already learned, was dead.

In the materials seized at Hofmann's home, George found a newspaper obituary dated January 7, 1952, reporting the death of Ansel J. White, a construction engineer, in Lodi, California, at the age of eighty-five.

He called the cemetery listed in the obituary, where an attendant told him that at the time of White's death he had a daughter who lived in Angels Camp, a small California town in the western foothills of the High Sierras.

After several telephone calls to Angels Camp, George discovered that White's daughter had long since left the old gold-mining town, and he traced her to another small town, halfway across the country, Blue Eye, Mississippi.

When he reached her by phone, George asked if she knew whether any relatives of her father had ever bought a Bible at a Mormon antique store in Carthage, Illinois.

"I don't think he'd ever met a Mormon," she said. Besides, she added: "Nobody referred to my dad as Ansel. Everybody called him Joe."

She said she was his only living relative in 1954 and *she* had never bought a Bible or anything else in Carthage, Illinois, because she had never been there.

When Forbes and George arrived at the Carthage home of Dorothy Dean, they suspected Hofmann had somehow managed to alter her mother's account book and forge White's name to establish his provenance for the Cambridge Bible, and they wanted to borrow it so that Throckmorton and Flynn could look for evidence of alterations.

But after welcoming the investigators from Utah with a look of suspicion, Dorothy Dean refused to give up the ledger. She had enjoyed her minor role in Mormon history. She had liked Hofmann; she didn't like the detectives.

George, who had a knack for lowering the guard of even the most hostile people he interviewed, asked gently if she would remember whether Hofmann had mentioned the name "White" before or after he saw her mother's ledger. She thought about it a minute and said the name didn't come up until after she discovered the name in the ledger.

"Are you sure?"

"Yes," she said, apparently suspecting that her visitors doubted her mental acuity at the age of eighty-five.

She said there was something about the whole transaction that still bothered her: She had thought about it many times and believed her mother would never have sold a family Bible to anyone; her mother was a *religious person* who would not give up a Bible.

There was something else that bothered her.

When she was a child her mother had told her the story of how her grandmother—Joseph Smith's sister Catherine—and her family had been traveling during the middle of the nineteenth century on the Mississippi River, moving to a new home, when their raft was swamped and sunk.

When the raft sank, she said, *everything* the family owned was lost except a cow. Her grandmother's Bible had to have gone into the river along with everything else the family owned, Mrs. Dean said.

Although Dorothy Dean had refused to let them take the ledger to Salt Lake City, George and Forbes had something else to take back with them: her story about the swamping of the raft in the Mississippi. It would play well to a jury, they agreed.

Before leaving Carthage, the detectives toured the restored jail where Joseph Smith and his brother had died and other Mormon landmarks in nearby Nauvoo.

For Forbes, the visit was as moving as his pilgrimage to the Hill Cumorah. He sat on the banks of the Mississippi and thought of his grandfather who, as a child, had looked out on the same vista, and he wondered what it was like to have been forced by persecuting mobs to flee such a lovely place.

* * *

Two days later, George and Forbes interviewed Lyn Jacobs and Rick Grunder at Grunder's home near Ithaca, New York, a few miles from the Cornell University campus. Grunder had rented one of the three bedrooms in the house to Jacobs after Jacobs had insisted he had nowhere else to go and needed a place to live isolated from the tumult surrounding the bombing investigation in Salt Lake City.

Jacobs and, to a lesser extent, Grunder had long been suspected of being Hofmann's collaborators. Jacobs not only was a better penman than Hofmann but was considered smarter and more knowledgeable about church history and was widely known among collectors to be an expert restorer of documents.

Jacobs had told the detectives that he had Mormon friends who had acknowledged their homosexuality, but he knew of no plot by homosexuals to embarrass the church by undermining its story of Joseph Smith and the gold plates and substituting one rooted in the lore of black magic.

It was true, he said, that some gay Mormons had grievances against the church, but he insisted that he knew nothing about the bombings. And to repeated questions, he said he was sure Hofmann was not gay or bisexual.

As they drove away from the big wooden A-frame cabin in the woods, Dick Forbes asked George: "Think it's possible one guy could have really done all this by himself?"

"I'm beginning to think so," George answered.

57

It was in a small town beside a lake in the wooded hills of New Hampshire that the detectives finally unraveled the mystery of the salamander letter.

Since the beginning of the investigation, the most famous and controversial of Mark Hofmann's documents seemed to have a provenance as solid as the granite peaks of the Wasatch Front: Dealer Elwyn Doubleday said the letter from Martin Harris to W. W. Phelps had been part of a collection of stampless covers from New York State that he had liquidated for the estate of a collector, Royden Lounsbery. The covers had been saved for generations by descendants of Oliver Phelps, a relative of W. W. Phelps's who lived in Palmyra. Doubleday said he had sold the salamander letter along with other stampless covers from the Palmyra area to William Thoman, the Cortland, New York, dentist and dealer in stampless covers.

Before arriving in Alton Bay, New Hampshire, Dick Forbes and Michael George paid a second visit to Thoman to look over his records and, as a result, as they approached Doubleday's two-story white home situated behind a picket fence on the main street of

Alton Bay, they suspected they already knew the solution to the mystery.

Doubleday was a tall, youthful-looking man in his forties with a bushy head of dark hair. Scholarly, introspective and friendly, he led them to a second-story garret in his house that served as the headquarters and warehouse of Doubleday Postal History.

Stuffed floor to ceiling with books, stampless covers, envelopes and boxes stuffed with more postal memorabilia, it was like a museum. At one side of the office was a huge oak chest filled with small cubbyholes and glittering with brass—an antique, early American post office, Doubleday explained.

Doubleday said he had been bewildered by the attention that had befallen him since the news surfaced that he was the source of the salamander letter. He had been interviewed by network television reporters and featured in newspaper articles and representatives of the Mormon church had arrived at his doorstep urging him to give the church—not Hofmann—a first look at any future letters he found from the Palmyra area. Friends of Hofmann's—Lyn Jacobs, Rick Grunder, Shannon Flynn and other collectors—had pressed him to sell *them* the letters before showing them to the church. The church, he told George and Forbes, had even sent missionaries to visit him.

After Forbes and George relaxed him with small talk, Doubleday agreed to trace the history of the salamander letter:

He said that after his friend Dick Lounsbery had died March 10, 1982, Lounsbery's widow had asked him to dispose of what—to collectors of American postal marks and stamps—was a legendary collection. It took him several months to catalogue it and produce a catalogue that was sold to collectors for $50.

Because they were overshadowed by more important items in the collection, the catalogue did not include more than 20,000 stampless covers Lounsbery had collected and they were offered separately to dealers and collectors.

Many of the covers, Doubleday said, bore the oval postmark of Palmyra, New York. On January 14, 1983, according to his records, he sold a large selection of the letters to William Thoman for an average price of $25.

"Are you sure of the date?" George asked.

Doubleday scanned his file of correspondence with Thoman again and said he was certain.

In 1984, Doubleday continued, he was contacted by Jacobs, who was then acting as a document scout for Hofmann and who asked him what stampless covers he had in his inventory. Subsequently, Mark Hofmann called, introduced himself and said he believed he might have discovered a historically important letter that originated in the Lounsbery Collection.

Doubleday told the investigators that this had not surprised him. The collection was so large he had not taken time to examine the letters he sold to dealers and collectors.

Hofmann, he recalled, inquired if there were any marks on the letters that would identify them as part of the Lounsbery Collection.

Doubleday said Lounsbery had written a code in pencil on each item in the collection and suggested that Hofmann look for it. Hofmann later called him back and said he had been unable to find the mark; but he said he had checked with a photographer who had made a picture of the letter, and the photographer said he had erased it. Doubleday and Hofmann agreed the letter had come from the Lounsbery Collection.

"Did Hofmann ever buy any covers from the Lounsbery Collection directly from you?"

"No," Doubleday said.

Michael George and Dick Forbes looked fleetingly at each other. It was the answer for which they had hoped.

When they had examined William Thoman's records, they discovered that his last transaction with Mark Hofmann—for the sale of several stampless covers—was in March 1982, nine months before Doubleday had begun selling the Lounsbery Collection.

The only way Hofmann could have gotten a letter from the Lounsbery Collection was to have purchased it directly from Doubleday.

Doubleday repeated that he had never sold any stampless covers directly to Hofmann.

When George and Forbes reviewed the sequence of events for Doubleday, he agreed they were right: The salamander letter couldn't have come from the Lounsbery Collection.

Hofmann, he said, must have invented the story after learning about the collection and then calling to ask about the coding. Aware that some of the letters had come from relatives of W. W. Phelps, Doubleday had jumped to a wrong conclusion and unwittingly collaborated in the creation of a false provenance for the letter.

Fortified with this information, Michael George and Bob Stott visited the Brigham Young University campus in a bid to win over the historians who had insisted Hofmann's documents were genuine and who were likely to be called at the trial to testify on his behalf. But they were unsuccessful. Almost without exception, the historians argued that the contents of the salamander letter and other documents Hofmann had found were too consistent with reality to be forgeries; they meshed precisely with other evidence that showed Joseph Smith was involved in money digging, folk magic and occult practices that were a part of his times.

"What validates the Martin Harris letter historically," said Dennis Michael Quinn, the BYU historian who had been one of the most eloquent critics of efforts by the General Authorities to censor historical accounts of the church, "is the reference to a salamander."

Anti-Mormons in Palmyra who derided Joseph Smith's story about the angel Moroni, he said, asserted the Prophet had originally claimed the gold plates were guarded by a toad, but Quinn told Stott and George this was impossible.

"The word *toad,*" he said, "has a very satanic meaning, but the salamander has a divine meaning to it."

It was only after the salamander letter was found, he said, that researchers discovered the importance salamanders had played in the lore of nineteenth-century folk magic. It would have been impossible for a forger to know about the relationship beforehand, he said.

As they drove back to Salt Lake City from Provo, Stott said he thought probably nothing short of Hofmann's confession would convince some historians that the salamander letter was not genuine.

"I'm not sure even that would convince some of these guys," George said.

* * *

On September 21, Stott recorded in his journal:

We still have five months before the first trial. However, we are
getting a false sense of security because there is certainly enough
work that we need the five months for. The investigators have
slowed down and are doing other cases and both David and
Gerry have other cases. And although I have not had as many
cases, I still have things to do. The main thing is to keep my
enthusiasm and direction going. Probably the biggest problem is
with Ted Cannon, my boss. Since he made a decision about four
months ago not to run for office his whole personality has
changed. It's almost as if all of his inhibitions have been lifted
from him and he has become a very strange and weird person.
He seems to delight in mixing things up at the office and causing
a lot of frustration. He delights in surprising people and wreck-
ing the continuity. He has made many changes in the spur of the
moment which has upset many people. He has kind of reverted
back to some of his earlier days. At times he has taken up smoking.

   He has a great need and desire to talk dirty and swear and to
talk about other people and to dominate and control the conversations. Sometimes he comes in to the office looking almost like a
bum. Unshaven, hair messed up, clothes not matching, shirt tail
out. And the next day he will come in with a nice suit and all
spiffed up. His behavior is so bizarre and weird that almost everyone comments on it and almost to the point of working underground, just waiting for Ted to leave the office so things can
perhaps get back at level keel. The office's reputation is at an all-
time low because of the way that Ted has been acting. . . .

Michael Christensen, the prosecutor whom Ted Cannon had
spoken against in the Republican primary election, had easily defeated Cannon's deputy, Roger Livingston. Cannon had felt betrayed by members of his staff who supported Christensen, and
even his closest friends said he had become eccentric.
Livingston's defeat meant that if Cannon was unsuccessful in
obtaining a judgeship, Livingston would be unable to appoint him

to head the County Attorney's civil division after the election, which was Cannon's backup plan.

Cannon had other problems: His second marriage was falling apart. He had lost interest in the church. Worse, he had heard rumors that political enemies were trying to have him indicted by the grand jury. If that happened his dream of a judgeship would be lost forever, he knew, even if he was eventually acquitted. Yet Ted Cannon's problems were only beginning.

On September 22, *The Salt Lake Tribune* reported that the Valley's distinguished crusader against pornography and onetime bright star of Utah politics had been accused of trying to seduce one of his employees and of threatening to fire her if she did not submit. Shauna Clark, the twenty-five-year-old secretary who had once claimed Cannon flirted with her, accused him of requiring her to drive his golf cart at a tournament and of threatening to fire her after she refused to accompany him to his home after the tournament. She also contended Cannon had rubbed against her and made lewd suggestions to her.

At a press conference, Cannon called her allegations part of a campaign to destroy him politically. He said he may have joked with her but his remarks never exceeded the level of banter that went on in all offices and it was not intended to be taken seriously. Cannon pointed out that Shauna Clark's boyfriend was the brother of a member of his staff who had campaigned for Michael Christensen and claimed Christensen had engineered the attack against him.

Christensen conceded that he had arranged for the interview in the *Tribune* but contended it had to be done. "The problem that we have," he said, "is we don't have a mechanism in place in which we can remove an elected official like Mr. Cannon when it becomes evident that he has become irrational."

The question of exactly what was said or intended in Ted Cannon's exchanges with Shauna Clark would remain in dispute. But during the weeks that followed the people of the Salt Lake Valley would demonstrate a capacity for exacting justice on a fallen leader as decisively and expeditiously as their frontier forebears.

58

In the woods of Montana, after weeks of hunting for him, the prosecutors found Roderick McNeil, the reclusive inventor who was reputed to have developed a process capable of precisely dating an ancient document.

Of all the experts who had examined and approved Hofmann's documents—from dealer Kenneth Rendell to the cyclotron physicists at the University of California to the document sleuths at the Library of Congress and the FBI laboratory—none had answered a fundamental question about their authenticity: *When was the ink placed on the paper?*

George Throckmorton and Bill Flynn told the prosecutors that a forger could easily obtain samples of centuries-old paper and manufacture and age iron gallotannic ink artificially; if a skillful forger could mimic handwriting effectively, he could make a document that not only looked genuine but was difficult to prove a forgery.

Rod McNeil, a short, stocky, bearded man in his early thirties, had been a professional inventor since he was a teenager. Previous research had suggested to him that ink left not only a visible mark on a piece of paper but an invisible atomic tail: With the passage of time, ions from the chemical components of the ink migrated into the paper at a rate directly proportional to time. If the minute migration of the ions could be measured exactly, he decided, it might be possible to determine when a document was written.

Shortly before Michael George found him working on a new research project in Montana, McNeil had developed a method to do so. It utilized a device known as a scanning auger microscope to measure the invisible migration of ions from particles of iron used in iron gallotannic ink. The method was so precise, McNeil said, that it was possible to determine when ink was placed on an ancient document to within twenty years or so.

Over a period of several months during the summer and fall of 1986, McNeil examined several of the documents Mark Hofmann had sold to the church.

None, he said, had been written before 1970.

One by one, the team of investigators preparing for the multiple trials of Mark Hofmann had reached back into history to discredit the provenance of some of Hofmann's most celebrated documents, anticipating testimony by historians who would testify—insist— they were genuine.

After the interviews with William Thoman and Elwyn Doubleday, George and Forbes were confident that they could destroy Hofmann's provenance for the salamander letter. Charles Hamilton would deny Hofmann's story that he was the source of Joseph Smith's 1825 letter about a "clever spirit." They thought they could undermine Hofmann's claim that the Bible containing the Anthon Transcript had come from the antique store in Carthage owned by Dorothy Dean's mother. With the help of Scotland Yard detectives, Forbes had located a bookshop near Bristol, England, where Hofmann during his mission had purchased a 1668 Cambridge Bible, almost certainly the same Bible in which he claimed the Anthon Transcript had been found.

Destroying Hofmann's provenance for the Thomas Bullock Collection, however, had eluded them.

The Bullock Collection, he said, had produced the Joseph Smith III Blessing, a large amount of valuable pioneer Mormon money and the letter secreted in the First Presidency's Vault in which Bullock had accused Brigham Young of seeking to destroy the Blessing of Joseph Smith III.

To Mormon scholars, the Bullock Collection had been almost as legendary a lost Holy Grail as the McLellin Collection. For decades, they had heard rumors about a cache of papers left by the man who was Joseph Smith's secretary during the final years of his life and Brigham Young's scribe during the epic trek by the Saints to the Salt Lake Valley. When Hofmann hinted in 1981 that he had acquired documents from a descendant of Thomas Bullock who lived in Coalville, a small town north of Salt Lake City where Bullock had settled after the trek, the news did not surprise the scholars. Subsequently, Hofmann presented a notarized affidavit to Church Archivist Donald Schmidt from Alan Lee Bullock, who listed his date of birth as September 22, 1918, and certified he had been the source of the Blessing.

Yet no one had ever seen Alan Lee Bullock, including Schmidt, who promised Hofmann to keep his identity secret.

In the church's genealogical records, Dick Forbes discovered a man named Alan Lee Bullock who had an identical date of birth and was living in Colorado. When Michael George contacted him, Bullock said he was not related to Thomas Bullock and had never heard of Mark Hofmann until the bombings. He said he was a member of the church, however, and Hofmann might have seen his name in the genealogical records.

Bullock's testimony would undermine Hofmann's account. But the prosecutors feared Ronald Yengich might produce a descendant of Thomas Bullock who would support Hofmann's story, and this concern sent Michael George on his own search for the Bullock Collection. It led him to Coalville, the town where Bullock had died more than a century before.

In the city's telephone directory he found a listing for a subscriber named Maybell Bullock. When he called the number, an elderly woman answered and identified herself as the widow of one of Thomas Bullock's grandsons. She was in her nineties and not feeling well. No, she said, she did not know anyone named Alan Bullock, but said that when she felt better she would be glad to go over her family's history and genealogy with George. He decided not to press her for more information and said he would call back later.

In late September, he was reading the obituaries in *The Salt Lake Tribune* when he spotted the name of Maybell Bullock.

He scolded himself for not following up the lead sooner, then noticed that her funeral was scheduled the following day. The obituary identified a married daughter of the deceased woman who lived in Coalville, and he telephoned her.

He apologized for calling her at a time of grief and explained his interest in her family: He said he was trying to discover if anyone in the family had ever owned a collection of papers owned by Thomas Bullock, her ancestor who had been a scribe for Joseph Smith and Brigham Young.

Maybell Bullock's daughter said that her mother's death had been expected and that she would be glad to talk to him. And yes, she said, the family did own some of Thomas Bullock's papers. Some had been given away over the years to historical societies, but those that remained were in the possession of her brother who lived in Colorado. She said he was flying to Salt Lake City for their mother's funeral and offered to ask him to bring the papers with him.

The following day, George held the Bullock Collection in his hands. As the family of Maybell Bullock gathered for her funeral, he questioned each of them: None had ever heard of Alan Lee Bullock; none had ever seen a blessing given by Joseph Smith to his son; none had sold any documents to Mark Hofmann; all said they were certain their father, who died in 1981, had not done so either.

The family allowed George to take Thomas Bullock's journal with him so that it could be used, if necessary, as evidence against Mark Hofmann.

It contained page after page of barely legible, tightly written script that described in poignant detail life among the Saints in Nauvoo and preparations for their exodus to Zion. On June 27, 1846, Bullock wrote:

It is now two years this day since Joseph & Hyrum were martyred, & what a tremendous alteration has taken place in Nauvoo, surely it has fallen, is fallen—wherever you now look, Taverns, Groceries, Bowling Alleys, Ten-pin Alleys—Whorehouses, Lawyers & Doctors salute your eyes and ears, the reeling Drunkard, the boisterous laugh, the giddy dance, confusion and riot rule supreme—hundreds I might say thousands of houses empty where once happy Saints dwelt, sung & prayed. Fences nearly all down—gardens laid waste, fruit trees destroyed by cattle & all. In the last few years this spot has been translated from a wilderness to a garden & the most delightful spot on the River and is now again running to its native wildness & desolation. . . .

Bullock's journal described lynchings and vicious attacks on the Mormons by torch-carrying mobs, and disease, hunger and devastatingly cold winters. It depicted a casualness about death that sent a chill through George: A child would die in the morning, her coffin would be finished by noon and she would be buried at 3. After recording these events, Bullock would pick up the narrative of his life as if nothing unusual had happened.

Yet on almost every page of the journal there were expressions of hope and optimism that life would be better on the other side of the Rockies.

As George looked at the yellowed pieces of paper that comprised the chronical of a man's life, he sensed some of the excitement that Brent Ashworth and other collectors must have felt when they had held similar documents recording the saga of the Mormons.

For probably the first time since the investigation began, he thought, he was holding a real lost document from the Mormon past.

On October 1, 1986, the legal apparatus of Salt Lake County began to go after Ted Cannon with a fury.

After several days of closed hearings, a committee of the Salt Lake County Commission, the county's governing board, concluded he had sexually abused Shauna Black and urged him to leave office before his term expired, in three months. Although the committee conceded that Cannon might have been the victim of attempted "political revenge" and that he had a reputation "for a lack of seriousness and joking" that made it impossible to determine his genuine intentions toward the secretary, it said its investigation of her allegations confirmed that he had engaged "in both verbal and physical conduct of a private, sexual nature toward Ms. Clark."

Eight days later, Cannon was indicated by the special grand jury on six felony and four misdemeanor counts of forcible sexual abuse, sexual harassment, criminal defamation and misusing public funds by assigning one of his employees to political errands. The charge of criminal defamation was the first brought in Utah in more than fifty years; it stemmed from his comments three years earlier alleging that a local television reporter used cocaine.

Cannon surrendered his office while repeating that he was the victim of a vendetta. Virtually none of the county Republican leaders who had once courted his support came to Cannon's rescue. It was as if they had consented to his political execution.

"This is a shabby and degrading end," he said, "to a career of thirteen long years as a public-service lawyer. I accept responsibility for my intentional acts, of course, but I want you to know from me that the worst day I ever lived I did not deserve the vicious hatchet job I am today being called upon to endure."

The problems disrupting the Salt Lake County Attorney's Office as it prepared for the trials of Mark W. Hofmann were not over yet.

In the November general election, David Yocum, a local defense attorney who was the Democratic candidate for County Attorney, easily defeated Michael Christensen, whose tenure in a department tarnished by multiple investigations had worked against him at the polls. For several years, Yocum and Gerry D'Elia, one of the rising stars of the County Attorney's Office, had hated each other. Their feud began when D'Elia prosecuted some of Yocum's clients and enmity for each other spilled into the courthouse corridor where they nearly got into a brawl.

Yocum had been in office no more than a few days when on November 26, 1986, he removed D'Elia from the Hofmann case and transferred him to the department's office in southern Salt Lake County—Siberia.

Stott appealed to Yocum to reassign D'Elia to the Hofmann case: The first trial was scheduled to begin in three months, and D'Elia had carried at least as much of the weight during the preliminary hearing as Stott and Biggs and he was needed for the trials. But the new County Attorney resisted and told reporters he wanted to reduce the size of the prosecution team so it would not appear his office was "ganging up" on Hofmann.

Two weeks later, Yocum and D'Elia revived their public feud during a conference of Utah prosecutors. D'Elia, still the unreconstructed street fighter from New York, accused Yocum of being "in a drunken stupor" and criticized his integrity. Yocum denied his allegations, accused him of insubordination and, among other things, said D'Elia's hair was too long.

The next day, D'Elia resigned from the County Attorney's Office.

59

"Ron," Bob Stott said when he called Ronald Yengich in early December, "if we're ever going to talk, we ought to do it now."

In a kind of mating dance in which each partner concealed his level of desire while waiting for the most advantageous moment to consummate the transaction, Stott and Yengich began to send tacit signals to each other about the possibility of entering into a plea bargain following the end of the preliminary hearing. But both knew it was fruitless to negotiate one until Ted Cannon was out of office. Cannon blamed Yengich for his fall from grace. It was Yengich who, after Cannon twice failed to convict one of his clients, a former Democratic county official, of misusing public funds, had orchestrated a campaign in the press that caused him to be branded a petty and vindictive prosecutor. He would never make a deal with Yengich. Besides, Cannon said that if Hofmann was guilty of two of the most vicious murders in the history of Utah, prosecutors had but one choice—convict him of first-degree murder and seek his execution.

Cannon's abrupt departure suddenly accelerated the mating dance.

For months Stott had suspected that Yengich and his partner, Bradley Rich, had decided, consciously or unconsciously, that the case would never go to trial: In Stott's opinion, they had not interviewed many important witnesses, they had not submitted requests for some of the evidence against Hofmann that prosecutors were required to give them and they had not yet filed certain court motions that might invalidate evidence seized at Hofmann's home.

Stott suspected Yengich would be receptive to negotiating a plea agreement not only because of the weight of the evidence that had been presented against Hofmann at the preliminary hearing but because Hofmann's family could not afford to meet the full expense of his defense. Hofmann had once promised Yengich he would pay his debt by selling the Oath of a Freeman. But Yengich, like others before him who were promised the same thing, had learned that this was not to be the case.

Hofmann had lied often to Yengich since his arrest. This had not surprised or even annoyed him. Yengich expected his clients to lie, not only because they might be guilty of the charges against them but because of other reasons—to protect someone, for example. Still, when Stott, D'Elia and Biggs had unfolded their case against Hofmann at the preliminary hearing, Yengich had been impressed and surprised by the evidence against Hofmann. For weeks afterward, Mike Hansen was the topic of a good deal of gallows humor in his office.

As the first snows of winter blanketed the Valley, Yengich holed up at his home and for almost a week reviewed the evidence against Hofmann while measuring his opportunities to obfuscate the prosecution's case and sow seeds of doubt among jurors.

He decided the evidence of forgery and fraud against Hofmann would be very difficult to defend against, but the evidence of murder was circumstantial and could be attacked; indeed, he suspected he had a good chance of an acquittal on the murder charges.

Yengich and Stott had both been criminal lawyers long enough to know that Stott's telephone call in early December was inevitable.

It was the way lawyers did business. Each knew the strengths and weaknesses of his own case, the strengths and weaknesses of his opponent's case. They knew how the script would play out in court and could guess at the outcome; experience had taught them what their advantages, what their risks, would be in the court-room.

Both believed that Hofmann could be convicted of fraud and forgery, but that the murder case was a kind of roll of the dice whose outcome was unpredictable. Both knew they could remove their respective risks by entering into a plea agreement.

Above all in the minds of Bob Stott and Ron Yengich there was a practical consideration: If the case was ultimately not going to trial because of a plea aggreement, why should they do all the work necessary to prepare for it?

Stott knew the most important prize that he had to offer Mark Hofmann was his life, and he decided that it was a price he was willing to pay.

Even if he were convicted of first-degree murder, he didn't be-lieve Hofmann would be sentenced to death. The evidence of mur-der against him, especially the murder of Kathy Sheets, was cir-cumstantial and not easy to present to a jury. Hofmann was a young father without a previous criminal record, and as vicious as the bombings were, Yengich could portray his acts as the aberra-tional behavior of an otherwise nonviolent person. It was unlikely anyone would ever send Hofmann to stand in front of a firing squad.

Still, Stott knew that neither Hofmann nor Yengich could be sure of that—and this uncertainty was the lever that he intended to manipulate to persuade Hofmann to plead guilty.

To prevent leaks to the press, Stott and Yengich agreed to meet secretly without Biggs or Rich. Their plea negotiations began in Yengich's office and continued in his car as they drove around the Salt Lake Valley while Yengich picked up a set of uniforms for a softball team his office sponsored.

For a long while, the mating dance continued.

Yengich insisted the prosecution's murder case was weak and vulnerable. He volunteered that even though he wasn't being paid he expected to take the case to trial. Nobody should suggest money had anything to do with his willingness to talk about a plea bar-gain.

Stott was poker-faced. He interpreted the remarks as proof

Yengich *was* concerned about having to defend Hofmann at a trial that could last four or five months and not be paid for it.

"Here's our bottom line," Stott said:

In exchange for not seeking the death penalty, Hofmann had to plead guilty to murder and to at least two counts of fraud and forgery, including forgery of the salamander letter, and he had to admit that all of the documents listed in the charges against him were forged.

"What if he gives you a co-conspirator?" Yengich asked.

Like the prosecutors, Hofmann's lawyers had been amazed by the apparent scope of the forgery case assembled against him and believed—as had the prosecutors—that he might be part of a larger conspiracy.

"If he can come up with somebody else and we can confirm it independently," Stott said, "we'll consider a better deal."

Yengich pressed Stott to accept a guilty plea to manslaughter instead of murder. It would enable Hofmann to tell his parents and friends that he hadn't intended to kill Steve Christensen or Kathy Sheets.

"There's no way we can do it on manslaughter," Stott said. "It's got to be murder."

Yengich inquired if Stott would accept a plea providing only a single life sentence, an advantage to Hofmann when he went before the state Board of Pardons, which ultimately determined how long inmates spent in Utah prisons.

Stott agreed to consider it.

Yengich responded with a sweetener: If Stott was willing to accept a plea to two counts of second-degree murder—one with a life sentence and one carrying a penalty of one to fifteen years in prison —he would try to persuade Hofmann to meet with the prosecutors and explain in detail what he had done and how he had done it.

Stott liked the idea: Without a trial, he knew that mystery would linger for generations over the documents that had made Hofmann famous and with it would linger gossip about a cover-up. But he told Yengich he was skeptical that Hofmann would abide by such a deal.

When they met again, Yengich said Hofmann had accepted the deal and agreed to demonstrate his willingness to live up to it by meeting with the prosecutors even before the plea bargain was formally signed.

At that, a tentative deal was struck. Stott said that before it could be consummated he had to get the consent of his new boss, County Attorney David Yocum, the police department and the families of Steve Christensen and Kathy Sheets.

Stott asked Yengich if he thought Hofmann would really go through with the deal. When Yengich said he was sure he would, it surprised Stott; during the preceding year, he had come to suspect that Mark Hofmann, more than anything else, would not want to admit to his father that he was a murderer.

Very soon, he learned that he was right.

He also learned that his father wanted Mark executed if he was guilty of murder.

60

When Ronald Yengich arrived at the County Attorney's Office without an appointment a few days later and said it was urgent that he see Stott immediately, the prosecutor expected trouble. But he did not expect to be told the plea agreement was off.

Bill Hofmann, Yengich said, believed in the doctrine of blood atonement. If Mark had killed an innocent person, his father said he had to admit his guilt and be executed, and until they could resolve the issue, the plea bargain was off.

Stott and David Biggs were stunned. Hofmann was scheduled to meet with them the following day, and then the plea bargain was to be announced in court.

Hofmann, who had been unable to admit to his parents that he was a killer, had hinted to them that he might plead guilty in order to end the anguish he had created for the family by forging documents. But his father said that if Mark was not a murderer, he and the members of the family would devote the last breath in their bodies to proving he was innocent.

If he *was* a murderer, he said, he had to admit his guilt, request a firing squad and have his blood spilled to atone for his sin. It was the only way he could be reunited with the family in eternity.

"Can you help us?" Yengich asked. Stott said he would see what he could do.

Assisted by the church, he found a statement by a church leader declaring that blood atonement "can only be practiced in its fullness in a day when the civil and ecclesiastical laws are administered in the same hands." Despite what many of its members believed, the statement implied that the practice of blood atonement was considered inappropriate until church and state were combined.

After Yengich said he would give the statement to Hofmann, Bob Stott wondered if he were the first prosecutor in history who had ever been enlisted to persuade a father that his son should not be executed by a firing squad.

Several days later, on January 7, 1987, Stott and David Biggs drove to Yengich's home in a middle-class neighborhood of Salt Lake City and knocked on the front door. Yengich's dog barked at the knock. Yengich opened the door and the prosecutors saw Hofmann standing a few feet behind him. They did not shake hands.

Yengich led them to his dining room table and then, as the four men sat around the table sipping fruit juice and eating sweet rolls, the former missionary confessed that he had killed Steven Christensen and Kathleen Sheets.

The prosecutors began the interview by asking Hofmann about his childhood. Michael George had advised them to break the ice by putting him at ease with innocuous questions before asking him about murder.

But Stott and Biggs discovered quickly that Hofmann *wanted* to talk about the murders.

He said he had done it all himself. No one else had been involved in the murders or the forgery of documents.

Words spewed out of his mouth as if he had a mental checklist and was in a hurry to complete it in proper order. He said he had always been interested in explosives and had built his first bomb when he was in elementary school after discovering a formula for black powder in *The World Book Encyclopedia.*

Then Hofmann discussed building the bombs that killed and

mutilated Steven Christensen and Kathy Sheets as matter-of-factly as if he had been talking about mowing his lawn.

He described shopping for the mercury switches and battery holders for the first two bombs at the Cottonwood Mall Radio Shack store, visiting a toy store to buy model rocket igniters, then waiting at a hardware store while threads were cut in the ends of two twelve-inch lengths of one-inch galvanized pipe.

Then he told how he packed the lengths of pipe with black powder.

"They were very simple . . . very simple to build," he said. "Why did you put nails around the bomb at the Judge Building?"

Hofmann replied that he had read somewhere that wrapping nails around a pipe bomb made it more lethal.

As he continued, Stott and Biggs felt an ugly lump form in their stomachs: Hofmann was *boasting* about the bombs that had taken the lives of Steven Christensen and Kathy Sheets.

He was condescending, even arrogant about the bombs.

Describing the meeting in his journal, Stott recollected:

It was an amazing scene. He was very concerned about the details and he wanted to go over the details time after time after time with us and he would relate minute, small details that seemed important to him, as if he wanted to make sure we believed him and verified it and to show how much he had thought things out.

He wanted to let us know that the pipe bomb was his own construction, that he pretty well thought the thing out himself. He was very, very proud of it and even drew a diagram for us showing how really simple the pipe bombs were. It was just basically identical to what Jerry Taylor, our ATF expert, figured out from the debris.

After almost two hours, Yengich said it was time to end the interview. Hofmann looked at him impatiently and said he wanted to finish his account of assembling and testing the bombs. Yengich prevailed and they recessed until the morning.

As he left Yengich's house, Stott, the meticulous prosecutor who had been criticized for being too cautious, too conservative, even too dull, could think to himself: After fifteen months, it was *over*. He had *won*.

His strategy had worked. If he had listened to the federal prosecutors who didn't believe Hofmann was a forger, if he had listened to the Salt Lake City Police Department officials who had pushed him to file charges against Hofmann before he was ready, they would not have unraveled the intricate scheme of forgery and fraud that had produced two murders. The story Hofmann was unfolding was exactly what he, Biggs, D'Elia, Cannon and the investigators had thought it would be. From now on, Stott thought, everything else would seem anticlimactic.

After they returned to the County Attorney's Office, David Biggs asked Stott: "Did you see *any* sign of remorse or guilt in Hofmann?"

"No," Stott said.

The following morning the four men met again around the dining table. Stott and Biggs brought a carton of milk and doughnuts for the group to share while Hofmann continued his chronicle of horrors.

He said he decided to kill *someone* on October 4, the day following his late-night visit with Steve Christensen at the home of Hugh Pinnock. He said he didn't know *whom* he would kill, but murder was the only avenue he saw open to him that could relieve the mounting pressure he was under to pay his debts. One way or another, he said, he had to kill to buy time until the Oath of a Freeman was sold.

Hofmann said he first thought about killing Tom Wilding, who was pressing him hardest for money. Then he considered Brent Ashworth, implying that he might try to link Ashworth's death to a disappearance of the McLellin Collection.

Then, Hofmann said, he began to consider Steve Christensen as a candidate for extermination.

After buying the components for the bombs the following day, Hofmann said, he confirmed their design with an electrical lighting tester he purchased at the Radio Shack store in the Cottonwood Mall. He connected flashlight batteries to a mercury switch and tilted it ninety degrees; when the light on the test instrument flickered, he said he knew an electrical circuit had been completed and, if it had been connected to a bomb, the bomb would have exploded.

On October 10, Hofmann said, he drove to an isolated desert area twenty miles west of Salt Lake City for another test of the design. En route, he was stopped by a policeman for speeding. The desert was too wet and muddy and he returned home.

The next day, Hofmann said, he returned to the desert and found a dry spot hidden from the road by a small hill. He ran a fifty-foot electrical cord to a model rocket igniter that was connected to a piece of pipe stuffed with black powder. Then he touched the opposite end of the wire to several flashlight batteries and the bomb exploded with a sound that rumbled like a gunshot across the alkaline desert wasteland.

Hofmann said he was now certain the bomb he had designed would accomplish the mission for which it was intended.

Next, he had to decide whom he was going to kill.

61

It was not until after midnight on October 15—as he assembled the bombs in his basement—that Mark Hofmann decided to whom he was going to deliver his fatal parcels. If he killed Steve Christensen, he decided, Christensen would not be around to inform Tom Wilding that the $185,000 payment for the McLellin Collection was not intended for Wilding's investors. And most important, Christensen would not be available later in the day to authenticate the McLellin Collection. The sale of the Collection would be postponed and at least temporarily he would be relieved of pressure to produce a collection of documents that did not exist.

Hofmann must have been shocked, Biggs thought, when church leaders informed him a few hours after the bombings that they *still* expected him to proceed with the sale of the McLellin Collection the following day, despite Christensen's death.

From Hofmann's point of view, Biggs thought, the execution of Steven Christensen and Kathy Sheets had accomplished nothing. He had killed two people and the church still demanded that he produce the McLellin Collection.

Hofmann explained that his goal in leaving a bomb addressed to Sheets was to create a diversion and confuse the police. He said he was aware of the financial problems at C.F.S. and believed Sheets's murder, coupled with Christensen's death, would focus attention on the company and away from him.

As if to make it clear to the prosecutors that he was not stupid, he said that Kathy Sheets's death had done exactly that—at least for a while.

After deciding who his victims were to be, Hofmann said he wrote the names of Gary Sheets and Steve Christensen on cardboard boxes containing the two bombs, looked up Sheets's address in a telephone directory and drove to his home about 3 o'clock on the morning of October 15.

He said he entered the driveway in the darkness, got out of his van and left his first package standing upright near the garage door. He was amazed, he said, when he later learned that Gary Sheets had driven his BMW out the driveway hours before the death of his wife and wondered why it had not detonated the bomb.

A different thought passed through the mind of David Biggs: Shortly after Sheets drove out of the driveway, the parents of a child who participated in a car pool with Sheets's fifteen-year-old son drove up the driveway. The bomb, he thought, could have annihilated a carload of teenagers.

Hofmann said he wanted to correct Treasury agent Jerry Taylor, who had testified at the preliminary hearing that the bombs did not have safety devices to render them harmless while being transported. He said he had designed the bombs with a gap in the circuitry that served as a safety device: Two wires extended from each bomb and were taped to the outsides of the packages. After placing the bombs where he wanted them, he twisted the wires together, completing the circuit and arming the bombs. When they were tilted, the electrical circuit was closed and the bombs exploded.

After leaving the bomb at the Sheets home, Hofmann said, he returned to his own home. When he walked into the house at about 3:30 A.M., his daughter was crying and his wife, who was accustomed to his working through the night in his basement office, asked him to console the child. She went back to sleep, but Hofmann said he did not go to bed at all that night.

Shortly before 6:30 A.M., he said, he drove to downtown Salt

Lake City and parked outside the Judge Building. He rode the elevator alone to the sixth floor, confirmed the location of Christensen's office, returned to his van and collected the second bomb. On his second elevator trip to the sixth floor, he was accompanied by three passengers—jewelers Bruce and Hal Passey and a woman whom he described as good-looking; it was the first time the prosecutors had heard about the existence of this other potential witness on the elevator.

At the sixth floor he left the elevator and placed the bomb against the door of Suite 609, twisted the two safety wires together and left. He said he did not see Janet McDermott or anyone else on the sixth floor.

Hofmann said he returned to his home and arrived just as the chimes of a living-room clock were announcing that it was 7 o'clock. Dorie Hofmann, he suggested, had passed a lie-detector test, establishing the alibi that he was at home with her all night, because he had been there when they spoke at 3:30 and again at 7 o'clock, and because one of his sons had told her he had spent the night working in his office.

Hofmann said he placed only about half as much black powder in the bomb that he left at the home of Gary Sheets as in the bomb left for Christensen. Because it was intended only to divert attention to C.F.S., he said he didn't really care if it killed anyone.

On the other hand, Stott thought, *he hadn't cared if he did kill somebody.*

He thought of the horribly mutilated body of Kathy Sheets, then thought of Janet McDermott, who had come so near to picking up the bomb at the Judge Building.

"Weren't you concerned someone else might pick up the bomb and get killed instead of Steve Christensen?" Stott asked.

"It really didn't matter," Hofmann said. "Even if Steve wasn't injured or killed, he would have never figured out it was me."

What a curious answer to his question, Stott thought. Biggs asked why he decided to use bombs rather than other weapons for the murders.

After hesitating for a long moment, Hofmann replied that he did not have enough nerve to point a gun at someone and shoot him face to face—he wanted to be as far away as possible when his victims died.

"Why did you use 'Mike Hansen' so much and wear your letterman's jacket to the Judge Building?" Biggs inquired. "Weren't you afraid people might remember it?"

"I probably wore the jacket when I bought all the stuff for the bombs, too," Hofmann said.

"Maybe subconsciously I wanted to leave some clues. I don't know; maybe I felt, if people were mad enough to come after me, I'd give them some clues. Maybe I wanted to tempt fate."

He said he first used the name "Mike Hansen" in 1979 when he checked out a book at the Utah State University library and had slipped into the habit of using the alias whenever he wanted to conceal his identity.

Hofmann said he decided to build a third bomb on the evening of October 15, after church leaders had pressured him to come up with the McLellin Collection even after the death of Steve Christensen.

The prosecutors asked whom the bomb was intended for.

"Me," Hofmann answered.

He said he was distraught and worried that he would be caught and his family would be embarrassed.

He said his plan was to kill himself in an explosion that produced a lot of debris, including a piece of papyrus and other documents that other people would surmise were parts of the McLellin Collection.

"I wanted to leave a mystery surrounding the McLellin Collection," he said.

Neither Stott nor Biggs believed Hofmann's story that he intended to commit suicide with the third bomb.

Stott thought it was probably his plan to destroy a group of documents that he could claim was the McLellin Collection. But Hofmann, he believed, intended the bomb blast to look like an unsuccessful attempt on his life.

Biggs thought the third bomb was intended for another victim, possibly Brent Ashworth, who usually met Hofmann in Salt Lake City on Wednesday afternoons a few blocks from where Hofmann's car was parked. If Ashworth had not skipped his regular rendezvous with Hofmann, it would have been an easy thing for Hofmann to lure him to the car with the promise of an opportunity to see the McLellin Collection. Another possibility was Al Rust, whose murder Hofmann could have used to explain his inability to produce the McLellin Collection.

Stott suggested they talk about the salamander letter.

"That's a forgery," Hofmann said before Stott could say another word.

Yengich announced that it was time to break up the meeting, but Hofmann said he wanted to continue, and he did.

As the topic shifted from murder to forgery, words flowed out of Hofmann, once again, in a torrent: He said he had stolen the paper he used to forge the letter from an eighteenth-century book in the University of Utah library; he said he had made his own engraving of an 1830 postmark, and wrote out the words supposedly addressed by Martin Harris to W. W. Phelps based on his own beliefs about Mormon history, not the history the church offered its members. Joseph Smith's letter to Josiah Stowell that President Hinckley purchased from him was also a forgery, he said—as was the Anthon Transcript, the Joseph Smith III Blessing and many other documents he had sold.

"What was going through your mind when you got the results back from the experts who said these documents were genuine?" Stott asked.

Hofmann said he was not worried in the least: He *enjoyed* having experts look at his documents; he knew what tests they performed on documents and knew he could deceive all of them.

Hofmann said he had never had any doubt the Oath of a Freeman would pass the examination by the Library of Congress.

"You'd be surprised at what I did to make it look genuine," he said.

His only mistake, he added, was asking DeBouzek Engraving to make an engraving of the Oath instead of making it himself.

"I got lazy and too impatient."

If *he* had made the plate for the Oath of a Freeman, Hofmann said, no one would ever have been able to prove it was forged.

Hofmann spoke of Kenneth Rendell and Charles Hamilton with contempt and ridicule and boasted that he had fooled them time and time again. "It was easy," he said, and added that forensic document examiners were no better at detecting forgeries than document dealers.

Stott was so overwhelmed by Hofmann's conceit that he wanted badly to prick his egotism.

He said that prosecutors had just received the results of a new chemical analysis of paper and ink conducted by an expert in Montana—Roderick McNeil—who had determined that the ink of Hofmann's best-known documents had been placed on paper no earlier than 1970.

Hofmann looked at Stott and Biggs dubiously.

He didn't believe it, he said.

Then an expression bordering on relief appeared on Hofmann's face. He said he remembered McNeil; he had read about him; he knew about his testing methods.

It was impossible, he said, for McNeil to have detected his forgeries.

62

As Bob Stott and David Biggs approached Ronald Yengich's home shortly before 7 A.M. on January 22, 1987, the streets were dark and covered with slush and snow. A chilly wind was whipping across the Salt Lake Valley, and the frosty slopes of the Wasatch Front were shrouded in a white, cotton haze.

Despite the gloomy weather, Stott and Biggs were in a euphoric mood. After Hofmann answered a few more questions, they were all to appear in court at 11 A.M. and Hofmann was to plead guilty and be transported immediately to the Utah State Prison.

As they turned a corner near Yengich's home, they saw Hofmann's van parked outside the house and prepared themselves for a diatribe from the defense lawyer.

The night before, reporters had gleaned from someone in the law-enforcement establishment of Salt Lake County that the bombing case was about to be brought to a dramatic climax. As they drove to Yengich's home, the airwaves crackled with speculation that Hofmann intended to plead guilty that morning to the murders of Steven Christensen and Kathleen Sheets.

By habit, the four men took their same places around the table.

And just as Stott and Biggs had expected, Yengich was primed for attack.

Even before they sat down, he began railing at them for permitting news about the plea bargain to reach the press.

"Do you know you're putting Bill Hofmann through hell?"

Yengich said Mark had still not told his father that he was going to plead guilty.

"He was going to tell his family last night," he shouted. "Then they all heard about it on television, and Mark couldn't do it."

Since childhood, Mark had had a special relationship with Bill Hofmann, a relationship compounded, probably in equal parts, of love, awe and fear. His strong-willed father had looked on Mark as nearly a perfect son, one who memorized pages of Mormon scripture at six, who lived according to the values of the church, who served a mission, had become a devoted father himself and seemed destined to become a General Authority—perhaps even the Prophet.

When Mark had expressed doubts about the church, his father had told him such doubts were better left unspoken, and he had gone on his mission so he would not disappoint his parents. Now, he was unable to hurt them by admitting he was a killer.

Yengich rose out of his chair and angrily paced around the table. Talking rapidly at the top of his voice, he attacked reporters and the prosecutors for being insensitive to Hofmann's parents and said it was not fair to put them through such torture: They shouldn't have to read in the paper or hear on television that their son was a murderer.

"Bill Hofmann is a good man," Yengich said. "He doesn't deserve this. He's a *decent* man; he reminds me of my own father. It's just brutal to torture him like this.

"Screw the goddamned press," he said. He was not going to let the press control what he did and he wasn't going to let Hofmann enter his plea that morning. They'd do it tomorrow—maybe.

One reason why some Salt Lake County prosecutors disliked Ron Yengich was a belief that he treated all of life as a competition and, whatever the circumstances, he wanted to dominate events.

As Stott and Biggs listened to his harangue, they were impassive: It was another instance in which Yengich's ego was offended because he had been unable to control events. Then it occurred to both at once what Yengich was trying to do:

The lecture wasn't aimed at *them,* it was aimed at Hofmann.

Yengich was trying to make him aware of the suffering he was causing his parents by not having the courage to admit he was a murderer. Stott looked across the table to see if Yengich's message was getting through. Hofmann's fleshy face showed no emotion.

When Yengich cooled off and sat down, the prosecutors resumed their interview of Hofmann.

Stott asked:

"Where did you get the idea for the word *salamander?*"

Hofmann said the 1833 anti-Mormon book *Mormonism Unveiled* contained an affidavit from one of Joseph Smith's neighbors who said Smith's father once told him that when his son found the gold plates in the Hill Cumorah they were guarded not by an angel but by "something like a toad."

Hofmann said he had changed *toad* to *white salamander* to make the letter sound more interesting and make it more valuable.

"Were you trying to create history?"

"In a way, yes," Hofmann said.

Although the church refused to acknowledge it, he said, Joseph Smith was deeply involved in folk magic and used seer stones to search for buried treasure. There was plenty of historical evidence, he went on, that demonstrated that the church's account of the coming forth of the Book of Mormon was fictitious and that Joseph Smith invented his account of the discovery of the gold plates.

He said he had merely written a letter that Martin Harris *might* have written. It was consistent with history as it happened, not with what the church claimed was history. And, he added, the word *salamander* had economic value. It was a simple equation: Controversial documents brought more money. If the church didn't buy a document and hide it, he said, a collector would want it.

Hofmann was interrupted by a knock on Yengich's front door. Yengich left and returned a few moments later.

"Mark, your father's here."

Hofmann's face blanched, and he slumped into his chair. "Get rid of him," he whispered with a hiss.

"I don't want him in here," he said.

"Don't let him in."

Bill Hofmann, wearing a long black overcoat that made him look like the mortician he once was, was standing near the front door and looking at the prosecutors seated with his son. Yengich walked back to him and led him to his car, then returned to the dining room table.

"It's your fault this family is going through hell," Yengich shouted at the prosecutors as he sat down.

"That's a damned good man out there, a *damned good man.* That man's been hurt. He's been hurt bad. Why couldn't you keep your damned mouth shut so I could have gotten this done so it hurt as few people as possible?"

Silently, Stott and Biggs understood what was going on:

Yengich had *invited* Bill Hofmann to his house. He must have decided that the only way Mark would tell his father about his guilt was to be forced into a confrontation.

After a few minutes, there was another knock on the door. It was Bill Hofmann again.

Stott, Biggs and Hofmann went into the kitchen while Yengich answered the door and invited Mark's father to wait in the living room.

Biggs and Stott were almost finished with their interview. A few minutes later, they prepared to leave Yengich's home. To reach the front door, they had to pass through the living room.

Bill Hofmann, a small, slender man with short dark hair, was sitting on a sofa. As they filed past him, he looked up curiously, searching their eyes for clues to the purpose of this meeting with his son. Stott and Biggs nodded at him, and both said, "Hi, Bill."

Mark Hofmann's father returned the greeting with a half-smile, then turned his head toward the kitchen, searching for his son.

As Stott and Biggs walked out of Yengich's house, two cars were pulling to a stop at a curb across the street. They watched as members of Mark's family—Dorie Hofmann, carrying her youngest baby; his aunt; and several other relatives—got out of the cars and walked toward Yengich's house.

The prosecutors nodded hello to the group, and the members of Hofmann's family responded with quick and polite nods.

Yengich had orchestrated their visit, too, Biggs and Stott agreed.

He must have called Mark's family to his house to force him to admit to them that he was a murderer.

Dressed in the dark suit of a missionary, with his father and his lawyers beside him, Hofmann arrived at the courthouse a few minutes before 11 on January 23, 1987. A pack of waiting reporters shouted questions at him as he passed.

"How do you feel, Mark?" a reporter asked.

"Obviously I feel sorry for what happened; obviously I feel worse for my family," he said, "but I think we'll all live through it all right. Other than that, I wouldn't like to make any public comment."

One reporter persisted.

"What effect do you think your documents will have on the church?" he asked.

Hofmann interrupted his stride slightly and looked at the reporter full in the face, smiled slightly and said:

"I don't think it has affected it overly."

Then, limping only slightly from the injury to his right knee, he walked up the steps of the courthouse and entered a circular courtroom whose walls were finished in imitation wood paneling and decorated with pictures of the Utah wilderness.

The room was jammed. All the seats were taken and chairs had been placed in the aisles to accommodate an overflow crowd that was anxious to witness the final act of the drama that had mesmerized the Salt Lake Valley for so long.

Mark turned around and looked at the crowd. His eyes caught those of Dorie Hofmann, who was seated beside his father, and several other relatives, but expressed no recognition when they passed over Terri Christensen and Gary Sheets.

There was almost a religious quality to the events that were about to unfold in the courthouse.

Mark Hofmann had come to be held accountable for his sins in front of those he had trespassed against.

More than thirty relatives of Kathy Sheets and Steve Christensen had accepted invitations to be in the courtroom for this last act.

Terri Christensen, Mac Christensen and other members of Steve Christensen's family looked out on Hofmann from the jury box, as if they had been summoned there to pass judgment on him. Seated a few feet away were Gary Sheets, Kathy Sheets's daughters and other members of her family.

The wives of the prosecutors who had fought for so long to convict Hofmann were also in the courtroom, as were Michael George, Dick Forbes, George Throckmorton, Ken Farnsworth and Jennie Glover. Absent from this final act were two of the most important players in the drama, Ted Cannon and Gerry D'Elia.

Utah Third District Judge Kenneth Rigtrup, who was confined to a wheelchair by polio, wheeled himself into the courtroom and took his place behind the bench, then read a list of the reduced charges against Hofmann: two counts of second-degree murder and two counts of theft by deception, including forgery of the salamander letter and the fraudulent sale of a cache of documents he did not own, the McLellin Collection.

A judge, Rigtrup explained, was not the originator of a plea agreement: He was only the instrument through which it was executed. Rigtrup was distancing himself from criticism of the agreement that he rightly anticipated would later come from residents of the Salt Lake Valley who argued Hofmann should have been executed.

One by one, the judge asked Hofmann how he pleaded to the charges. In response to each question, Hofmann answered in a low voice that could barely be heard in the rear of the courtroom:

"Guilty."

Declaring that he believed the plea agreement would serve the interests of justice, Judge Rigtrup said he intended to approve it.

Hofmann, he said, had already admitted his guilt during meetings with the prosecutors and had pledged, as a condition of the agreement, to meet with them again to further discuss his crimes.

Rigtrup said Salt Lake County's law-enforcement agencies had been apprised of the agreement and approved it "with some disagreement," a reference to Sheriff Pete Hayward, who was among those who believed Hofmann should be executed.

The judge said the families of Steven Christensen and Kathleen Sheets had also given their consent to the plea agreement.

"They have a need and a substantial desire," he said, "to close this chapter of their life."

After signing a document admitting his guilt, Hofmann was

asked by the judge if he wanted to say anything before he passed
sentence on him.

"No," Hofmann said.

Because of the nature of Utah's sentencing laws, the judge said,
he did not determine how long a defendant would spend in jail
even after he handed down a life sentence:

"The judge puts 'em in jail. How long they stay becomes the
power and prerogative of the Board of Pardons."

But he said he planned to make a recommendation to the Board
of Pardons because of the nature of Hofmann's crimes: He had
killed blindly and indiscriminately. Kathleen Sheets, he said, died
simply because she picked up a package addressed to her husband.
Another innocent bystander, Janet McDermott, had nearly been
killed by the bomb addressed to Steven Christensen.

Rigtrup looked down at Hofmann, then across to Terri Christensen and Gary Sheets, and said:

"I will recommend that you spend the rest of your natural life in
the Utah State Prison."

It was over.

Bob Stott had given permission for Hofmann to spend half an
hour alone with his family after the hearing to make his good-byes,
and Judge Rigtrup ordered the courtroom cleared for the meeting.
But at the last moment Hofmann told Yengich that he did not
want to face his family and asked to be taken immediately to the
Utah State Prison.

As Hofmann was led away in handcuffs, David Biggs wondered
to himself whether Hofmann had yet had the courage to admit to
his parents that he was a killer.

Yengich handed a mimeographed letter in Hofmann's handwriting to relatives of Steve Christensen and Kathleen Sheets after the
hearing. It was an apology and request, with religious overtones,
for their forgiveness.

When Bob Stott saw the letter, the first thing he noticed was that
several words in Hofmann's letter were misspelled, just as they
were in the letters he had signed with the name of Joseph Smith.

Epilogue

In the months following Mark Hofmann's courtroom admission of his guilt, former Salt Lake County Attorney Ted Cannon, the man who directed his prosecution, also went to jail. He was convicted of defaming a television reporter who he had once suggested might be involved in drug dealing and pleaded no contest to two misdemeanor charges stemming from the allegations that he had made inappropriate sexual advances to a secretary in his office. "My life is ruined," he told reporters before spending twenty-five days in a rural Utah jail where his cellmates were petty thieves and drying-out winos. In a court brief, Cannon blamed his behavior on a mental disorder that had temporarily caused him to have manic-depressive symptoms. Secretary Shauna Clark sued Salt Lake City for $1.2 million for alleged sexual harassment and eventually settled her claim for $66,000.

The University of Utah sent an appraiser to Texas to inspect the McLellin Collection, the cache of documents that had led indirectly to the killing of Steven F. Christensen and Kathleen Webb Sheets. After the appraiser proposed that the documents were worth no more than $25,000—not the $185,000 church leaders had helped Hofmann raise in a desperate effort to keep them from "the enemy"—Otis L. Traughber, Jr., decided not to sell them, and the McLellin Collection remained locked in his safe-deposit box in Houston.

Terri Christensen and J. Gary Sheets, lonely and confident that someday they would be reunited with Steve and Kathy for eternity in the Celestial Kingdom, remarried within sixteen months of the bombings. As a federal grand jury launched an investigation into the affairs of C.F.S., Sheets resumed the vocation that had supported Kathy and him as newlyweds, selling insurance. His children and friends in his ward rallied around him and predicted that, before long, Gary Sheets would be a financial success again.

For Brent Ashworth, the pain inflicted by Mark Hofmann's forgeries lingered long after his former friend went to prison. He had lost more than $200,000—his retirement nest egg and more—to Hofmann. But it was not his financial loss that haunted Ashworth. It was a sense of guilt and abandonment. Once, he had been convinced that God had chosen him to take Hofmann's faith-promoting letters to the world, and he had fulfilled his mission faithfully: He had traveled the country, holding up the letters before thousands of Mormons and non-Mormons as tangible evidence that the Book of Mormon was true. Church leaders had made him a hero. But after they learned the letters were forgeries, he felt they not only abandoned him but scorned him for contributing to their embarrassment. Worse, Ashworth was haunted by a sense of guilt that, however unintentionally, he, like Mark Hofmann, had been a fraud. "I wish I could have exchanged places with Steve Christensen," he told an acquaintance two years after the bombings.

During the spring of 1987, in accordance with the terms of his plea agreement, Hofmann met several times at the Utah State Prison with prosecutors Robert Stott and David Biggs and offered them a primer on how to forge historical documents.

Hofmann said the texts of the salamander letter, the Joseph Smith III Blessing, Joseph Smith's letter to Josiah Stowell, and the other Mormon documents that had made him a celebrity were figments of his imagination, rooted in his belief in what *must* have happened more than a century before, based on Fawn Brodie's book *No Man Knows My History, Mormonism Unveiled,* and other nineteenth-century histories of the church.

After securing samples of the handwriting of Smith and other early Mormon leaders, he said, he practiced copying their writing until he was expert at it. Then he stole sheets of blank paper from nineteenth-century library books and used blank sheets from authentic stampless covers to forge the letters. The ink he made himself, using a formula for iron gallotannic ink similar to that in Charles Hamilton's book, *Great Forges and Famous Fakes.* To age the ink artificially, he oxidized it chemically—exactly as investigators Flynn and Throckmorton theorized he had.

Hofmann admitted that some of his forgeries had amateurish touches: The counterfeit Anthon Transcript was stuck into the old Cambridge Bible with white Elmer's Glue thickened with wheat paste and darkened with ordinary charcoal, and it should have been detected as a forgery, he said.

But he boasted that he had gone to great lengths to make some documents: After discovering bugs had eaten their way through a paper bag in which he stored wheat in his basement, he placed the bugs between several sheets of paper and discovered that he could use them to simulate the dark holes and tracks bored through old books by nineteenth-century bookworms.

He said he produced the Oath of a Freeman, his crowning achievement, by first using a Xerox machine to make photocopies of a library facsimile of Stephen Daye's *Bay Psalm Book.* With a razor-edged knife, he then cut out hundreds of letters and floret symbols from these copies and glued them to a sheet of paper, arranged as he imagined Daye might have printed them. Then he made a photocopy of the sheet of paper and ordered a photoengraving of the sheet made at DeBouzek Engraving. To mislead document examiners into believing the Oath of a Freeman had been printed with Stephen Daye's movable printer's type, he rounded off the edges of some of the letters on the zinc engraving with steel wool and ground other letters down with an electric grinder, giving each a different appearance. When he was finished, he printed the Oath in his basement by inking the engraving plate and clamping it to a stolen sheet of seventeenth-century paper chosen, he said, because its chain lines were almost identical to those in the paper upon which the *Bay Psalm Book* was printed. When he made ink for the Oath, Hofmann said, he burned a piece of seventeenth-century leather to extract its tannic acid. If examiners later used the carbon 14 dating technique employed by archaeologists to date prehistoric fossils, he said, the ashes of the old piece of leather would have made the ink appear to be 350 years old. Hofmann said he chemically applied a fungus to the paper on which the Oath was printed to create the kind of yellowed stains often found on old documents. And once it was printed, he put the Oath in a glass chamber and subjected it to the burst of an electrical spark; the spark generated ozone, a colorless gas, which bleached and oxidized the ink, making it appear to be more than three centuries old.

Hofmann was alternately forthcoming and uncommunicative during the interviews. As a teenage coin collector, he said, he had discovered a form of alchemy: Using an electroplating instrument, he added a *D* to an ordinary dime, mailed it to an important organization of coin collectors for an appraisal, and was told it was worth thousands of dollars because it bore a rare mint mark from the United States Mint at Denver. A skeptical dealer, astonished that a collector barely into his teens owned so valuable a coin, sent it to numismatic specialists at the U.S. Mint in Washington. They confirmed it was genuine.

Hofmann said he decided that if *experts* had said the coin was genuine, it *was* genuine. Therefore, he was not cheating anyone to whom he sold counterfeited coins.

He suggested to the prosecutors that he had been able to pass a lie-detector test because he had learned as a teenager to hypnotize himself and conceal his emotions. "I don't give myself away very easily," he said. "I can look someone in the eye and lie. . . ."

Although Hofmann spoke at length and candidly about his methods of forgery, he refused to say much about his dealings with the church or to comment about any specific documents that he had forged beyond the handful cited in the original indictments against him. Whenever the prosecutors' questions moved very close to these topics, his lawyer, Ronald Yengich, advised him not to answer. Yengich knew the Utah Board of Pardons would soon decide how much time his client was to spend in prison, and he did not want Hofmann to implicate himself in any further crimes—or further antagonize the church that dominated Utah's power structure.

Thus, as the interviews came to an end on May 27, 1987, many questions about Mark Hofmann and his crimes remained unanswered.

Perhaps no one would ever know, Charles Hamilton said, how many documents Hofmann had forged or how many signatures he had mimicked. Like everyone else in the world of buying and selling rare documents, he wanted to know. "Mark Hofmann was unquestionably the most skilled forger this country has ever seen," the man who wrote the book on forgers told a reporter, "not just because he was a good technician. He got away with it because he had a knack for making people like and trust him. He fooled me, he fooled Ken Rendell, he fooled the whole world. He packaged himself as a bespectacled, sweet, unobtrusive, hard-working, intelligent scholar dedicated to the uncovering of history. We now know he was something more than that."

On August 6, 1987, more than one thousand members of the faculty and other people, Mormons and non-Mormons, entered Brigham Young University's cavernous Marriott Center basketball pavilion for an all-day conference to review the Mark Hofmann affair and ponder, among other things, the question: Why had he been so successful a forger?

One of the first speakers, prosecutor Robert Stott, blamed his success on the gullibility of Mormon historians who believed Mormonism had roots in folk magic and frontier mysticism and were too eager to accept his documents as genuine simply because the documents supported their preconceptions. Several historians in the audience rose angrily to denounce Stott's interpretation of events. They said they had taken every reasonable step to ensure that the documents were genuine and said academics were not equipped to detect skillful forgers.

Two scholars offered a different view: They suggested that an atmosphere of historical paranoia had helped give rise to Mark Hofmann. The church was split, a BYU librarian observed, between those who wanted to close its archives because they feared enemies of the church would mine them for damaging information and those who insisted that truth was an overriding virtue and should be revealed regardless of the consequences. "Hofmann," he said, "managed to take advantage of this tension and suspicion by playing on the worst fears and needs of both groups." What was one to expect in a society in which scholars had to ransack desks and otherwise steal documents in order to complete their research projects? he asked tacitly. "Perhaps it is a shorter step than we imagine from stealing documents or using unauthorized manuscripts to *inventing* them."

Richard Howard, the Historian for the Reorganized Church of Jesus Christ of Latter-day Saints who first lost and then won the race for the Blessing of Joseph Smith III, suggested that the roots of the Mark Hofmann affair reached into his childhood, when he was told to smother the questions that he had about his faith. Religious leaders, Howard said, too often ignore or scorn young people who "develop what seems to be an inordinate curiosity about the real past that lurks behind the stories of heroes and villains that for the most part makes up 'official' church history. I for one stand committed to be that someone who cares enough about intellectual rigor and integrity to encourage the asking of such questions." Asked by someone in the audience if he intended to ask the Utah church to return the valuable Mormon Book of Commandments that he had exchanged for the forged Blessing of Joseph Smith III, Howard said he would not.

"A deal's a deal," he said.

For all the heartache that he had caused its leaders, Mark Hofmann, in the end, left undamaged the church's miraculous story of the coming forth of the Book of Mormon: The church could say truthfully that his tales of salamanders and clever spirits, which had provoked a crisis within the church and a wave of ridicule outside it, had been created out of whole cloth. In the months and years following the bombings, record numbers of young Mormon missionaries—some thirty-five thousand a year—traveled to every corner of the earth, continuing to retell, again and again, Joseph Smith's glorious story of being led by an angel to a cache of gold plates buried by an ancient people in upstate New York. And as they spread Smith's optimistic doctrine of eternal progression, with its promise that *every man* could become a god with sovereignty over his own star, planets, and principalities, church membership passed the 6.5 million mark.

Still, Mark Hofmann had not left everything unchanged within the Church of Jesus Christ of Latter-day Saints. Whatever else they had done, Hofmann's documents had stimulated a burst of historical inquiry regarding Joseph Smith's youthful enthusiasm for magic and the occult and it did not wither after his conviction. New, even harsher barriers to scholars' access to its archives were imposed by the church after the scope of Hofmann's crimes became apparent. Nevertheless, the Mormon Underground flourished as never before. The Mark Hofmann affair had emboldened many scholars to penetrate deeper and deeper into recesses of the Mormon past that its most conservative leaders wanted left unexplored, and it was unlikely that those in the Church Administration Building would ever be able to contain fully the fires of intellectual curiosity that Hofmann had helped fan.

On January 28, 1988, Hofmann sat down at a wooden table in the Utah State Prison. Seated across from him were three members of the Utah Board of Pardons. In a brightly lighted conference room, Dorie Hofmann was seated nearby and, next to her, Bill Hofmann. There was also a large group of reporters in the room.

The parole officials—two men and a woman—were to decide how many years Mark would spend in prison because of his crimes. His lawyers had proposed that, as a first-time offender, he should be sentenced to seven years; privately, they thought the best they could get would be a term of twenty years.

On the table in front of the parole officials was the report of a prison psychologist who had measured Hofmann's IQ at 137 and concluded after an examination that he was sane but "inordinately self-centered and possibly narcissistic." There was also a letter on the table from Hofmann himself in which he tried to explain his motives for murder and forgery. "As far back as I can remember," it began, "I have liked to impress people through my deception. In fact, some of my earliest memories are of doing magic and card tricks. Fooling people gave me a sense of power and superiority. I believe this is what led to my forging activities. . . ."

Hofmann said he found it more difficult to explain why he had killed Steve Christensen and Kathy Sheets: "In October, 1985, it seemed like everything started to collapse around me. I could not come up with the money to pay off investors to keep from being exposed a fraud . . . the most important thing in my mind was to keep from being exposed as a fraud in front of my friends and family."

Under questioning by the board members, Hofmann said that when he left the bomb near the garage of Gary Sheets's home it had not mattered to him whether it exploded or not. Chilled by his detached and businesslike explanation of the event, the chairwoman asked him to elaborate. "As strange as it sounds," he answered, "it was almost a game as far as . . . I figured it was a fifty-percent chance that it would go off and a fifty-percent chance it wouldn't; at the time I made the bomb, my thoughts were that it didn't matter if it was Mrs. Sheets, a child, a dog . . . whoever" was killed.

The members of the parole board left the room, and twenty-seven minutes later they returned with a verdict: "Mr. Hofmann, we are impressed that you exhibit a callous disregard for human life and that the killings were done to cover other criminal activities. . . .

"By majority vote, the Board has decided that you shall serve your natural life in prison. . . ."

The file was not yet closed, however, on the Mark Hofmann affair.

Two months after Hofmann was informed at the age of thirty-three that he would have to spend the rest of his life behind bars, two inmates at the prison told guards that he had asked them to murder the three members of the Board of Pardons.

When security officers questioned him, Hofmann denied the story and claimed the inmates had invented it. Under some circumstances, the officials might have discounted the reports as fabrications of prison informers bent on currying favor with administrators. But the two inmates did not know each other and lived in different units of the prison, and they told a remarkably similar story: Before he went before the Board of Pardons, Hofmann said that if he was not given a favorable sentence he wanted the board members executed, preferably with bombs. If the inmates could arrange with someone outside the prison to murder them, they said, Hofmann promised to pay at least $10,000 for the job—money that he said was safely hidden outside the prison unbeknownst to his wife.

Extra police patrols were assigned to keep homes of the Board of Pardons members under surveillance and Hofmann was questioned again. But, wearing the inscrutable mask that had once been so familiar to his clients, he continued to deny the prisoners' claims.

When investigator Michael George of the Salt Lake County Attorney's Office was told about the allegations, he decided to reopen his investigative file on Hofmann. Then something happened that made the issue suddenly more urgent: A letter Hofmann had mailed to his wife was intercepted at the prison; when it was opened, prison officials discovered that it was coded in a meaningless gibberish of letters and numbers. The implication was clear: If Hofmann couldn't hire someone at the prison to do his bidding, perhaps he was trying to contact someone on the outside to kill the members of the Board of Pardons.

George decided to visit the prison, a clay-colored, triple-fenced fortress that sprawls like a small city across a grassy plain north of Provo, in hopes of completing not one but two missions: He wanted to learn the truth about the purported assassination plot, and his mind was still brimming, more than two and a half years after the bombings, with unanswered questions about the original case.

When the slender, bearded investigator, who was three years older than Hofmann, was led into a prison meeting room to confront him, he was shocked by what he saw: Hofmann, in his dark blue prison jump suit and sandals, had lost forty pounds and he was completely bald. His shaved head gleamed under the fluorescent lights in the room as brightly as if it had been a mirror.

For almost an hour, Hofmann emphatically denied that he had discussed a new bombing plot with anyone: "I don't know anything about it."

As he repeated the sentence again and again, George recalled one of Hofmann's remarks during his interviews with prosecutors Stott and Biggs: *"I can look someone in the eye and lie."*

George's ability to extract information from criminal suspects by disarming them with a soft-spoken style of interrogation that, to some, must have seemed as if it bordered on friendship was a legend in Utah. In a celebrated case three years earlier, he had persuaded Marc Schreuder, a New York prep school student, to admit that—at his own mother's request—he had murdered his grandfather, the wealthy owner of a chain of Utah auto-parts stores. As he persistently but gently pressed his questions on this warm afternoon during the first week of April 1988, Mark Hofmann, like Schreuder, began to open up.

Yes, he finally conceded, he *might* have discussed with other inmates the *possibility* of killing members of the Board of Pardons. Then he admitted that he *had* done so, but quickly added it hadn't been *his* idea: Other inmates had proposed the idea to him. They had offered to arrange the killings for him. While he *might* have shown interest in their proposal, he said, it was only because he wanted to get along with fellow inmates, and he would never have carried it out. Then George showed him the coded letter.

Hofmann's complexion turned as white as the snow that still covered the upper slopes of the Wasatch Mountains. George asked him to decode the letter, but he refused.

"If I did, it would incriminate other people, and I can't afford to be labeled a snitch in here."

The evidence was too inconclusive to warrant filling additional charges against a prisoner facing a life sentence. If Hofmann had really considered blowing up the three members of the Board of Pardons, he wouldn't do it now. George decided to turn to the second of his missions: to seek answers to some of the questions that had been on his mind for so long.

"Mark," he said, "you've admitted that the salamander letter and the Oath of a Freeman and some of the other Mormon documents were forged. Would you talk to me about your *other* forgeries? People all over the country, document dealers and collectors, are asking us whether this document or that document was forged. . . ."

Hofmann was silent for several moments. Then, he said:

"It's probably time I got that behind me."

He began a discourse that lasted almost two hours and continued, as George took notes, for five more hours several days later:

The scope of his forgeries was beyond anything anyone had imagined.

With a handful of exceptions—mostly documents he had taken in trade from clients—Hofmann said virtually *every* document he had sold was forged.

He said he had sold documents to collectors and dealers around the country with forged handwriting of at least eighty-three American and European historical figures and early Mormon leaders, including, among many others, George Washington, John Adams,

John Quincy Adams, Daniel Boone, John Brown, William (Billy the Kid) Bonney, Andrew Jackson, Mark Twain, Nathan Hale, John Hancock, Francis Scott Key, Abraham Lincoln, John Milton, Paul Revere, Miles Standish, and Button Gwinnett, a Georgian whose death shortly after he signed the Declaration of Independence had made his signature the rarest and most valuable of any early American leader.

He said he had forged so many names, "I can't remember all of them," then identified his customers, which included America's most prestigious auction galleries and autograph dealers and collectors from coast to coast.

"Once," he said, "I sold an Emily Dickinson—I just made up a poem and signed it—and I'll be darned if a year later I saw the poem published in a magazine as a 'newly discovered poem' by Emily Dickinson."

Charles Hamilton, George thought, was right: Hofmann must be the most prolific forger in American history. All over the country, perhaps the world—in private safes and museums and framed on collectors' walls—there were forged historical documents that their owners regarded as genuine.

"How many documents, in all, did you think you forged?" he asked.

Hofmann said the number ran into the hundreds but he did not know the answer. "Whenever I needed the money, I just forged something," he said.

George asked how much money he had made as a forger.

He said he had never kept records of his transactions and could only guess.

"Probably at least $2 million," Hofmann said.

He said he never thought of himself as defrauding the collectors or dealers to whom he sold the documents. As far as they knew, the documents were genuine. They got their money's worth. George thought of the Salt Lake Valley teenager who had convinced himself that in counterfeiting a valuable mint mark on a coin, he was creating a *genuine* rare coin.

Hofmann said he had been bewildered by the attention that had been devoted to the murders of Kathy Sheets and Steven Christensen. In words that sent an icy chill through George, he said, "I don't feel anything for them. My philosophy is that they're *dead.*

They're not suffering. I think life is basically worthless. They could have died just as easily in a car accident."

As if wanting to strengthen his argument, he added:

"I don't believe in God. I don't believe in an afterlife. *They don't know they're dead.*"

He must be a sociopath, George thought: He seemed utterly devoid of a conscience.

"Why did you decide to plead guilty?" George asked.

Hofmann said that after the preliminary hearing he realized his conviction was probably inevitable and that a plea bargain was in his best interest.

"You don't see me sitting on Death Row, do you?"

Hofmann, George thought, must have set different standards for the worthlessness of human life when his own was at stake. He asked how Hofmann liked his life in prison.

"I love it down here," he said. "I'm basically a loner; I always have been. I've been alone all my life; I've never had many friends. I'm in my cell twenty-three hours a day, I have lots of time to read, I've got a TV. I like being alone. Prison suits me to a T.

"I always wondered if and how I'd get caught," he volunteered while George was framing his next question. "It was almost a game: I wanted to see how good I was . . . I'd do little things to the documents, make mistakes, to see if I'd get caught."

George asked him to explain the curious transaction in which he paid Deseret Book more than $100,000 for his forgery of the letter purportedly written by Joseph Smith to General Dunham shortly before he died in the Carthage Jail, then resold it to Brent Ashworth for less than $20,000 in cash.

"Things were going downhill at the time," he said, "and I wanted to reestablish my reputation. I'd promised to get it back for Brent, and if I did I thought he'd defend me when I needed help and it would help my reputation."

Hofmann stuck to his claim that he intended to commit suicide on October 16, 1985.

Regardless of what prosecutors believed, he said, "the third bomb was for me."

He said that after learning from television reports that he might have been identified at the Judge Building the previous day, he decided that suicide was the only way he could avoid embarrassing his family.

George listened quietly but was not convinced. He believed Hofmann nearly killed himself in a mistake, that he had planned to lure Brent Ashworth to his car and blow him up, along with a potpourri of papyrus and other old documents in the car that he would then claim was the McLellin Collection. That would have ended the pressure he was under to deliver the nonexistent documents.

"Have you admitted to this day to your father and Dorie that you really are a murderer and a forger?"

Hofmann grinned. "I've told them and, intellectually, they've got to know it's true," he said. "But I think it's still hard for them to accept it as the truth."

After more than seven hours, there was still one topic Michael George wanted to discuss.

He had long suspected that before the bombings Hofmann was planning to forge the lost 116 pages of the Book of Mormon, the work called by Joseph Smith "the keystone of our religion." He suspected Hofmann was driven by a rage against the church rooted in angry feelings of disillusionment and betrayal.

By producing a document transparent with errors or filled with creatures of the occult, Hofmann could have rocked the foundations of the church and its multibillion-dollar business empire. He might even have destroyed it.

Everything he knew about Hofmann suggested that this was his ultimate objective, and he asked him if it was.

"Yes," Hofmann answered matter-of-factly. "It was all set up and ready to go."

If he hadn't gotten so deeply in debt because of the expected windfall from the Oath of a Freeman, Hofmann said, he would have carried out the scheme.

"I could have done it any time. I *would* have done it. In fact, I should have done it sooner. I got too lazy."

Hofmann said that long ago he had become convinced that Joseph Smith, Jr., was, like himself, a con man, and the Book of Mormon was simply a product of his imagination. In *completing* the Book of Mormon, he said, he would have been doing nothing more than what the Prophet himself had done—and would have gotten rich, too.

"Everything was in place."

"Amazing," George said.

Hofmann said he had paid a college friend thousands of dollars to catalogue every word in the Book of Mormon, enabling him to emulate its structure and syntax.

Experts had accepted his handwriting as that of Martin Harris, the scribe who transcribed and then lost the 116 pages. And he had engineered it so that each of the samples of Harris's writing that he had written appeared to have a separate and independent origin, never himself.

Lyn Jacobs, for example, was believed to be the source of the salamander letter. Deseret Book said its copy of the *Book of Common Prayer* that supposedly contained Harris's handwriting had been in its possession, locked in a safe, for years.

"Ingenious," George said.

One of George's investigative techniques was to inflate the egos of people he interviewed and to encourage them, sometimes with flattery, to think they were smarter than he was. But as the long conversation continued in the small room starkly furnished with a table and two chairs, he was genuinely impressed by the preparations for and the scope of Hofmann's grandest scheme.

Hofmann said the salamander letter and the Josiah Stowell letter, with their superstitious references to the occult, had been accepted as genuine and would back up his version of the lost Book of Lehi. When he forged it, he said, he intended to include references to money-digging and folk magic that were consistent with the letters.

Thus, he said, they would have added further weight to his version of the lost 116 pages, which he said would have thoroughly undermined Joseph Smith's story of the gold plates and the angel Moroni.

"Let me ask you this," George said. "I've heard that the church might be willing to pay $25 million for the 116 pages. Do you think that's right?"

"I don't think that figure would have been unreasonable," he said. "They were willing to pay me $10,000 just for my notes from a *forgery,*" Hofmann said, referring to Brent Ashworth's assignment from a friend in the Church Office Building to obtain a copy of the missing 116 pages Hofmann was rumored to have found in Bakersfield, California.

"What would you have done with the 116 pages if you'd forged them?"

"They would have gone to the church," he said.

George wondered if, after extorting a fortune from the church, Hofmann would have then leaked damaging portions from the lost manuscript to anti-Mormon groups as he did after forging the salamander letter.

Sure, he would have, George decided.

One more question troubled the investigator.

"Mark, does the church have any of your documents that we don't know about yet, that they never told us about?"

"Yes," Hofmann said.

"You got most of 'em," he added, but the church had several of his forgeries that had not been made public, including some, he said, that church officials might not realize originally came from him.

"Are there any other documents in the First Presidency's Vault that the church hasn't told us about?"

Hofmann's face became blank and the slightest hint of a blush appeared on his glistening white scalp.

As George waited for him to answer, his question seemed to hang in the air, the words echoing between the narrow walls of the small room.

Several long moments passed before Hofmann shook his head affirmatively. Yes, he said, there was *one*.

George asked him what the document was.

"I don't really want to talk about it," he said.

George fought to convince him: It didn't matter now, he said; he might as well get everything out in the open and be done with it. But this time George's powers of persuasion failed him.

Suddenly subdued, Hofmann became silent again, then said:

"I just don't want to talk about it."

Perhaps, Mike George said to himself, there would be some questions about the bombings that shook Salt Lake City during the middle of October 1985 that would never be answered.

"Let me tell you my theory about this case," he told Hofmann a few moments later. "I believe in God. I'm not LDS but I believe in God and the hereafter. You probably won't agree with me because you don't believe in God. But I believe the reason you didn't die when the bomb went off was because God wanted you to live so that we could do the investigation and find out that all those documents you sold were forgeries and set history right. If you had died, nobody would have ever known they were forged. I think that's what God intended."

Hofmann let him finish and then he smiled:

"You're right," he said. "I don't agree with you."

ACKNOWLEDGMENTS

I want to acknowledge a debt of gratitude to my editors and colleagues at *The New York Times,* especially Richard Witkin, my mentor and friend; A. M. Rosenthal, Max Frankel, Arthur Gelb, David R. Jones, Edward Klein, Soma Golden, John Lee, Warren Hoge and James Greenfield. All, in differing ways, directly and indirectly, made it possible for me to write *A Gathering of Saints.* In Salt Lake City, the number of people who gave of their time and helped guide me through a culture that I found at once fascinating and rich in paradoxes is too large to cite here. But I want especially to thank Kenneth Farnsworth, Terri Christensen, Brent Ashworth, Ted Cannon, Robert Stott, Richard Forbes, David Biggs, Gerry D'Elia and George Throckmorton. Many members of the Church of Jesus of Latter-day Saints welcomed me into their homes with openness and kindness, and to all of them I extend my deepest thanks. In New York, Charles Hamilton tutored me patiently about the complexities of the rare document business and Justin Schiller shared with me his experiences with the Oath of a Freeman.

Above all, I express my gratitude to Michael George, a man of extraordinary intelligence, warmth and humanity who, more than anyone else, helped me understand the intricacies of an enormously complicated murder investigation and the complex society in which it took place.

As ever, I owe a great debt to my wife, Sandra, for her love and patience during the preparation of this book. My friend Jonathan Coleman was a source of counsel and sound advice, as was my agent and friend, George Diskant.

Alice Mayhew, the editor of the book, provided inspiration and keen editorial guidance throughout its development. Others at Simon and Schuster who, in various ways, made its publication possible include Richard Snyder, Charles Hayward, Eric Rayman, George Hodgman, Stephen Messina, Marcia Peterson, Vincent Virga and Ursula Obst. My thanks to all of them.

ROBERT LINDSEY

Index

ABOUT THE AUTHOR

ROBERT LINDSEY, who was born in 1935 in Glendale, California, was for twenty years a reporter and correspondent for *The New York Times*. His first book, *The Falcon and the Snowman*, won an Edgar Allan Poe award in 1980. He lives in Carmel, California.

PICTURE CREDITS

1. Ben Martin/*Time*
2. no credit
3. Library of Congress
4. Library of Congress
5. no credit
6. Library of Congress
7–10. no credit
11. Tom Smart/*Deseret News*
12–15. no credit
16. Wide World Photos
17. Lynn Johnson/*Salt Lake Tribune*
18. Ravell Call/*Deseret News*
19. Paul G. Barker/*Deseret News*
20. O. Wallace Kasteler/*Deseret News*
21. Ravell Call/*Deseret News*
22. Ravell Call/*Deseret News*
23. no credit
24. Tim Kelly/*Salt Lake Tribune*
25. Wide World Photos
26. Don Grayston/*Deseret News*
27. Tim Kelly/*Salt Lake Tribune*
28, 29. Ravell Call/*Deseret News*
30. no credit
31. O. Wallace Kasteler/*Deseret News*
32. Tom Smart/*Deseret News*
33. Ravell Call/*Deseret News*
34. Paul Fraughton/*Salt Lake Tribune*
35. Paul G. Barker/*Deseret News*
36. Ravell Call/*Deseret News*
37. Tom Smart/*Deseret News*
38. Charles Hamilton
39–42. no credit
43. Jeff Aured/*Salt Lake Tribune*
44. Paul Fraughton/*Salt Lake Tribune*
45. Tim Kelly/*Salt Lake Tribune*

DELL NONFICTION BESTSELLERS